THE LIFE AND LOVES OF CARY GRANT

THE LIFE AND LOVES

OF

CARY GRANT

A BIOGRAPHY BY

LEE GUTHRIE

DRAKE PUBLISHERS INC. NEW YORK•LONDON

Published in 1977 by
Drake Publishers, Inc.
801 Second Avenue
New York, N.Y. 10017

Library of Congress Cataloging in Publication Data

Guthrie, Lee.
The life and loves of Cary Grant.

Filmography: p.
1. Grant, Cary, 1904- 2. Moving-picture actors and actresses — United States — Biography. I. Title.
PN2287.G675G8 791.43'028'0924 (B) 77-6201
ISBN: 0-8473-1613-0

Printed in the United States of America

this book is for Blanche Guthrie

(our Aunt Ditty . . .)

in loving gratitude

for all those Saturday lunches and matinees

back in the Forties

Contents

ACKNOWLEDGEMENTS

I am indebted to David Ragan, author of the comprehensive *Who's Who in Hollywood, 1900-1976* (Arlington House) and editorial director of Macfadden Entertainment Magazines, for his generous assistance.

The theatre archives of the New York Public Library at Lincoln Center proved indispensable to my researching the early days of Mr. Grant's Hollywood career.

Much of the material in the early chapters is based on Cary Grant's three autobiographical sketches which appeared in *Ladies Home Journal* in 1963.

Finally, I must thank my friend, editor *extraordinaire* Jim Hoffman, for first suggesting to me that a book-length treatment of Cary Grant's life and career was long overdue.

THE LIFE AND LOVES OF CARY GRANT

Prologue

CARY GRANT. HIS VERY NAME conjures the kind of authenticity that is rare in today's world of here-today-gone-tomorrow, instant throwaway celebrities. In fact if it weren't for Cary Grant, the very word *celebrity* would have lost much of its meaning. The media need stars and so they create them—and then discard them with equal facility.

In an age that seems bent on glorifying the crude, the barbaric, and the self-indulgent, Cary Grant is still around to prove that it's really better to be stylish, civilized, and gracious.

In an absurdly youth-oriented culture, he casually shows that old age is a state of mind and that, truly, you live until you die.

It's been twelve years since he made a film, but the movie offers keep pouring in, despite his repeated statements that movie-making is behind him.

"Let the tall, dark, smooth-haired guy stay where he is on the late-night TV," says Cary. "He was very immature compared with me, but I quite liked him."

The moviemaking years were from 1932-1966—longer than nearly anyone's. He made seventy-two films, most of them box office hits. David Thomson's *Biographical Dictionary of Film* says quite simply and categorically that Cary Grant "is the best and most important actor in the history of the cinema." It's just not possible to do better than that.

The early years were hectic. Half of those seventy-two movies had been made in the first seven years of his Hollywwod career. His thirty-sixth movie—the numerical midpoint of his career—was released in 1940. It was *My Favorite Wife*, co-starring Irene Dunne.

There were to be four wives—Virginia Cherrill, Barbara Hutton, Betsy Drake, and Dyan Cannon—but he won't tell you which one was his favorite.

"I loved and enjoyed them all," he says.

They all left him. He's not sure why.

To this day he keeps mementoes from three of them on a gold chain around his neck: a cross from Betsy Drake, a Saint Christopher Medal from Barbara Hutton, and a Star of David from Dyan Cannon.

He won't single out a favorite leading lady either, although you sense that his affection for Ingrid Bergman is perhaps stronger than for all the others. There were so many leading ladies, beginning with Mae West who chose him from a crop of Paramount unknowns to be the leading man in her first Hollywood movie, *She Done Him Wrong*.

The others are a very nearly complete list of all the major American movie actresses. A partial listing includes: Sylvia Sidney, Marlene Dietrich, Myrna Loy, Loretta Young, Katharine Hepburn, Constance Bennett, Jean Harlow, Irene Dunne, Jean Arthur, Carole Lombard, Rosalind Russell, Joan Fontaine, Ginger Rogers, Ann Sheridan, Deborah Kerr, Grace Kelly, Sophia Loren, Eva Marie Saint, Doris Day, and Audrey Hepburn.

He was always a loner. He needed and demanded privacy and solitude. He went to few parties and gave fewer.

He wasn't always able to subdue the dark side of his character. Friends reported depressions, black moods, and outbursts of temper.

Now, in a protracted middle age (how can one think of Cary Grant as *old*?), he seems to have come to terms with the insecurities and doubts that once plagued him.

He's lasted so long he's had to develop a sense of humor about his age. A magazine writer at work on his profile once wired him:

"How old Cary Grant?"

Cary promptly wired back, "Old Cary Grant fine. How you?"

He became a father for the first time when most men are becoming grandfathers. It changed his life. His daughter, Jennifer, is perhaps the first female person he has been able to love without doubt, ambivalence, or ambiguity. It has restored him.

His voice and his clipped British accent have been a stock imitation of the stand-up comedians for years. "Judy . . . Judy . . . Judy," they say and we instantly recognize it. But really, what he said was "Julie . . . Julie . . . Julie . . ." to Carole Lombard from his hospital bed. The movie was *In Name Only*. The year was 1939. That's how long his legends last.

To women he gives the impression that he would be a friend and a pal as well as a sensitive and extremely competent lover.

To men he is strangely non-threatening. He appears to be a fellow who would be glad to tell you his secret of success with women—if he could just figure out what it was.

Like many natural aristocrats his beginnings were modest, his early life troubled by family strife. The solution was work. And he's been working ever since, at one thing or another.

Somewhere, in all of us, is the persistently held belief that life should be graceful and lighthearted and fun—that life at its best would be like a Cary Grant movie.

Perhaps it is the role he has played in keeping that vision alive that makes us so terribly fond of Cary Grant.

1

Bristol and the English Music Halls

IN 1904 THE OFTEN CLOUDY SKIES over Bristol looked down on a staid and prosperous seaport, bustling with the trade of a still intact British Empire. In London, one hundred miles away, the stuffy conventions and rigid social mores of the Victorian era were being questioned and sometimes discarded by a rebellious younger generation.

The "dear old Queen," as her more informal subjects called Victoria Regina in her later years, had died peacefully in 1901 after a sixty-four-year reign that saw Great Britain become the unquestioned mistress of the high seas, as England forged an Empire on which the sun never set. Now, in 1904, Victoria's playboy son, Edward VII, sat on England's ancient throne and kept the lights of Buckingham Palace blazing in sharp contrast to his mother's famous austerity.

A group of young writers and painters were living in the placid Georgian houses that lined the squares of a quiet London neighborhood known as Bloomsbury. Fresh from Cambridge, they were preparing to turn the arts upside down and inside out.

But life for the working poor had changed very little. In Bristol there wasn't even the reflected glitter of Buckingham Palace balls, nor the charged atmosphere provided by intellectual and artistic innovation. Life was organized around work, and the daily struggle to make enough money to pay for the bare necessities of life. To do this relentlessly, year after year, without drunkenness, scandal, or violence was known as "respectability."

* * * * * *

Elias Leach was tall and slim, and his eyes often wore a sad, resigned expression. He was a handsome young man with a gentle look about him. His wife, Elsie Kingdom Leach, brought different traits to their marriage. She was diminutive, with black hair, olive skin, and a firm set to her jaw. She was determined to rise in the world, and, in those days, that meant that she would have to somehow infect her easygoing husband with her own ambition and motivate him to work hard and rise, like Horatio Alger, by dint of his own efforts. They had no wealthy or upper middle class parents to provide advantages for them. They'd have to make their own breaks, like countless other young couples before them. Elias Leach's job as a presser in a Bristol clothing factory paid very little, and progress in the company was agonizingly slow. Now it was more important than ever that things go well for them, for Elsie was pregnant again, a pregnancy that now, in its final weeks, was especially difficult.

Elsie Leach worried that the bone-piercing chill in the old stone house where they lived would somehow reach the baby she carried. She had already lost one child, a beautiful little boy, perfect in every way, except for the violent convulsions that had killed him when he was just two months old. The thought of losing this baby as well was a thought she couldn't bear, and yet there it was, staring her in the face during every waking moment.

There was another thought that Elsie Leach couldn't face. Maybe it wasn't the damp and the cold that had caused her little son to die. Maybe she had done it. Maybe she was responsible. When she hadn't been on her feet taking care of him, trying to get a few drops of milk into his small body, rocking him to sleep so he could build up enough strength to endure the next wave of convulsions, she sat by his bed, anxiously watching his tiny chest rise and fall in laboured breathing. It was as if she were forcing him to live by the strength of her own will. Weeks of this round-the-clock nursing had left Elsie Leach very close to collapse herself. Her worried husband summoned a doctor. He came, pronounced the baby's condition stable, and ordered Elsie to bed for at least one full night's sleep. Elsie had doubts, but, after all, the doctor himself had said it would be safe for her to sleep for a bit. Gratefully she fell on her bed, too exhausted to undress, and slept for hours. Sometimes she wished she had never awakened. When she did, they told her the baby was dead.

And now as her second pregnancy came to term, Elsie found herself experiencing the most intense emotions and feelings she'd ever known: a joyous anticipation of the new life, a haunting fear for the new baby's health, and a soul-destroying guilt over the death of her first child.

Finally, late in the afternoon of January 17, 1904, the pains began. Her sisters and her mother gathered at the tiny house on Holfield Road and performed the ancient tasks and rituals of birthing. Elias tried not to upset his wife with his own fears and occupied himself by keeping the fires in all the fireplaces blazing. At 1:00 A.M. a robust, black-haired baby boy arrived on this planet. He cried lustily and nursed voraciously. They named him Archibald Alexander Leach and had him baptised as soon as possible in the Anglican Church.

Archie Leach. A name as English as steak and kidney pie. Who in that small stone house in the provincial city of Bristol could guess that Archie Leach would grow up to become Cary Grant, that most indestructible of American movie stars, the epitome of international glamour and sophistication: a complex, contradictory, shrewd, and strangely vulnerable man?

* * * * * *

Weeks, then months, passed, and young Archie Leach showed not a trace of the illness that had struck down Elias' and Elsie's first child. His appetite was excellent. He gained weight right on schedule, and he slept soundly through the night. Still, it was impossible for Elsie not to worry. She hovered over Archie like the proverbial mother hen. Somehow she thought that if she could keep him a baby, she would always be able to protect him from danger.

On especially cold days she took him to her mother's house for his bath. Archie's grandmother had a coal stove in the kitchen, and Elsie could bathe her son in the little enameled bathtub in front of the fire and thereby lessen his chances of catching a cold. One of those sessions with soap and towel in his grandmother's kitchen was to become the earliest memory of young Archie Leach. He remembers that he was "a squirming mass of protesting flesh," because the bath in front of his grandmother terribly violated his sense of modesty. He wonders how a mere baby could already have such a painful "sense of embarrassed shame."

In those days boy babies and girl babies wore the same thing: dresses and long curls. It was customary for boys to leave the dresses behind at about the time they started to walk. Then they would wear long stockings and short pants. The curls lasted a bit longer. Often, a little boy, depending on how much power his father had in the home, would not get a boy's haircut until he was three or four years old.

Elsie kept Archie in dresses and curls months longer than the other little boys in the neighborhood. Elias had learned that when it came to their son, his wife and decided she was the absolute and final authority. He knew it was pointless to protest, especially when it was so clear how much she loved the boy, and how disastrous it would be if any harm should come to him. So Elias let Elsie have her way. Archie was unhappy even after he was put into short pants. By this time all the other boys were in long pants. Sometimes Archie felt he'd never catch up.

When Archie was two years old, Elsie somehow engineered a move to a larger house, an amazing feat considering that she had barely been able to make ends meet while living in the small stone house on Horfield Road. Like wives from time immemorial, however, Elsie Leach had learned how to make money stretch to miraculous amounts when it had to pay for a better life for a child. The new house had a garden, and under a huge old apple tree, Elias Leach built his little son his very own swing. Archie loved owning the swing but was terrified of actually using it. His father's gentle shoves seemed quite foolhardy to the little boy who was not to conquer his inborn fear of heights until much later in life.

After he had lovingly and carefully built his little boy a swing, Elias Leach began to restore the garden which was badly overgrown and hadn't been properly tended in years. He weeded and cultivated the existing beds of fuchsias, hollyhocks, geraniums, and primroses. He added daffodils, crocuses, lilies of the valley, and a vegetable garden for Elsie's kitchen: carrots, green beans, radishes, onions, and squash.

On summer Sunday afternoons he set up a trestle table under the wide branches of the apple tree, and Elsie served the traditional Sunday dinner of roast beef and yorkshire pudding. Between mouthfuls, Elias would jump up to check on his vegetables, as if he expected a few of them to ripen during the early part of the meal so they might be eaten before it was over.

Archie was later to remember those peaceful Sunday afternoons as the happiest days he and his parents were ever to know.

When he wasn't exploring the garden and the fields beyond, Archie turned his inquiring mind to whatever happened to be close at hand. His mother's pinking shears fascinated him. How *could* they make that delightful edge on everything they touched? One morning when Elsie was out in the garden, young Archie took the magical pinking shears and put a fancy edge on everything he could get his hands on, including his own nightshirt, his father's magazines, and his mother's best tablecloth.

Perhaps it was this childish curiosity which convinced Elsie that her little boy was unusually intelligent. In any case when he was only four and one half years old, she persuaded the local schoolmaster that Archie belonged in a classroom, even though he was six months away from the usual beginning school age. Frightened and fearful he began school the same day, wearing a sailor suit and sitting at a little wooden desk. In front of him sat a pretty little girl with long, blonde curls. Archie wanted to talk to her, but everytime he thought of something to say, he was overcome with shyness and soon forgot the clever remarks he'd planned to impress her with. He was very good at ABC's, clay modeling, and crayon drawing. He was terrible at arithmetic and talking to pretty little girls.

* * * * * *

But the ability and willingness to perform for a crowd was something Archie Leach knew how to do from a very early age. One night Archie was awakened out of a deep sleep by his slightly tipsy father who took him downstairs to the parlor where he and his wife were entertaining their friends. Holding the sleepy child on his shoulders, Elias prompted him to repeat the poem he had just learned by heart in school. Young Archie, wrapped in a blanket and rubbing the sleep out of his eyes during the entire performance, dutifully recited "Up in a Balloon So High." Everybody applauded, but unfortunately Archie had learned only one poem at this time, so he had no material for an encore.

* * * * * *

All children are beautiful, but Archie Leach was an unusually handsome little boy. An early photograph shows a sweet-faced, dark-haired child solemnly gazing into the camera with a look that is both intelligent and wary. He is wearing knee socks and short pants and a long-sleeved, turtleneck sweater against the cold and damp of the English winter. His legs are straight and sturdy. And like his father, Elias, his eyes are a bit sadder than a boy's eyes should be.

How does a child, with neither guidance nor experience of the world, begin to understand that his parents are not as happy as they should be, that he is lonelier than a child should be? Mother, father, and home seem as necessary to a young child as the air he breathes. How does a child begin to confront the terrifying knowledge that *something is wrong at home*?

At this time, Archie knew nothing about the baby that had died while his mother slept. He knew nothing of her guilt and self-reproach. The trouble that Archie was first aware of was the increasingly bitter arguments about money.

Elias never earned enough at the clothing factory to provide all the things that Elsie wanted her son to have, and she let her husband know it repeatedly. Elias soon learned that the best thing to do was simply to let Elsie say whatever she wanted. It was pointless to argue with her. Perhaps Elias sensed his wife's accusations that he was not providing enough for his family were in some mysterious way a defense against her own sense of guilt over the death of their first child.

But young Archie was confused and frightened by the increasing tension. He wondered if he was somehow to blame, and he tried extra hard to be a good boy. But it was impossible to escape the effects of his parents' unhappiness. He later remembers:

"I seemed to be caught in a subtle battle which eventually took residence inside my own slowly forming character."

Archie was loved but "seldom ever praised," and praise is as necessary to a child's well-being as good food and restful sleep. But the conventional wisdom of the Victorian child-rearing practices, still holding sway in Bristol in the early twentieth century, held that praise as well as hugs and kisses were somehow corrupting and would result in a "spoiled" child.

The Leaches had to show their love for their son indirectly. He was given middle-class niceties like piano lessons. He was taught the behavior that would allow him to make his way in the world. Archie Leach was taught to "speak only when spoken to," that his father was "not made of a mint of money," and that "money doesn't grow on trees." He was taught to clean his shoes before entering the house, to hang up his school coat and cap as soon as he got home, and to take proper care of his clothes because, as Elsie put it, "they're not made of iron."

There were other lessons in the same vein that Archie had to master if he were to grow up to be the fine gentleman that his mother wanted him to be. He learned to "polish my shoes, to raise my cap politely and automatically to adults of both sexes, to pick up my feet, to resist wiping a perspiring brow or a running nose on my coat sleeve, according to seasonal necessity; to pretend delight while my father sang one of his party songs, "I Dreamt I Dwelt in Marble Halls."

On other occasions, in his untrained baritone, Elias sang "The Man Who Broke the Bank at Monte Carlo," trying to mimic the style of whoever was the currently popular music hall singer. By this time, having whipped the garden into shape, Elias started cultivating a small growth of whiskers above his upper lip that had blossomed into a luxurious cavalier's mustache. Archie would watch, rapt, as his father drank cup after cup of steaming tea without ever getting so much as a drop on his stylish mustache. How on earth did he do it? At noon on Saturdays, Archie ran up the road to meet his father coming home from work. The game was that Archie had to pretend that he didn't know his father had stashed a few pieces of hard candy in his pockets. So Archie, bursting with eagerness, would quietly walk along hand in hand with his father for several minutes. Then Elias would smile and let the boy search his pockets for the treat he'd brought.

* * * * * *

Archie continued to be flustered by the presence of his female classmates, but he made up for lack of courage with girls by the ferocity with which he threw himself into the boys' playground games. When the other boys asked him to play goalkeeper on the football team, Archie's delight knew no bounds. English football is similar to soccer: a ball kicked through the goalposts is a score. The goalkeeper guards the goalposts and deflects (if he can) the ball so the other team won't score. Archie's school did not have goalposts on the playing field, just chalk lines crudely marked on jagged stone fences at either end of the playground. After several weeks of crashing into those stone walls in his attempts to keep the opposing team from scoring, Archie began to entertain the slight suspicion that being goalkeeper wasn't quite the honor he'd thought it was in the beginning.

But he kept at it. The bloody knuckles, the scraped knees, and the torn clothes were as nothing to the cheers and applause of his teammates when, leaping through the air like a dancer, he made a difficult save. Archie Leach had learned that much loneliness can be assuaged by praise and applause.

Perhaps that was his motivation when he talked his parents into letting him have a party, so that he could show all the other neighborhood children the magic lantern he'd got for Christmas. The lantern was complete with shiny breastplate, gold braid, officer's epaulets, and tin sword. Except for the splendid hussar's costume he'd received the year before, this was the best present he'd ever had. A "magic lantern" was a simple slide projector using a candle as the source of light. Elias hung a sheet against the wall of a spare room for use as a screen and then ran the show while Archie, who had decided in which order the comic slides should be seen, tried to give a running commentary that he intended to be memorable for its high level of hilarity. Unfortunately most of Archie's guests believed themselves to be every bit as funny as he was, and Archie couldn't be sure that the laughs he was getting were really his.

It was shortly after the famous magic lantern party that Elias Leach came home one night with the news that he had been offered a higher-paying job at a factory in Southampton that was making soldiers' uniforms. World War I was still over a year away, but war industries all over Europe were gearing up. Everybody knew it was just a matter of time. Elias felt he had to take the job. It paid considerably more than he was making at the Bristol factory, and maybe the extra money would improve his marriage. It also appears that when Elias took the job in Southampton, while his wife and son stayed behind in Bristol, it was a kind of trial separation. By this time there was very little communication between Elias and Elsie. Perhaps some distance between them would ease things a bit. Then, if the new job worked out, they could join him later.

Elias' fellow workers at the Bristol factory gave him an engraved pocket watch as a going-away present. Shortly after Elias left, Archie and his mother moved into a larger house. The increased rent was made possible by the room and board fees paid by two of Archie's cousins, young women who had just gone to work as secretaries in a Bristol shipping firm.

As soon as summer vacation began, Elsie put her son on the train to Southampton to visit his father. Archie thought his father seemed gayer and happier then when he'd left Bristol. Still the new arrangement lasted only a few months. Even with the increase in his father's wages, there wasn't enough money to support two households. Elias came back to Bristol and his old job. The family moved again, to a less expensive house. There were enough rooms in the new house to accommodate the paying cousins.

One of the cousins had a brief fling with an elegant young man who passed himself off as a titled Italian count. (Or were they just trying to tease young Archie?) Title or no the young man possessed a motorcar, a marvelous device that was still pretty much a rarity in Bristol—at least among people you were likely to know. It was in this vehicle that Archie Leach got his first automobile ride. And he dearly loved it.

The car was long and open, for "touring." Archie sat up on the back seat like a visiting monarch and begged his cousin to drive through the section of town where he would most likely be seen by the other boys in school.

Archie was definitely blossoming. That same year, at the age of nine, he fell hopelessly in love for the very first time. The young lady, daughter of the local butcher, was pretty, just a bit on the chubby side, and very flirtacious. When you are nine years old, love affairs are conducted with an entirely different set of conventions than grown-ups use. You let it be known that you "like" a certain boy or girl. You think about your beloved a great deal. You go out of your way to sit next to this person in school assemblies. But to actually talk to your loved one? Good heavens, it would be unheard of. The primary source of pleasure in the relationship is simply to be in relatively close proximity to your beloved. Or to get him or her to notice you. Or to be able to look at him when you ordinarily would not have a chance to.

Whenever Archie Leach's mother asked him to run an errand for her, he would always make sure that it took him by his beloved's house. Ah, if he could just catch a glimpse of her vivacious presence, then all the extra blocks he had trotted out of his way in order to see her would be well worthwhile. And sure enough, luck was with him. There she was, playing a solitary game of jacks in her front yard. He saw her. She saw him. Neither gave the slightest indication that they were madly in love. Archie Leach walked very slowly past her house. How marvelous to be near her. Then she was out of his sight, and he couldn't stand it. He casually turned his head to keep her in view. Soon he was walking down the brick sidewalk with his body going in one direction, and his head facing in the exact opposite direction. Archie Leach's beloved, who was well aware that he was feasting his eyes on her, tossed her curls and continued picking up jacks even though her heart was pounding so hard she was afraid he'd be able to hear it. Archie walked full tilt into a metal lamppost with such force that it very nearly knocked him unconscious. Now he understood what it meant in the comic strips when the hero was belted by the bad guy and "saw stars." He staggered to the curb and sat down. Actually he sort of crumpled into a heap. When he regained his composure enough to continue with his mother's errand, he got up and continued on his way without looking back. He would never, never be able to look at her again. He was mortally embarrassed. Alas, Archie Leach's first love affair was over, nipped in the bud by an ill-placed lamppost.

Love affairs did not end with such humiliation in the movies, and maybe that is one of the reasons that Archie Leach loved them so much. Both his mother and his father occasionally took him to the movies. Every Saturday afternoon "with a shrieking turbulence of assorted children clutching small bags of sweets and licorice strands," Archie stood on line to pay his tuppence admission to the local cinema. Once inside the children sat in a kind of giggly attention while Charles Chaplin, Ford Sterling, Rosco Arbuckle, and Mack Swain cut their comedic capers across the small, flickering screen. Bronco Billy Anderson was the reigning cowboy star.

Numerous pushing, shoving, and shouting contests broke out over the relative merits of various stars. Everyone had a favorite. These Saturday afternoons at the movies—arguing, cheering, and laughing—were the only times in Archie Leach's life in which the unrestrained expression of honest emotion was allowed. No wonder he loved them so much. They were "the high point of my week."

When Archie's mother took him to the movies, they usually went to the Claire Street Cinema, the poshest moviehouse in Bristol. The management served tea while the film was being shown, along with dainty little cakes and pastries, and fancy pastry forks to eat them with. It was in the Claire Street Cinema that Archie Leach saw his first talking pictures. Actually what he saw was the usual silent film, with a separate sound recording that was supposed to be synchronized with the film, but seldom was. Even so it was a grand and amazing thing, and Archie intently watched what seemed to him to be a technological innovation almost too wonderful to believe.

Elias took him to a much less expensive moviehouse known as the Metropole. The seats were hard and the floors were bare. The ripe aroma of well-worn galoshes filled the air. The Metopole most certainly did not serve tea and pastries. Archie loved it. Elias took his son to the movies nearly every week. First they stopped at a tobacconist's shop and bought some pipe tobacco: men were allowed to smoke at the Metropole. (Ladies did not smoke at all.) Then father and son bought a small bag of apples and a little bag of peppermints. If Archie had been an especially good boy, Elias would buy him a small bar of chocolate.

What they watched so faithfully every week was the latest installment of a serial called *The Clutching Hand* which always ended with the hero or leading lady within seconds of certain death. But the next week when Archie and his father took their seats, they knew that somehow a way out would be found. And it always was.

* * * * * *

A passionately longed for day had finally arrived. Archie Leach was going to have his first pair of long trousers. And he would be able to wear them to the annual church bazaar and open-air carnival. Archie had an important responsibility at this big community event: he was going to be the official ticket-taker on the merry-go-round. And how impressive he would look in his white flannel trousers.

His mother worked on them for a week, fitting and refitting them as Archie stood patiently in her little sewing room. It never occurred to him they wouldn't be perfect. The long-anticipated day rolled around, and Archie proudly put on his long pants, luxuriating in the way they felt on his legs which had so long been encased in the traditional English schoolboy's black kneesocks. He walked with his parents to the churchgrounds and proudly took up his post at the merry-go-round.

At first he tried to ignore his burgeoning awareness that something was wrong. But in the end his steadfast refusal to face the facts disintegrated before the evidence of his own eyes. The truth was that the trousers that Elsie had so carefully made just didn't measure up. They didn't fit right, they didn't look right, and the flannel was not as nice as the material in the store-bought ready-made trousers that all the other boys were wearing. The carnival was ruined for Archie and his once-important job of ticket-taker now seemed like a prison sentence he had to serve until the bitter end.

* * * * * *

The few months that Elias had spent earlier that year in Southampton had not eased the strains in the marriage. Actually things were worse than they'd ever been. Archie, even though he was only nine years old, could observe for himself their growing unhappiness. There had been a moment when he was scarcely more than a baby when a flash of lightning had awakened him, and he had seen his parents, their arms around each other's waists, outlined in the window where they stood watching the storm. And the little boy had felt shut out and alone in the face of their affection and unity. But those days were long past. Now his father came home from work exhausted in both mind and body, went to bed right after dinner. His mother withdrew into herself more and more. Archie would have been glad to endure her scoldings and tongue-lashings if only she would seem like her old self again.

When Archie came home from school that fateful Friday afternoon, he knew instantly that some-thing was terribly, terribly wrong. The house was too quiet. There was a raw, unfinished feeling in the air. It would have been an upsetting homecoming for an adult. For a nine-year-old boy, it was terrifying, a terror that almost immediately went underground and imbedded itself in his unconscious mind. If he was to blame for his parents' alienation from each other, what could he possibly make of the fact that his mother had apparently vanished? Her clothes were gone too. His cousins told him that she had gone to the seaside for a few weeks, and he tried desperately to believe them. But he knew, in that wordless way of knowing that children have, that she had not gone to the seashore. But where had she gone? And was it his fault? If it wasn't his fault, whose fault was it? Did she just not love him anymore? Was that it? No one gave the bewildered boy any answers. That, too, was part of the Victorian morality. What you didn't talk about simply didn't exist.

The weeks went by, and Archie tried to hold up his end of the charade, all the time wondering when his mother would return. If she would just come back, he resolved that he would not ask her what had happened. Finally Archie realized that she wasn't coming back, not then, not ever. Her absense made a void in the child's life and produced a sadness of spirit that he'd never known before. No matter what he did to take his mind off his sorrow, it wouldn't go away. It was only years later that Archie Leach learned that his mother, the first love of his life, had suffered a nervous breakdown. Twenty long and lonely years would pass before he saw her again.

* * * * * *

Elias looked after his son as best he could, but he worked long hours at the clothing factory, and much of his attention was absorbed by worry over his wife's health. Even though a young physician named Sigmund Freud had begun his life's work in Vienna, his discoveries about the causes and cures of mental and emotional illness were still confined to a small circle of continental professionals. In provincial England Elsie Leach's condition was a mystery to the medical profession, even though not many of them had the grace and humility to admit their ignorance.

Elias wanted life to go on as normally as possible and, of

course, the young women cousins were an enormous help. But as the months went by, it became apparent that trying to run the household, as well as work at his job, was more than any man could handle, especially when it became apparent that Elsie would not be coming home soon. Elias began to face the fact that she might not ever be coming home.

When his nieces moved away from Bristol, Elias knew that he couldn't manage alone and he did what his mother had been urging him to do for months: he moved Archie and himself into her house so that she could look after Archie during the long hours between school letting out, and Elias' homecoming from work.

Mrs. Leach lived in a fairly roomy house. Archie and his father had a sitting room on the first floor, with bedrooms at the rear of the second floor. Mrs. Leach had a sitting room at the rear of the first floor, with her bedroom at the front of the second floor.

Of course they shared the kitchen, but with such an arrangement of the available space, the three of them were not tripping over each other. Archie, in fact, did not see a great deal of his grandmother except for the meals they all took together on the weekend when his father was home. During the week Archie found something to eat on his own and was left pretty much to his own devices.

It was during this period that Archie began to imagine that he could never be clean enough. He began to wash himself constantly, a habit that continued far into adulthood. The usual psychiatric explanation of compulsive washing is that the person imagines himself guilty of a terrible, almost unforgivable deed and is desperately hoping that the repeated cleaning of the physical self will somehow wash away the stains he imagines are embedded in his soul. Almost certainly Archie Leach was convinced, deep down, that he was responsible for his mother's disappearance. Remember, he still did not know what had happened to her or where she was. For awhile the guilt the boy felt represented a serious hazard to his own mental health.

But the summer he was ten years old, an event occurred which proved to be a godsend to Archie Leach, even though for the rest of the world, it was the worst tragedy that had so far befallen the human race. On August 3, 1914, German troops invaded Belgium. World War I had begun. When school started in September, Archie and the other lads in his Boy Scout troop were made Junior

Air Raid Wardens and had a pass from the Home Office to prove it. Should an air raid occur, each boy was expected to don his Scout uniform and quickly run to the district assigned him, climb up the gas lamppost, and extinguish the flame by shutting off the gas valve.

Whoever planned the program had not taken the rather obvious and simple step of matching up the Scouts' home addresses with the location of the street lamps they were assigned to extinguish. Archie Leach's district, for example, lay a good twenty minute run from his grandmother's house, a period of time that gave a distinct advantage to any lurking German aircraft.

But in World War I Bristol was spared. Every night before going to sleep, Archie carefully hung his uniform on a chair by his bed, "ready to jump into it and out of the house at a moment's notice." But, mercifully the call never came, the sirens never wailed. In World War II, however, Bristol would not be so lucky.

* * * * * *

In the years after the disappearance of his mother, Archie tried very hard to conduct himself as he knew she would have wanted him to. There were two reasons for this, both of which he was *almost* aware of. If he was a good boy, maybe she'd come home and if he lived according to her precepts she did not seem quite so far away.

Paradoxically Archie Leach brought home better report cards after his mother disappeared than he had during the years she was there, prodding him to do better, checking to see if he had, indeed, done his homework correctly and neatly.

When he was twelve years old, his diligent application to his studies paid off, just as Elsie had always told him it would. He passed the examinations required to win a scholarship to Fairfield, an academically rigorous prep school near Bristol. Up till now all the schoolteachers Archie had known were women. Now, at Fairfield, all his teachers were men, and there was a different one for each subject.

Archie promptly joined the cadet corps and immensely enjoyed wearing the very grown-up looking uniforms that corpsmen were allowed to wear. He threw himself into his school work with even more enthusiasm. Winning the Fairfield scholarship had whetted his scholarly ambitions. Archie sometimes sat at his desk and thought about the scholarships he would win in the future, one of which would take him to Oxford or Cambridge, England's two great universities. But economic reality soon intervened and dashed Archie's hopes. The incidental costs at Fairfield were proving to be a major burden: the school uniform and cap, gym fees, books, and bicycle-shed fees. Archie had to seek out upperclassmen who could sell him books secondhand. He, in turn, had to take very good care of his texts so that he could resell them at the end of the term. Archie had grown up knowing what things cost. He did not need his father to tell him that if a local prep school cost so much more than they'd expected, going to university was out of the question.

Again the war provided an outlet for Archie's energies, enabling him to put his disappointment to the back of his mind. When the school year was ending, Archie applied for war work anywhere in England that he could be of service. Those were the middle years of the Great War. Boys as young as sixteen were going into the Army. And Boy Scouts like Archie, twelve to fifteen years old, were being put to work all over the country.

He was assigned work as a messenger and guide on the docks of Southampton. It was a sobering experience. When he was hardly more than a child, Archie saw thousands of young men file onto ships that would take them to the trench warfare in France.

Archie soon learned that the boys who reached France were the lucky ones. The troop ships left at night. When Archie was on gangplank duty, he issued life belts to hundreds of young men who would be dead before morning. The lumbering transport ships were easy prey for the German submarines that patrolled the English Channel. Rows of bare sheds lined the Southampton docks and the men sat on the ground while waiting for their ships to be called. Some of them were not only making their second trip, but were returning after having already sustained serious wounds in the trenches. Archie remembers one Guardsman who had lost an arm and part of a leg in two previous combat sesions. And here he was on crutches, trying to manage his kit with one hand, and trying to rejoin his mates at the front.

The Scouts ran errands for the waiting soldiers who weren't allowed to leave the dock area. It was part of the spontaneous code of honor that had grown up among the Scouts that, under no circumstances, did you accept money for these small favors. But the grateful Tommies would sometimes press a regimental badge or button on the boys. These trinkets, of course, soon became treasured status symbols and were proudly displayed on the belts of their Scout uniforms.

It was a summer that contained tragedy, excitement, and adventure in a very concentrated dose. Back at school Archie was restless and bored. He had been infected with wanderlust, and suddenly Bristol seemed like a cage that he very much wanted to break out of. But how?

He began hanging around the Bristol docks, a drab area of the city that had never interested him before. Now he saw the seagoing schooners and steamships in a different light. These ships could take him, he knew, out into the great wide world, where all sorts of wonderful and intriguing things happened all the time. On Saturdays, when the other boys were playing cricket, Archie Leach wandered around the docks for hours, watching the ships being loaded, watching them slowly move down the Avon River toward the open sea.

He had shot up like a weed during the summer in Southampton and was now considerably taller than most boys his age. One Saturday morning, almost on a whim, Archie presented himself to the captain of the finest and biggest schooner in the harbor and applied for a job as a cabin boy. He almost got it. The captain was much taken with the wide-awake and intelligent look the boy had about him. He looked to be the type you wouldn't have to follow around to make sure he did things right. Archie was sent home to get his birth certificate and his parents' permission. Alas, he could get neither: he had lied about his age (he wasn't 18 yet, only looked it), and he knew that his father would never give his permission anyway.

So he tried to find something at school that would occupy his mind and still his restlessness. Little did Archie Leach realize how very close he was to the chance meeting that would forever change his life.

* * * * * *

Chemistry was one of his favorite classes. When the weather was too bad to play outdoors, Archie would putter around the chemistry lab. He was especially interested in electricity, but the science professor was reluctant to let him experiment with the various wires, resistors, and voltmeters without adult supervision. Quite simply it was much too dangerous. The boy could have wrecked the school's electrical system, started a fire, or killed himself.

The regular chemistry professor didn't have time to oversee Archie's experiments, but in the face of Archie's eagerness to learn, a local electrician, who'd been hired as part-time assistant in the chemistry department for the express purpose of helping set up electrical experiments, offered to take him the following Saturday to visit backstage at Bristol's newly built Hippodrome Theatre. The electrician (his name is forgotten so let's call him Tom) had installed the new theatre's electrical system. Archie eagerly said that yes, he'd love to go.

The electrician and Archie arrived at the Hippodrome on the following Saturday. The matinee was in full swing when they entered the backstage doors. Suddenly a lonely and troubled boy found himself, for the first time in his life, completely and totally bewitched. Why had no one told him such a magical world existed?

"I found my inarticulate self in a dazzling land of smiling, jostling people wearing and not wearing all sorts of costumes and doing all sorts of clever things. And that's when I *knew*! What other life could there *be* but that of an actor? They happily traveled and toured. They were classless, cheerful and carefree."

Coming from a background that was classbound, morose, and anxiously careful of the smallest detail of living, Archie Leach was convinced that he had somehow, mysteriously, entered Heaven. After that incredible afternoon one thought was uppermost in Archie's mind. What did he have to do in order to take his rightful place in that wonderful backstage world? He never, not for a moment, doubted that was where he belonged. It was hard to stay in the drab, everyday world of school, homework, and sports now that he knew, beyond the shadow of a doubt, that another glittering world existed.

Several weeks later on an winter icy day that had come unusually early that year, Archie was walking, deep in his own thoughts, toward the bicycle shed. A classmate, in much more of a hurry than Archie, sideswiped him as he hurried past. Archie, taken completely off guard, fell flat on his face. The warm salty taste of blood flooded his mouth. The inside of his upper lip was badly cut. He didn't discover until minutes later that he had also broken off half of one of his front upper teeth. His heart sank. He knew this would mean another bill for his father to pay, and there were already so many bills.

A classmate came to the rescue. He told Archie about the dental school on the other side of town where they would pull out a bad tooth for free, so that the fledging dentists could practice on real people. Archie had the rest of the tooth removed. The problem now was that he had to be careful not to laugh or smile in front of his father. He pulled it off and then noticed a few weeks later that the rest of his teeth were growing together to fill up the gap that had been left when he'd lost the front tooth. Astonishing! But after the wonders he'd observed backstage at the Hippodrome, nothing, absolutely nothing, seemed impossible.

* * * * * *

Archie began to spend every available moment hanging around the Hippodrome. Some of the regulars thought he'd been given a job. But no, Archie was quite willing to work for free if they'd just let him stay.

Then Tom came through again for him. He arranged an introduction for Archie to the manager of the Empire, Bristol's other theatre. Archie Leach was officially invited to assist the men who worked the arclights from tiny, precarious platforms high up on either side of the stage. There was no pay, of course, but for Archie the glory was quite enough. One night Archie decided to leave his regular post and help out the man who ran the big center stage spot from the second balcony.

The featured attraction was "The Great David Devant," a famous and innovative magician. Many of the illusions that he invented are still being used by magicians today. The list, however, does not include the one Devant was using the night that Archie Leach was working the center spot.

He hadn't expected to be in charge of the unwieldy piece of equipment for even a moment. But the man running the big spot had asked Archie to hold it steady for a moment while he had a cigarette. The man should have known better. Lights for the magicians' acts were carefully rehearsed and for a very good and obvious reason: if people saw what was actually happening in the shadows, the illusion of "magic" would be totally destroyed. And that was bad for business.

Archie proudly took over the big light. It was heavier than he thought. He'd have to make a special effort to hold it steady. Archie was absolutely intrigued by "The Great Devant." How *did* he manage all those tricks?

Suddenly a blinding flash of light provided an answer. Archie, wrapped up in attentiveness to Devant's act rather than his task of holding the spotlight steady, had let it slowly slip downward. The light hit the mirrors hidden under the table Devant was working on, thus ruining the trick. If looks could kill, the one The Great Devant shot toward Archie Leach at that moment would have made the talented magician guilty of possessing a deadly weapon. The official operator initiated his young helper into a whole new style of cursing and yanked the light out of his hands. Archie Leach's brief career as an electrician at Bristol's Empire Theatre was over.

* * * * * *

So it was back to the Hippodrome and another appointment with destiny. Playing the theatre that week was a troupe of young knockabout comedians and acrobats known as "The Penders." Their mentor was Bob Pender, a former Drury Lane clown and a man who, years before, had been one of the biggest draws the English music halls had ever known. He was, in other words, a pro.

Archie could not believe his luck. The boys in Pender's troupe were only slightly older than himself. A few of them, actually, looked a bit younger. Backstage gossip had it that Pender was having a difficult time keeping his company together: as soon as they turned sixteen, many of the boys were going off to join the Army. He was having a hard time finding replacements.

There was no doubt in Archie's mind about what he had to do. He was only thirteen, but somehow he had to find a way to join Pender's troupe. The thought of simply presenting himself to Bob Pender never crossed Archie's mind. Nothing so precious could be gained easily. Everybody knew that.

Archie decided on an end run. He wrote a letter to Bob Pender as if he were his own father. He enclosed a snapshot and wrote several paragraphs on what a talented and hard working son he had.

The results of Archie's plan were even better than he'd hoped for. Not only did Bob Pender answer the letter with amazing promptness, he enclosed railway fare to Norwich where the troupe was then performing, so that Mr. Leach's talented son could be interviewed and auditioned.

Sleep was impossible that night. Archie packed and repacked his suitcase just to have something to do. Would morning never come? What if he finally fell asleep near dawn, overslept, and missed the train to Norwich? What if his father saw him leaving with a suitcase? He couldn't take a chance that, having come this far, his scheme could be ruined by mere chance. It just wouldn't be fair. So in the middle of the night, Archie tiptoed down the stairs and carefully let himself out of the house where his grandmother and father lay sleeping, unaware of the boy's hopes, dreams, fears, and needs.

Walking through Bristol's deserted streets at 3:00 A.M, Archie Leach was profoundly impressed with his own daring. All his life he had been taught that it was necessary to do what other people (always grown-ups) told you to do. And now here he was, thirteen years old, doing exactly what he wanted to do. It was a nice feeling. Scary, but very, very nice.

The train to Norwich pulled in at 6:00 A.M. Four hours later Archie was asking directions from the Norwich stationmaster to the theatre where "The Penders" were playing. When he arrived backstage Bob Pender was putting his boys through their daily workout.

Pender's wife, Margaret, a former dancer and ballet mistress for Paris' Folies Bergere, took Archie in tow until the gymnastic session was over. Then the two of them sat their new prospect down for a bit of a chat. Could they see his birth certificate? No: unfortunately, he'd left it at home. Did he have any experience as a performer? Well, no. Surely a bit of training in acrobatics? Afraid not, but eager to learn. And willing to work very, very hard, if he were apprenticed to the troupe.

They bought it. Right on the spot Bob Pender wrote out in longhand, a brief contract which said that, in return for his services as a performer in "The Penders," Archie Leach would receive his room, board, and ten shillings a week. On paper Archie Leach was an actor. Now all he had to do was learn how to be one on a stage.

Margaret Pender, whom Archie Leach always remembered as a kind and generous woman, got Archie settled into the same boarding house where she and Bob were staying. If it wasn't possible for the entire troupe to stay in the same house, the Penders always made sure that the younger and more inexperienced members of the troupe stayed with them.

The next morning, on a bare, splinter-ridden stage in a cold provincial theatre, Archie Leach began to study tumbling, acrobatic dances, and the various bits of business that music hall performers had to master. Archie was starting from the very bottom.

Those first days were painful. Compared to the other boys in the troupe, Archie felt clumsy and inept. But after about a week Archie knew that, while he was still a long way from being good enough for an audience, he had shown substantial improvement. He was learning quickly, just like he had promised Bob Pender he would, and Archie knew that it wouldn't be long before he, too, would be in front of the footlights.

But Elias Leach, unable to take time off from work to search for his missing son, had been spending every spare moment talking to Archie's teachers and classmates, hoping to find a lead as to where he'd gone. Finally he was introduced to Tom, the electician, who told him about Archie's fascination with backstage life, and one of the stagehands at the Hippodrome told him that he'd overheard Archie ask the theatre manager several weeks ago for the address of Bob Pender and his troupe of teenage acrobats.

It all fell into place. The theatre manager checked his schedules (he had them for most of England's major acts), and told Elias that the following weekend, "The Penders" would be performing in Ipswich.

When the Ipswich stage-door keeper told Archie during the Saturday matinee that his father was waiting in the alley, Archie tried to tell himself that, after all, his father had been bound to find him sooner or later. No point in further struggle. The jig was up. The game was over. Back to reality.

But as he walked to the stage-door, he wildly cast about in his head, trying to come up with the words that might, just might, convince his father that this is where he belonged. Fate, which had been dealing Archie Leach aces for some time now, dealt him another.

Before either Archie or his father had had time to utter any hasty or foolish words they'd later regret, along came Bob Pender. Stocky, jovial, likable Bob Pender. He had a Masonic emblem dangling from his watch chain, just as Elias Leach had a Masonic emblem dangling from *his* watch chain. This meant they were brothers. If Elias Leach had been entertaining any ill will toward the man for whom his son had run away from home, it immediately vanished.

While Archie sat on the back steps of the theatre wondering what was going on, his father and Bob Pender retired to a nearby pub to discuss Archie's future. After a few ales they decided that Archie should finish his basic education. That would take another two years. Then he could rejoin "The Penders" as a full-fledged, legitimate member.

Archie and his father returned to Bristol on the next day. On Monday, Archie Leach, now a bonafide adventurer, rebel, and daredevil, was back with his classmates at Fairfield. Archie saw no need to tell them that he hadn't actually been on stage yet. Whenever he got a chance, he demonstrated his complete repertoire of new skills: cartwheels, handsprings, nip-ups, and spot-rolls.

Then Archie discovered that, without new material, you lose your audience. After they'd seen his antics a number of times, his classmates were no longer impressed. He had to think of something different.

In singing class one day Archie was mouthing, in a very exaggerated and comic manner, an especially popular art song of the day, "Who Is Sylvia, What Is She?" It is a song with sentiments guaranteed to cause uneasiness, hence mirth, among teenage boys. Archie threw himself into his self-appointed role of singing comedian, or rather, non-singing comedian. For, in spite of all his emoting, not a sound emerged from his wide-open mouth. Still he was a hit. The titters of an appreciative audience were spreading throughout the ranks of the boys lined up on risers for their daily instruction in the fine art of song.

Suddenly something whizzed through the air inches from Archie's face. The teacher had thrown a bunch of keys at his unorthodox competition. Had this exasperated man's aim been more accurate, Archie Leach might well have lost his remaining front tooth that day.

After the brief taste he'd had in life on the road with "The Penders," Archie was incapable of settling down to his life as a schoolboy again. He wondered how he'd ever endured it at all. He wasn't really trying to be difficult, and he certainly didn't want to cause trouble for his father or anyone else. But why couldn't they understand that he had found his real life, and it wasn't in Bristol?

Every morning he set off for school, determined to sit quietly in class and pay attention. After all, two years wasn't forever. It wasn't as if his hopes had been completely cut off. But the closer he got to school, the faster his fine resolves faded. He cut more classes than he attended. The only sessions Archie could be counted on to attend were in physical education and gymnastics. He knew he had to stay in shape for the physically rigorous standards the Pender boys had to live up to.

One day Archie and another boy were cutting class together. Suddenly, they had a brilliant idea. Why not sneak over to the girls' side of the school and see for themselves what the girls' lavatories really looked like? They both agreed it was a truly splendid idea. Such an expedition might turn up secrets hidden for millenia by those elusive and crafty creatures known as girls. They set off.

Once in the corridor that held the mysterious chamber, Archie stood guard while his pal investigated its inner sanctums. Then it was his turn. Unfortunately, before he could get his bearings, a no-nonsense woman teacher grabbed him by the scruff of the neck and not only refused to turn him loose, but headed straight for the headmaster's office. Archie knew he was in bad, bad trouble. He'd been in Mr. Smith's office far too much in recent weeks. God only knew what his punishment would be this time.

The next morning he found out. Headmaster Augustus Smith was waiting when all the boys and girls had gathered in the assembly auditorium for morning prayers. Before they began he called out Archie's name and asked him to come to the stage. Once there he heard Headmaster Smith give an obviously well-prepared little speech in which he used words like "inattentive, irresponsible, incorrigible, and a discredit to the school."

It is not clear whether this was the usual method for expelling children from Fairfield, but it most assuredly was the method used for drumming Archie Leach out of the schoolboy regiment. And even though he didn't want to be at Fairfield anymore, it was an almost unbearably humiliating way to have to leave.

Archie was blinded by tears as he stiffly walked past the assembled students and went to collect his books and get his bike. He heard the sound of the rousing march that was traditionally played each morning when the boys and girls left the hall and hurried to their first classes. Being appointed piano-player for the day was a coveted reward for good grades or other scholastic achievement.

As he slowly pedaled away from the school that he had worked and studied so hard to be admitted to, he remembered that he had been named piano-player on several occasions himself. Now it seemed a long time ago.

* * * * * *

Elias Leach knew it was useless to find another school for his wayward son. He was fourteen now and could legally quit school. It was obvious that Archie's heart wasn't in his studies anymore. All he could think about was getting back to Bob Pender and living the life of a music hall gypsy.

Elias did not try to stop him this time. Three days after his expulsion from Fairfax, Archie Leach was back on a train, speeding toward his old troupe.

His real life had finally begun.

* * * * * *

Archie threw himself into learning the skills and techniques that the Pender boys were famous for: acrobatics, dancing, stilt-walking, tumbling, and pantomime. There were no lines to be learned. "The Penders" had to get their meaning across using non-verbal methods only, forcing the boys to learn two of the most important elements of stagecraft: timing and the art of physical gesture.

The boys had their morning work out whether they were touring the provinces or back at their home base in London. But wherever they were, there were hardly enough hours in the day for Archie to study all the things he wanted to learn about the theatre which, quite simply, was everything.

When he wasn't onstage himself, he watched the other acts from the wings, immersing himself in the methods used by other headliners. These long hours, spent observing virtually every music hall act then working in England, instilled in Archie Leach a deep respect for "the diligence and application and long experience it took to acquire such expert timing and unaffected confidence, the amount of effort that resulted in such effortlessness."

After he had acquired mastery of the basic physical skills required of all the boys in the troupe and actually had a small part in the show, Archie worked very hard to make everything he did onstage appear easy and relaxed. He wanted, of course, to acquire that same effortlessness he'd been observing in the headliners: the men and women who were known and loved all over the United Kingdom. His efforts to project effortlessness were so successful that sometimes he even began to relax a bit, in fact, as well as in appearance. When those blessed moments occurred Archie discovered, much to his delight, that he was actually enjoying himself on the stage in front of all those people. To think that he was getting paid for having such a good time!

* * * * * *

Shortly after Archie had made it into the act, he was initiated by several of the oldest boys into the fine art of theatrical makeup. They very carefully sat him down in the dressing room away from the mirrors and proceeded to demonstrate the wonders of greasepaint. One boy made up another so that Archie could see exactly how it was done. At the same time another boy put the same makeup (he said) on Archie. He was told to watch the other two boys *very* carefully so that he'd know how to do it once he was onstage himself.

When the makeup lesson was over, the other three boys said that Archie looked better in his stage makeup than just about anybody they'd ever seen. They sent him ahead to the neighborhood pub where they were all planning to have fish and chips so everyone could admire him.

"We'll be along in two shakes," the ringleader said. "You go ahead and save us a booth before the crowd hits."

Archie, resplendent and ridiculous with his bright blue nose, green eye sockets, and white mouth, would have done just that had he not been rescued by Don Barclay, an American performer fresh from the Ziegfeld Follies, who was trying out his act in the provinces before taking it to London.

Barclay took Archie to his own dressing room, cleaned off the absurd clown's face and advised Archie to saunter into the pub as if nothing untoward had happened.

"Yes, sir," Archie said.

"Just call me Don," Barclay offered.

"Yes, sir, Don," Archie said politely.

Barclay and young Archie Leach were on the same bill for two months and got to know each other quite well. Barclay took the boy under his wing, and Archie was glad to be singled out and given attention and interest from a man who was old enough to be a father figure. Bob Pender, after all, had twelve surrogate sons to look out for. The time he could spend on any single individual was necessarily limited.

* * * * * *

When "The Penders" were on tour, the local boardinghouses usually couldn't put up the entire troupe together. They'd be spread at several houses near the theatre, with the younger boys staying with Bob and Margaret Pender. In London, however, the entire troupe stayed together in the Penders' suburban home in Brixton. The boys lived dormitory style, and Archie had more adult supervision in his life now than he'd had when he was still at home. On nights when they weren't performing in London's Gulliver circuit of vaudeville houses, the boys had to have their lights out by 10:00 P.M.

They had to be washed, dressed, and downstairs for breakfast at 7:30 A.M. They had an hour to chat or read while their bacon, eggs, toast, and jam settled a bit, and then they began a long and grueling day of gymnastics, acrobatics, and working up new routines. When they were working, they played two shows a day, six days a week. Archie thrived on it.

His day of glory finally arrived. They were going to play Bristol's Empire Theatre, where Archie Leach had disgraced himself by ruining "The Great Devant's" act with a careless spotlight. The audience would surely be most of the boys and girls of Fairfield. He could hardly believe that only three months had passed since that humiliating day he'd been booted out of school. It seemed so long ago. Best of all it now seemed so unimportant.

Archie, after only three months, did not yet have a big part in the act, and he had not yet completely mastered the most difficult parts of the acrobatic and tumbling routines. But he didn't let that dampen his triumphal homecoming.

"I excitedly threw myself into a performance that made up in exuberance what it lacked in experience."

Fellow Masons Bob Pender and Elias Leach got re-acquainted at a Bristol pub, and Pender told Elias that Archie was coming along just fine. After the show Archie stayed at home instead of in the boardinghouse with the other boys. He remembers walking home through the quiet summer streets with his father and sensing how much pride and pleasure Elias took in his son's new life.

* * * * * *

English music halls were packed all through the Great War. People desperately needed relief from the grim reality of war and the often tragic news from the front. Frequently there were soldiers home on leave in the audience. Archie remembered the solemn young faces that he had seen boarding the troop ships at Southampton. He threw his whole soul and spirit into giving the kind of performance that would make them laugh and take their minds off what they'd seen in the trenches.

One night he succeeded beyond his wildest dreams. It was a skit called "The Spirit of the Theatre." Archie's role was to come leaping out of a trapdoor that was located just behind the footlights. He had managed about a third of a leap when the trapdoor sprang shut, pinning him inside from the chest down. In traditional show business tradition, the skit continued while Archie desperately tried to extricate himself from the immovable trapdoor. All the audience could see, however, was the panicky expression on his face and his wildly gyrating head just above the footlights. The theatre shook with laughter. Archie got far more laughs than he would have if the skit had played without incident.

* * * * * *

World War I finally ended on November 11, 1918, after nearly four and a half years of unbelievable butchery and killing. "The Penders" were playing a little town called Preston in Lancashire that night, and the theatre was virtually deserted.

After the show Archie and several of the other boys walked to the town square. The streets were full of people, but they were quiet and subdued. There was a strange lack of gaiety—possibly because Preston was such a small town that it was difficult to find a family that had not suffered the loss of a husband, brother, or son in this war that had been supposed to end all wars forever.

* * * * * *

By the time the fighting ended, Archie was making one pound a week. This was long before the erosion of the pound which was then worth nearly five dollars and in those pre-inflationary times was worth considerably more in purchasing power than it is today.

One morning before their limbering-up exercises, Bob Pender made an announcement. Rumors of a possible American tour had been circulating throughout the company for months. Ever since the war ended, Pender had been trying, without success, to set up an American tour. Maybe he had finally succeeded.

Indeed he had. Pender had managed to sell the show via press clippings and word-of-mouth to Broadway producer Charles Dillingham who planned to use them in a show starring Fred Stone, a onetime vaudeville headliner who had made the big leap to musical comedy on Broadway.

But there was bad news too. Pender told them he had only been able to get a contract and boat passage for eight boys. Twelve young men listened to this announcement with pounding hearts. Four of them would be staying behind. But which four?

They would not know for six weeks. Pender said he wanted to re-evaluate each member of the troupe, so that he could make as fair a decision as possible. After all careers and lives were at stake, and Bob Pender knew that. But the next six weeks were a tense and anxious time for "The Penders."

Every boy in the troupe worked extra hard, and Archie Leach was no different. He'd been playing two shows a day for nearly two years. But now he pushed himself even harder. When he wasn't performing, he was rehearsing, often by himself in a deserted theatre. He had worked his way up to a couple of featured spots in the show, and he now wanted them to be better than perfect.

They were. Archie Leach (who ever doubted it?) was one of the eight Penders who boarded the White Star Line's S.S. Olympic at Southampton on a bright July morning in 1920. As the big ship pulled away from England's lushly green summer shores, Archie Leach must have marveled at the sheer length and diversity of the long, long trip he had initiated—was it only two years ago?—when he had forged that letter to Bob Pender.

He had no way of knowing that the most crucial phase of his life's itinerary was just beginning.

The USA: the Vaudeville Circuit and Broadway's Great White Way

ARCHIE LEACH DID NOT YET KNOW what his trip to America held in store for him, but there was a remarkable omen of his future on board if only he had known how to read it. Shipboard gossip had it that none other than the fabled Douglas Fairbanks, Sr. and his new bride, Mary Pickford, were on board. Indeed they were returning to the states from their European honeymoon.

The next morning Bob Pender was putting the boys through their limbering-up exercises on the upper deck, when Archie Leach saw the great acrobat himself approaching. Fairbanks and Pickford kept to their staterooms more than the other passengers, primarily because every time they appeared on deck, they were immediately surrounded by dozens of adoring fans.

Fairbanks introduced himself to an awestruck Bob Pender, said that he had seen the troupe perform, and could he join them for their morning workout?

Close-up, Fairbanks was even more magnificent than he had seemed in all those Saturday afternoon matinees that Archie had attended so religiously as a child.

At thirty-seven, with his dazzling smile, deeply tanned, and as agile as a boy, Doug Fairbanks was at the peak of his physical prowess and soon proved it to a delighted throng of his fellow shipmates, as he tumbled about with "The Penders" in their morning work-out.

Later in the 5½ day trip, Archie had his picture taken with his idol during a game of shuffleboard. It seemed so unlikely that he, Archie Leach, should be standing next to this incredible actor and athlete, "this affable, gentle man, warmed by success and well-being," that he had to blink back tears. While the photographer adjusted his camera and Fairbanks stood patiently waiting to get back to his game, Archie, in a soft voice that no one else could hear, "tried with shy, inadequate words to tell him of my adulation."

* * * * * *

The day the Penders stood at the Olympic's rail as the big ship moved majestically up the Hudson to the forty-sixth Street pier was quite possibly the longest and most fantastic day in their lives. At least it seemed that way to Archie Leach.

First there was the Statue of Liberty and the glorious New York skyline. He had seen these twin symbols of the American dream often enough in photographs and in the movies, but seeing them with his own eyes was far more moving. London is a lovely city, but it is built on a marsh: skyscrapers are geologically impossible. As London's orderly squares speak of civility and grace, so the spires of Manhattan speak of energy, hustle, and a certain irrepressible brashness that won't take "no" for an answer. These qualities also existed to a high degree in Archie Leach. Up until now these traits in him had found expression only in his life as a music hall entertainer. He had never before responded emotionally to a physical landscape as if it were a kindred spirit. Now he did.

After the confusion of disembarkation and the by-no-means perfunctory searches of Customs, Bob Pender finally located, in the swirl of passengers, porters, and mountains of baggage, the man that Charles Dillingham had sent to meet them.

The troupe was taken directly to the Globe Theatre on Broadway, just north of forty-second Street. They were introduced, en masse, to the great Fred Stone and watched from a distance as

Stone, Bob Pender, and Dillingham held a lengthy conference in the middle of the Globe stage.

Finally Archie and the rest of the boys learned there'd been a change in plans. Dillingham wanted to use them in a huge variety show he was staging at the Hippodrome, then reputed to be the world's largest theatre. Everyone groaned, hoisted his luggage yet again, and headed for the Hippodrome on Sixth Avenue between forty-second and forty-third Streets. It is one thing to have heard that a theatre is "the world's largest." It is quite another to actually see a revolving stage that is one city block wide and a half-block deep. Like the English music halls the Hippodrome played two shows a day: a matinee and an evening performance. Every week more than ten thousand people lined up at the box office for tickets.

For these faithful patrons Dillingham was putting together a show unlike anything New York had seen before. Part vaudeville, part circus, the ambitious and unwieldy project boasted a cast of nearly a thousand people, including one hundred singers and an eighty-member ballet corps. Backing up this unheard of number of performers was an equally unheard of number of stagehands, electricians, and other non-performers. In addition to the human personnel were a wide variety of animals: horses, chimpanzees, a couple of giraffes, a few zebras, lions, tigers, and a pair of performing mules. Oh yes, and the inevitable dog act.

Pender and his lads stared in disbelief at the backstage chaos. Pender's heart sank. He was responsible for these boys. He had brought them far from home, and he did not see how the confusion that he was looking at could ever be made stageworthy by opening night. It was impossible. The show was bound to fail. Then what would he do? Would Dillingham put them back into Fred Stone's show? If he didn't, would they be able to find at least a few month's work? Enough to pay their passage back to England?

Well he would have to think about all that later. Now he and the boys had to look over the barnlike dressing room they shared with four other acts. Then, in the best show business tradition, they had to hurry up and wait for Dillingham to reappear again. He wanted to see their act.

Finally, after a dinner of corned beef on rye sandwiches and Kosher dill pickles, another first for the Pender troupe, Dillingham appeared and the boys went through their best bits.

When Dillingham signaled that he'd seen enough, the eight exhausted Penders flopped on the stage where they stood while Bob Pender spoke with Dillingham, sitting in the tenth row. The boys were beyond caring what the verdict was.

The verdict was that they had a great act, they should get a good night's sleep, he would see them tomorrow at 10:00 A.M, at which time they should be ready to do a complete run-through of the material. Nobody had enough energy left to groan. Bob Pender herded his little band of theatrical gypsies past a juggling act, a tumbling act, and a magician. The newcomers spilled onto Forty-third Street. Pender could only hope there'd been no mix-up with the rooms he'd rented.

He took four boys in one taxi, and Margaret took Archie and the remaining three boys in another taxi that was told to follow the first one. Their rooms were on Eighth Avenue, about three blocks from the Hippodrome, and everything, thank God, was in order. Bob and Margaret had a small studio apartment of their own and, across the hall, Archie and his fellow troupers settled into what was then called a Pullman apartment. Each room led into the next like the cars in a train. The boy in the end car turned out to be Archie Leach, who had to walk through everyone's car in order to go to the bathroom. Happily, however, this also meant no one had to walk through his room.

Margaret and Bob Pender said goodnight to their charges, and everyone gratefully fell into bed. This one day had seemed so long. Could it really have been just this morning, Archie thought, that they had steamed up the Hudson? It seemed like something that had happened months ago. He wondered if every day in America would be like this. Archie yawned and prepared to drift off into much needed sleep. Then the noise began. Or rather, he was suddenly aware of the noise that had apparently been there all the time. There was the traffic on Eighth Avenue. There were the periodic rumblings of the elevated trains on Ninth Avenue. There were sirens and ringing bells from the police station just around the corner. Was it like this all the time? Poor Mrs. Pender, she had looked so tired in the taxi. Would she be able to sleep? Would he, Archie Leach, be able to sleep?

The next thing he knew the sun was streaming in the windows, and Bob Pender was making his way through the apartment rousting everyone out of bed. Archie had learned that if you are tired enough, you can sleep anywhere.

Bob and Margaret made breakfast for everyone that morning. While they all enjoyed their morning tea, they went over a work schedule they had devised. The boys would take turns with cooking, cleaning, and shopping. While on camping trips with his Bristol Boy Scout troop, Archie had learned how to make stew. So when his weekly turn at the stove came around, there were no surprises. Everyone knew he'd get stew.

Much to Bob Pender's relief and surprise, Dillingham got his extravaganza in working order by the August 9 opening. This was the first theatre Pender had ever seen in which you had to punch a time clock, but he could see the sense in it. How else could you keep track of eighteen hundred people, all of whom were responsible for different aspects of the total production? An hour before the curtain was due to rise, you could tell at a glance if anyone was missing. If he was still missing thirty minutes later, you could arrange for replacements.

Best of all Dillingham's fast-paced, lively production was a solid hit. Within a few weeks after it opened, *Good Times* was sold out for months.

Archie's life settled into its usual pattern of hard work. His only free days were Sundays. Mostly, he spent them alone, walking through the streets of New York, immersing himself in that unique sense of unlimited possibility that Manhattan so often manages to impart to fledging actors, writers, and artists. There were double-deck open-air buses on Fifth Avenue then. Archie loved to board the bus at Washington Square, grandly ride up Fifth to Seventy-second Street and then down Riverside Drive. He took buses to the Bronx Zoo and to Coney Island, which, like everything else in America, was bigger and grander than its counterpart in England.

Archie Leach had always been a hearty eater and Coney Island was an ethnic feast. Every contributor to America's melting pot culture was represented at the Coney Island food stands. With his week's pay in his pocket, Archie could wander through the crowds and choose between hot dogs with tart, bright yellow mustard, thick hamburgers with "the works," pizza, egg rolls, blintzes, stuffed cabbage, halavah, knishes, bagels, fried chicken, corn on the cob, and, of course, the ubiquitous popcorn, peanuts, pretzels, and salt water taffy. But what he liked best about American food was ice cream. On Sundays Archie often had an ice cream soda for breakfast. Yes, breakfast. His lunch would be a couple of ice cream cones. And dinner would be one (or two) huge banana split, a delicacy that had not yet reached English shores.

* * * * * *

The weeks sped by in a comforting blur of work and camaraderie with the other Penders. They performed two shows a day and somehow fitted in all the big and small chores needed to keep their dormitory-apartment in working order. Archie, along with the other boys, washed his clothes in the big kitchen tub, learned to mend rips and tears, and to replace missing buttons. He learned to iron his shirts and press his trousers. Necessity was providing a complete home economics course for "The Penders."

After each evening's performance they explored the theatre district looking for good cheap restaurants. They'd find one, gather there for supper after the show for a week or two, and then, tiring of the new place, move on in search of another. Adolescent boys, even those who are performing in two shows a day, have to keep moving, or they just might explode from their own excess energy.

Archie Leach was still painfully shy around girls. During the years when most boys are getting to know girls in school or in their own neighborhoods, Archie was living a kind of monastic life on the road. The only woman he saw regularly was Margaret Pender who was a surrogate mother. The only girls he saw were in the audience. He was beginning to wonder if this bleak state of affairs would ever change.

Then he saw her. Gladys Kincaid was a member of the Hippodrome corps de ballet. She was a pretty, blue-eyed blonde, more generously endowed with bosom than dancers usually are and a year or two older than Archie Leach, who began to spend most of his backstage time trying to get a glimpse of the sprightly little dancer.

She knew Archie was watching her, and there were occasional shy smiles of encouragement. Archie knew she was watching when he performed and felt inspired to heroic efforts by her attention. Unfortunately neither of these otherwise talented youngsters knew how to make the first move.

As Christmas approached Archie was out of bed hours earlier than everyone else so that he could find a Christmas present for his beloved. Finally, after much trekking from store to store and much indecision, Archie found the perfect gift at Macy's: a multicolored coat, sweater, and scarf set. Gladys Kincaid must have been very surprised to get such a grand gift from a young man who hadn't even spoken to her yet, but at least now there was absolutely no mistaking his eventual intentions.

And who knows? If the show had run long enough, Archie's shyness with girls in general, and with Miss Kincaid in particular, might have been vanquished. Alas, *Good Times* did not run long enough for that hurdle to be overcome.

On the last night of the show, often a tearful emotional evening for cast members, Archie Leach was more despondent than most. He lurked about the time clock, hoping to give and get one last tender look. His troupe mates were already outside the stage door waiting for him, frequently sticking their heads inside the door to yell for Archie to get a move on.

Still he lingered. Finally his patience was rewarded. There she was. Gladys Kincaid and Archie hesitantly smiled at each other yet again. Archie's knees threatened to give way. He still didn't know what to say. Apparently neither did Gladys. Then they both spoke at once, "I hope I see you again." And it was over. She left for home, and Archie was left with a vast irritation at his shyness. He was nearly eighteen now. He could afford to buy his girl a nice Christmas present, and he hadn't even held her hand.

* * * * * *

In the show's closing weeks Bob Pender had received an offer from a booking agent of the B.F. Keith vaudeville circuit. Many of the other acts in the Hippodrome show did not find work for months, but the Sunday after the show closed, "The Penders" left for Philadelphia where they began a six-month tour of the famous Keith circuit, the most prestigious string of theatres in the entertainment world.

The tour took them to Chicago, Cleveland, Boston, and other big Eastern cities. Bob and Margaret Pender and their little band of well-behaved young men were much in demand socially during the tour. It was in the Twenties that both entertainers and sports figures became acceptable, even desirable, at fashionable dinner tables and other important local events, a development that not only stretched the Penders' food budget, but exposed the boys to a strata of American life they would not otherwise have seen. They might not have been in school, but they were definitely getting an education.

At the Keith Theatre in Washington, Archie Leach, the rest of the Pender troupe, and the Foy family, who were headlining the show, were presented to former President Woodrow Wilson. In ill health ever since he had collapsed in September, 1919 during his nationwide campaign to win public support for the League of Nations, Wilson watched the show from a back row seat. After the final curtain, aides pushed his wheelchair into the stage door alley where "The Penders" and the Foys were lined up to meet him. They all filed by, shook his hand, and listened with delight as their performances were warmly praised by a former president of the United States. It was a proud moment for everyone. Archie Leach was particularly struck by "the smiling simplicity of this kind man."

Archie also got an object lesson in the trials and tribulations of celebrityhood in Atlantic City. It was Sunday, and Archie had found a deserted strip of beach where he was basking in the sun and listening, with a noticeably pleasant lack of interruptions, to the sound of the waves pounding the shore and the occasional raucous cries of the big, white seagulls that looped and sailed overhead. Suddenly, he sensed he was not alone. Heading for the ocean and a swim was a powerfully built man in a green bathing suit. Archie was fascinated by the way the man's shoulder muscles literally rippled as he strode, arms swinging, toward the water. When the man glanced back at the boardwalk, Archie saw that it was none other than the great boxer, Jack Dempsey.

Archie watched, amazed, as dozens of screaming, shouting fans materialized out of nowhere, quickly surrounding Dempsey who had obviously wanted nothing but a quiet, relaxing swim and a few hours of solitude. Instead he was forced to spend his time shaking hands and signing autographs.

When the tour was almost over, Archie Leach ran into a good bit of trouble himself. "The Penders" were playing Rochester that week, and for several days Archie hadn't been feeling well. He had a slight fever and strange aches and pains throughout his body which was usually in tip-top shape.

Finally, when Archie couldn't shake it off, Bob Pender called in a doctor. The diagnosis was not a cheerful one: Archie was suffering from rheumatic fever and had to spend six weeks in bed. If he didn't follow this regimen, he could very likely end up with permanent damage to his heart.

Spirits were very low in the Pender troupe that night. Not only was Archie Leach an invaluable and irreplaceable part of the act, he was also a member of what had virtually become a family in the nearly two years they'd spent in America. Still, for both professional and financial reasons, the show had to go on.

Bob Pender redesigned the show and paid six weeks advance room and board to the woman who ran the boardinghouse where they'd all been staying. Bob and Margaret, who felt they were leaving their own son behind, told Archie to follow the doctor's orders exactly so that he'd be able to rejoin them in time for their stint at the Palace, the Times Square flagship theatre in the Keith Circuit and the goal of every vaudeville performer in the country.

The long recuperation began. Archie's only visitor was Jean Adair, a veteran showwoman who was beginning a long run at Keith's Rochester theatre just as the Penders were leaving. She visited the lonely boy everyday bringing fruit, candy, and the best gift of all, backstage gossip.

Somehow the six weeks passed, and the doctor gave Archie a clean bill of health. With a box lunch packed by his landlady, he boarded the train for New York City and the Palace. But somehow it was all a bit anticlimactic. Lying in bed all those weeks, he had realized that he was not going to end his American tour at the Palace. Oh, he'd go on with the rest of the guys, and he'd do his very best. That wasn't it. He just wasn't going to end his American tour at all. He was going to stay here. He'd made up his mind. Now the only problem was how to tell Bob Pender. He felt rotten, as if he were letting Bob down. But Archie Leach knew, in a way that was difficult to put into words, that his future lay here in America and not back in the music halls of England. Mr. Pender would just have to try to understand.

Having been a young man once himself, Bob Pender did understand. Unfortunately several of the boys had come to the same conclusion, including Bob Pender's own, much younger brother. Bob and Margaret Pender sailed for London with half the boys they'd started with. Pender had honed the eight-member troupe that he'd brought over on the Olympic—was it really two years ago?—to razor-sharp perfection. They performed as if they were a single entity, effortlessly picking up cues as if each knew what the other was thinking. And, in a way, they did. Now he'd have to start that process all over again.

Before he left Pender warned the lads that they'd not have an easy time of it. Summer was just beginning, a notoriously slow time in vaudeville. He also gave each boy return passage to England in case they changed their minds. But he knew they wouldn't. And he was, as always, right.

* * * * * *

That summer of 1922 when he was eighteen years old, Archie Leach learned a number of truths he hadn't been exposed to before. He learned there was a veritable abyss between performers who talked and performers who didn't. He was one of the ones who didn't—at least not yet—and he feared that he never would. He had absolutely no idea if he could, but he definitely wanted to try. How else would he know? The simple task of speaking a line (any line!) on a stage (any stage!) took priority over everything else. That was the next hurdle.

In the meantime he had to eat. The summer wore on, his modest savings dwindled away to nothing and soon, heart pounding, he began dipping into the money that Bob Pender had left for his return to England. It was like burning the bridges behind him.

It was a bad time. Every day he made the rounds of a dozen booking offices, and every day all he got for his trouble was the exercise. Bob Pender was right and then some: things weren't just slow in the summer, they came to a complete standstill.

Archie stowed his things with a friend and gave up his room at the boardinghouse where the troupe had stayed during their run at the Palace. He'd sleep for a night or two in the apartments of friends. He had made friends in show business, and he'd spend several nights in their offices. During this terrible time he was still, as a good-looking, personable young bachelor, being invited out to dinner, often at some very fancy houses.

One night a friend invited him to dinner at his father's house on Park Avenue. And could he please pick up lyric soprano Lucrezia Bori on his way there? When Archie Leach arrived at her apartment, she suggested they walk to the dinner party. She insisted she needed the exercise.

When they finally arrived at the party, Archie realized that she had made that suggestion because she sensed that taxi fare would have wrecked his food budget for a week. The gods continued their beneficence to Archie Leach that fine summer night. At the dinner, he met George Tilyou, whose family owned Steeplechase Park on Coney Island.

By the time the evening was over, Archie had nailed down his first and only advertising job. Until Labor Day he would patrol the boardwalk at Coney Island on stilts wearing a green and red uniform that would loudly proclaim the fun to be had at his employer's place of business.

That job, arduous and hazardous as it proved to be, was still a godsend. It kept Archie Leach going until fall. Things were bound to improve in the booking offices and he'd get himself a real job.

The pay was five dollars a day on weekdays and ten dollars on Saturdays and Sundays. That came to forty-five dollars a week, more money than he had ever made before, and he managed to save most of it. Archie knew that he'd get an onstage job when the theatrical season began in the fall, but there was no point in taking chances. Besides sometimes you had to pay for your own costumes. Sometimes you had to pay your own train fare to get to a city where you'd gotten a booking. He didn't want to ever find himself in the position of having a job offered to him but be unable to take it for want of a few dollars expense money.

In 1922 Coney Island was a delightful place, clean and properly maintained. The breezes off the Atlantic were cool and steady and by judiciously planning his schedule, Archie could usually manage to eat for free by turning up at his favorite food stands at mealtimes. Crowds always followed him, and the proprietors of the stands thought it a fair exchange to give Archie food in return for the customers he always brought with him, like a Pied Piper on stilts.

All in all Archie Leach's stint as a stilt-walker at Coney Island would have been a great summer job for an out-of-work actor if it hadn't been for the kids. In any group of children there are always two or three who will try anything.

Depending on whether your point of view is that of parent, bystander, teacher, or victim, these children are known as "high-spirited, working off excess energy, discipline problems, troublemakers or miserable little brats."

Precariously perched atop his eight-foot stilts, Archie Leach attracted hordes of miserable little brats that summer, all of them intent on toppling him from his lofty roost as quickly and unceremoniously as possible. No one could describe this almost constant warfare better than Archie Leach himself:

"There were all sorts of opening moves, and from my altitude I could follow the beginning of each maneuver, the strategy and deploy. I could predict that concerted rush, and spot the deceptive saunter resulting in the rear-guard shove; or the playful ring-around-the-rosy, with me as rosy, beaming daffily down on the little faces of impending disaster. I dreaded the lone ace who came zeroing in out of the sun, flying a small bamboo cane with a curved handle. One good yank as he whizzed past and he'd won the encounter hands down (*my* hands down), with full honors and an accolade from admiring bystanders.

"After a few graceful air-clutching staggers, it still took about three life-time seconds for me to topple—TIMBER!—and by the time I was spread-eagled on the street, those frolicsome urchins were yards away . . .

"Still, I occasionally outwitted them by grabbing a nearby awning, while parrying with an elongated wooden leg; but often some sturdy young squirt, joined quickly by volunteers of his cowardly gang . . . would grab the stilt's foot and tug steadily. It became an interesting speculation which would come away first—the awning, or me. Usually I came away first, resulting in an entirely different, much more entertaining, sort of flailing parabolic descent, known as a backward high gruesome."

The English are fervent lovers of summertime, but when the summer of 1922 finally came to an end, Archie Leach was one Limey who was very glad to know that it was over.

Archie had taken a small room near Coney Island for the duration of his job there, to save both commuting time and subway fare. Now, back in Manhattan, he again began haunting the booking offices. While both of them were waiting in an outer office, Archie met a young Australian named John Kelly who was trying to get work as a theatrical designer. To support himself in the meantime, he was making and selling hand-painted ties.

And soon Archie Leach was adding to his carefully nurtured

savings by helping Kelly make and hawk his flamboyant neckwear. (Kelly eventually succeeded in realizing his ambitions. He became Hollywood designer Orry-Kelly who years later, would win an Oscar for his work on *An American in Paris*, an MGM movie starring Gene Kelly and Leslie Caron.)

As October arrived so did good news for Archie. He and the remaining Pender boys were offered jobs in a new production at the Hippodrome that would be closely modeled on the original Dillingham extravaganza, *Good Times*. The new show would be called *Better Times*. Archie and the other Penders did several acrobatic routines.

Archie, who had diligently been working to overcome his shyness with girls, fell in love, again with a tall and lovely girl who was also appearing in the show. This time he and the young lady not only carried on animated conversations, they actually went out on dates: supper after the evening performance and occasional weekend parties.

At the beginning of their interlude, Archie took her home on the subway to the farthest reaches of Brooklyn. By the time he got back to his own Manhattan Boardinghouse, the tardy winter dawn was breaking. This left about five hours to sleep before he had to be at the Hippodrome for the afternoon matinee. Archie gave up the subway trips to Brooklyn, but not the young lady. He would put her on the subway and then meet the other Penders to work out final plans for the new act they were putting together. They wanted to be ready for vaudeville circuit when *Better Times* closed.

Their foresight paid off. *Better Times*, in spite of its onward-and-upward title wasn't nearly as successful as its predecessor. At first the boys couldn't get bookings in the top vaudeville theatres, and they spent Christmas week at the Lyceum Theatre in Duluth, Minnesota. Archie had once believed that nothing was more grim than an English winter. Now he knew better. The sub-zero winter winds roaring in off the prairie made the English winter seem like spring time.

Their fortunes improved after New Year's Day. They were offered a tour of Pantages circuit, second in prestige only to the B.F. Keith circuit, and soon they were on the road again for over a year, playing a series of weekly engagements that took them across Canada, down the West Coast, and then back across the U.S. to New York.

During this tour Archie Leach got his first look at Southern California. He loved it. Once again his path crossed that of Douglas Fairbanks, Sr. who invited the troupe to come to the United Artists studio and watch him work making the *Thief of Bagdad*.

It was a long tour and a successful one, continuing through the 1924 season. The tensions and hardships of life on the road, however, were beginning to take their toll. The clash of temperaments was becoming painful for everyone and without a Bob Pender to act as peacemaker, arbitrator and final authority in all disputes, the troupe slowly began to disintegrate.

After the final break Archie moved into the National Vaudeville Artists Club on West Forty-sixth Street. He had lost touch during the tour with the girl from Brooklyn and didn't feel motivated to find her now that he was back in town.

For several years Archie Leach picked up jobs whenever and wherever he could. He worked regularly, if not constantly, and began to make the slow, but steady transition from a wordless boy acrobat to a performer who delivers lines. He teamed up with several other young comics who lived at the NVA Club for weekend dates at small theatres in and around New York. These were places that wanted a couple of "live acts" to help bring crowds in for the silent movies that were their main fare.

These jobs didn't pay much, but Archie didn't care as long as he was learning how to deliver lines. He was the straight man in these duos, often a technically more difficult job than the one performed by the actor-comedian who actually got the laughs.

One day as he was walking in the West Forties, Archie spotted a familiar name on a billboard: Don Barclay, the man who had rescued the garishly made-up neophyte from his hazing by other and older Penders back in the first days of his theatrical apprenticeship in England.

He had seen Barclay once or twice when he'd first arrived in America, but then Barclay had gone on the road, and they had lost touch.

Archie remembered their first meeting in America. He called Barclay in his dressing room.

"Is that you, Don, sir? I'm in America!"

After Barclay's show, they met at a Broadway restaurant. Archie had begun ordering ice cream every chance he got. He was taller than the last time Barclay had seen him nearly two years before. Archie showed Barclay one of his first purchases in the New World: a black leather bow tie that was attached to a rubber band that remained hidden under his shirt collar.

He showed Barclay how you could pull the tie away from your neck and then let it snap back.

"Pretty snazzy, eh, sir?"

Archie blushed to think of it. He had been in American nearly five years now. He had long since discarded his snazzy black leather bow tie.

Barclay was delighted to see him and within weeks, they had worked out an act of their own that proved surprisingly successful over the next couple of years. Archie especially enjoyed their mind reading shtick.

From the audience Barclay would pick out a likely-looking candidate for some mild embarrassment. Archie would be on the stage. Barclay, with his hand on the man's shoulder, would ask Archie:

"Where is this man's father?"

Archie, hand to his forehead, would pretend to concentrate with great ferocity. Finally, he would reply:

"At this minute your father is in Denver, Colorado."

"Oh, no," the unsuspecting patron would say, "my father is in Memphis."

"You're wrong," Archie says triumphantly. "Your mother's husband is in Memphis. But your father is in Denver."

Archie always thought this bit was in bad taste, but it got such huge laughs that Barclay was always able to convince him that it should stay in the act.

* * * * * *

As those years in the mid-Twenties went by, Archie worked with more and more regularity, sometimes in New York, sometimes out on the circuit, sometimes with Barclay, sometimes with other partners. There was a time when he would have called that success, but not anymore. The pinnacle of success was broadway. That's where the top vaudeville performers ended up, and that's where Archie wanted to be. But he knew he'd never make it as a straight man, nor did he want to.

As so often happens, once this realization of what he really wanted was firmly evolved in his mind, outer events seemed to conspire to produce the very thing he wanted. One night Archie Leach was with his friend Max Hoffman, Jr. at a New York nightclub where Helen Morgan was appearing. Unlike Archie, Hoffman was already working regularly on Broadway, and Hoffman believed that's where his friend belonged.

In between sets of Morgan's poignant torch songs, Hoffman introduced Archie to Reginald Hammerstein, a director and younger brother of Oscar Hammerstein II. The two hit it off and, a few days later, young Hammerstein took Archie to meet his uncle, Arthur Hammerstein.

The meeting was successful. Archie got a substantial part in the upcoming Hammerstein operetta, *Golden Dawn*. He also understudied Paul Gregory, the leading man, in the ill-fated production, a World War I love story set in Africa. Louise Hunter and Olin Howland were the two principals. Archie played an Australian prisoner of war who was the show's backup love interest. His English accent easily passed for Australian to American audiences, and Archie, as well as everyone else in the cast, had high hopes for the show.

The out-of-town tryouts began in October. They played Boston first, and the critics were lukewarm. They didn't pan the show, but they didn't praise it either. Their Boston run lasted for two weeks, and Oscar Hammerstein II and Otto Harbach, rewriting constantly in a feverish attempt to create a hit, ordered daily changes in words, lyrics, timing, and placement. The cast grew more and more edgy.

But by Philadelphia everything seemed on an upswing. The Philadelphia critics were a bit more enthusiastic than their Boston colleagues, and everybody jumped on the slight improvement in their notices as a signal that everything was OK, they should quit worrying, they had a hit on their hands.

As it turned out they most certainly did not have a hit on their hands, and nobody quite knew why, because all the elements were there: a Hammerstein score, a Harbach book, experienced actors, and a competent and skilled director. But for some mysterious reason, the total production was less than the sum of its parts.

The Harbach-Hammerstein stamp sold six months of tickets in spite of lukewarm reviews. Then the show closed.

But Archie Leach had been noticed. He had definitely made the jump from vaudeville to Broadway and was clearly on his way.

Hammerstein offered Archie the lead in his next production, *Polly*; a show whose cast also included Inez Courtney, Fred Allen and, in the chorus, a newcomer named George Brent. Courtney was an ingenue who later achieved a modest success in Hollywood. Allen was a veteran of the vaudeville circuits who would one day become one of the top stars of radio in its prime era before television. Brent, a young Irishman, was also destined for leading roles in Hollywood.

In spite of this dynamite cast, *Polly* was in trouble from the beginning. The out-of-town tryout period stretched from two, to three, to finally, six weeks. But no amount of fiddling with the words, music or book made any difference.

In Wilmingtion a critic said:

"Archie Leach has a strong masculine manner, but unfortunately fails to bring out the beauty of the score."

He was replaced as leading man before the show opened on Broadway. This did not prove to be the terrible blow it might have been had the show been a success. *Polly* closed after a mere fifteen performances. Another ameliorating factor in Archie's failure was that his contract with Hammerstein required that he be paid four hundred dollars a week for six months no matter what the fate of the show.

This seemed a splendid situation at first. But within a month Broadway star Marilyn Miller wanted Archie to replace her leading man, Jack Donahue, in an already acclaimed hit, *Rosalie*. It was like having stardom handed to you on a silver platter. Archie couldn't wait to get started.

Unfortunately there was the minor technicality of his contract with Hammerstein. *Rosalie* was a Ziegfeld show, and Arthur Hammerstein and Florenz Ziegfeld were bitter enemies. Hammerstein wouldn't release Archie from his contract. Instead he sold it to the Schubert brothers.

Archie could hardly believe what was happening. For another five months, he was in possession neither of his life, his time, nor his talent. It was not a pleasant place to be.

Lee and J.J. Shubert have become super legends in a era of American entertainment that produced legends by the dozens. They owned dozens, maybe hundreds, of theatres in New York and the U.S. They also owned, via long-term contract or by outright purchase of the rights, numerous plays, operettas, and musical comedies. They also "owned" actors, writers, musicians, and composers.

Rumor had it that some of the actors who had been signed by the Shuberts were sent to the sticks and never heard from again. Archie Leach did not want to be sent to the sticks. He knew about them already, thanks just the same.

He needn't have worried. Less than a week after they had acquired legal title to his Hammerstein contract, the Shuberts summoned him to their Times Square offices. Archie was told that he had an important role in a big new musical they were planning. *Boom Boom*, with a book by Fanny Todd Mitchell and music by Werner Janssen, opened early in the 1928 theatre season. The female lead was a pretty young blond from Philadelphia named Jeannette MacDonald.

Archie Leach and Jeannette MacDonald proved to be a star-spangled combination. The critics loved *Boom Boom* and especially took notice of the handsome young Englishman.

By the time Archie opened in *Boom Boom*, he was no longer a neophyte on the Broadway scene. He was solidly entrenched in the new web of relationships, a new pattern of life. He had moved out of the National Vaudeville Artists Club into an apartment of his own. His everyday hangout spot was no longer the NVA Club restaurant and bar, but Rudley's Restaurant at Forty-first and Broadway.

In this frenetic heyday of Broadway, Rudley's was a gathering place for the discontents, the rebels, and the dreamers. Playwright Moss Hart was a regular there. So were writers Edward Chodorov and Preston Sturges; Sturges then ten years away from his 1940 Oscar for the screenplay of *The Great McGinty*.

Rudley's was also a good place to hear about jobs. George Murphy, who would later go on to starring roles in Hollywood, was still in the chorus and haunting Rudley's hoping to hear about auditions for more important roles. Humphrey Bogart, a young actor weary of frothy roles, was often seen nursing a cup of coffee for hours and complaining about his job as a "gopher" for producer William A. Brady.

Playwright and film writer Chodorov remembers that Archie Leach "was never a very open fellow but he was earnest and we liked him." Moss Hart later recalled that Archie seemed disconsolate in those years. But it's possible that Moss Hart misinterpreted Archie's shyness and willingness to listen. Or it may have been that Archie was simply tense, and perhaps a bit fearful about his future on Broadway.

Getting fired from *Polly* before it reached Broadway had been a tremendous blow to him. He had thought the show would be a hit. He felt he had thoroughly mastered the role he'd been given. Neither assumption had proved correct, and it had badly shaken his confidence.

His solid success in *Boom Boom*, however, gradually restored his self-esteem. One day, while strolling along upper Broadway, where all the automobile dealers had their showrooms, Archie Leach decided that he needed a car. After all he'd been earning between $350 and $450 a week for over a year now, and he could certainly afford it.

He wanted a Packard, then one of the most status-heavy cars one could drive. The model he wanted was a phaeton, a touring car, with a 143-inch wheelbase. It was like driving a small apartment, and Archie, who had never had a driving lesson in his life, at first found his new possession difficult to get around corners.

Archie got a few lessons from the salesman, but some vital information must have been overlooked. On his very first drive in the country, with two girls along to provide a properly appreciative audience, Archie lost control while turning a corner of a small Connecticut town and plowed into a parked car. It was a recently parked car whose driver was still behind the wheel.

Leaving his friends in the Packard, Archie quietly and rather desperately explained that he was not accustomed to driving such a long car. In a lower voice he added that, indeed, he was not accustomed to driving any kind of car at all, that he had really been showing off for the two pretty young women.

The middle-aged driver of the other car spent several long minutes contemplating what he'd just heard and then shrugged his shoulders and sent Archie on his way. It was, after all, a very small dent.

* * * * * *

And then it happened. The chance that Archie Leach had become more and more convinced he had to have: the call from Hollywood. Several months into *Boom Boom*'s run, Archie and

Jeannette MacDonald were invited out to Queens for a screen test at Paramount's Astoria studios.

The Jazz Singer, the first talking movie, had been a wild success the year before and Hollywood was desperate for real actors: people who both looked and sounded good. Archie Leach figured that he looked and sounded as good as anybody else. Besides he knew New York like the back of his own hand by now. He'd been in the States eight years and most of those years had been spent in New York. And during his years in vaudeville, he'd seen the rest of the country with a thoroughness that most American citizens would never experience. He'd even toured Canada all the way from Nova Scotia in the east, to British Columbia on Canada's western coast.

There was only one place that haunted him, that he couldn't get out of his mind. And that was Southern California. It wasn't just that Doug Fairbanks had invited him to the set to watch him filming the *Thief of Bagdad*. It was a sense he had during their run in Los Angeles that was strangely reminiscent of another time when he had walked backstage for the very first time at Bristol's Hippodrome Theatre. He had known immediately that was where he belonged. He felt the same way about California.

Now they had noticed him. Or so he hoped as he and Jeannette MacDonald drove across the Queensboro Bridge the morning the test had been scheduled. Even the best Broadway performers did not make as much money as Hollywood paid its actors and actresses. Then there was the issue of audience. You could make one movie, and it could be seen by hundreds of thousands of people all over the country. Hell, all over the world.

The actual test itself seemed to have been designed to provide irrefutable proof of the truth of Murphy's Law: if anything can go wrong, it will. The studio was freezing. The soundstage on which they were to perform was not lit properly. The technicians didn't seem to know what they were supposed to do. The lines they were given to learn didn't make any sense at all, and, in any case, they only had about fifteen minutes to prepare themselves. There was no director to block out the scene, and they were told there would be only one take. Rehearsal would be impossible.

What could they do except try to make the best of it? They muddled through and prayed that whoever had the decision-making power knew what the conditions in Astoria were.

At the age of four, Archibald Alexander Leach, later Cary Grant, displayed none of the *joie de vivre* which was to make him the king of sophisticated comedy in films like "The Awful Truth" (preceeding page) with Irene Dunne. He was doubtless already feeling the family tensions which would culminate in the mental breakdown of his mother, Elsie Kingdom Leach (shown here at a happier time in the mid 1960s) and her disappearance from his childhood life. His father, Elias Leach, whose appearance in this old family photograph seems almost a forecast of Cary's later jauntiness, was prevented by long hours of work, and worry over his wife's health, from giving his son the attention the boy required.

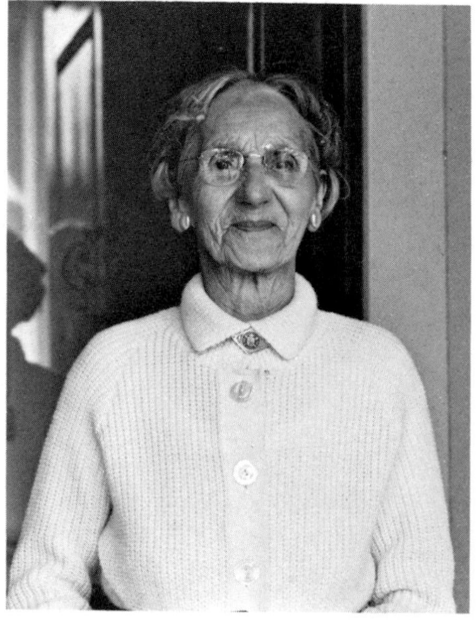

Above: Mae West gave him first big break in "She Done Him Wrong."
Below: Dating Virginia Cherrill before she became first Mrs. Grant.

Cary and Virginia had intended to get married in November of 1933, but Cary came down with a severe respiratory illness which found him spending Christmas, complete with champagne, in a hospital bed. They were finally married on February 9, 1934. Picture at left is one of the rare shots taken during their marriage which broke up a little more than a year later on March 26, 1935.

During the bachelor days which followed his first marriage, Cary's career took an important upward turn which found him playing opposite such top Hollywood stars as Myrna Loy in "Wings in the Dark." The screen persona which was to become definitive – cocky, zany, irrepressible – was already emerging in "Sylvia Scarlett," 1936. This was the first film in which he co-starred with Katharine Hepburn.

That's Edmund Gwenn peering over Cary's shoulder in "Sylvia Scarlett." The other "gentleman"? Believe it or not, Katharine Hepburn! She's more recognizable below in that perennially popular Grant-Hepburn classic "Bringing Up Baby." "Baby" was Kate's pet leopard.

By 1937, Cary was established as Hollywood's leading man about town. Ginger Rogers was only one of many glamor stars he dated.

It was big news in the late 1930s when Filmtown's most eligible bachelor became engaged to luscious young starlet Phyllis Brooks. The engagement was broken, however, before it led to matrimony.

They got the results a week later. Jeannette MacDonald was signed to a long-term contract and was to leave for Hollywood, as soon as *Boom Boom* closed, to star opposite Maurice Chevalier in Ernst Lubitsch's, *The Love Parade*.

Archie Leach was told that he would never make it in the movies: he was bowlegged and his neck was too thick. And how do you go about correcting those kinds of flaws?

* * * * * *

The following season the Shuberts had Archie scheduled for *Wonderful Night*, a spectacular remake of *Die Fledermaus* with Johann Strauss' music and a rewritten book by Fanny Todd Mitchell. Archie would be the male lead opposite Gladys Baxter. The show opened on October 31, 1929, at the Majestic Theatre.

Unfortunately, two days before, another spectacular event had occurred downtown. The stock market had resoundingly crashed through the paper veneer of American economic security. The country was in deep trouble, and everybody knew it. In good times *Wonderful Night* would have been a solid, money-making hit. These were not good times. Ticket sales fizzled out as theatregoers pulled in their belts and wondered how long the Great Depression would last.

The Shuberts then put Archie Leach into a road company production of *Street Singer* opposite Queenie Smith. He did not relish the thought of going on the road again, but Hollywood had receded on his immediate horizon and who could know how bad times would get? If work was available, the only sensible thing to do was take it.

The tour ended late in the spring of 1931. Archie was glad to be back in Manhattan and was not concerned when the Shuberts said they wanted to see him. He was sure that they had a good role in mind for him in the upcoming fall season. But the information the Shubert brothers had to impart that day, was that they were sending Archie to St. Louis for the summer. He would star in a series of twelve operettas in the St. Louis Municipal Opera in Forest Park.

It was terrific experience, and he was glad to have the work and the St. Louis summer opera was one of the few good out-of-town assignments available in those lean years. But it wasn't Hollywood. Archie was afraid that he'd miss out on a good part for the fall season if he wasn't in town. But there was little he could do about all these problems. He tried to forget them and threw his considerable talents, energy, and concentration into mastering twelve singing roles in just a few weeks. He wanted, as always, to do the best job humanly possible.

If the Midwest correspondent for Variety can be believed, he did just that. Variety's stringer wrote a series of long and glowing accounts of Archie's performances in *Rose Marie, Rio Rita, Irene, Nina Rosa, The Red Mill, Blossom Time,* and other staples of the summer operetta circuit.

On the strength of these accounts in Variety, Broadway producer, William Friedlander, wanted Archie to appear in a play he was mounting that fall in New York. Written by John Monk Saunders, *Nikki* was a World War I story about fliers at loose ends in Paris after the war's close. (Later, it was made into a movie, *The Last Flight*, starring Richard Barthelmess.)

The Shuberts gave their blessing to the venture and gave Archie a run-of-the-show hiatus from his contract with them. He played a character called Cary Lockwood opposite Fay Wray, who was married to playwright Saunders and was several years away from her meeting with King Kong in deepest darkest Africa.

Nikki opened on September 29, 1931 and closed about a month later.

Now what? Broadway, once the pinnacle of his ambition, seemed to be getting him nowhere. People were flocking to movie theatres and staying away from legitimate theatres in droves. Archie Leach knew that Hollywood was the wave of the future, and he knew that it was his future. But how to get there? How to make them notice him, expecially now that *Nikki* had closed, and he wasn't even working anymore.

Nowhere is it recorded what Archie was doing at the moment he decided that if Hollywood wouldn't come and get him, why, then he'd just have to go to Hollywood.

* * * * * *

His first movie role turned up even before he headed West. Casey Robinson, who would later write such screenplays as *Dark Victory* and *Kings Row*, was then making one-reelers at

Paramount's Astoria Studios. He was casting now for a ten-minute musical short feature called *Singapore Sue*. Archie Leach was one of the actors who showed up for the audition.

Robinson later recalled:

"I needed a leading man to play an American sailor. Among the young men brought to see me was Archie Leach, who had never been in front of a camera. I liked him and cast him without hesitation."

The other stars in the brief program filler were Anna Chang and Joe Wong, with Millard Mitchell as the other sailor in the Singapore saloon setting.

That assignment completed, Archie began winding up his affairs in New York. He would be driving to the coast with a friend, Phil Charig, a young composer.

There was just one stop to make that morning before Archie and Phil watched Manhattan fall away behind them on the George Washington bridge. Archie eased his Packard into a rare Broadway parking space just across from the Palace. Theatrical agent Billy "Square Deal" Grady met them at the curb and gave Archie the Hollywood office address of Walter Herzbrun. The idea was that Archie could have his mail forwarded there, but Herzbrun provided much more than a mailing address. He introduced Archie to Marion Gering, a former Broadway director. Gering took Archie to dinner at the home of B.P. Schulberg, then the head of Paramount Studios.

During dinner the conversation got around to the screen test that Gering was planning for his actress wife. Schulberg suggested that Archie make the test with her. *Singapore Sue* had not yet been released, and Archie didn't mention it. He'd had nothing but bad luck at Paramount's Astoria studios, and he didn't want to call attention to "Sue" without having seen it.

The test with Marion Gering and his wife was a completely different experience than the one he'd had with Jeannette MacDonald in the Astoria studio. They had time to memorize their lines, and Gering carefully set the lights and blocked out the six-minute scene. They rehearsed for two hours, and when the cameras were finally rolling, Archie felt relaxed and competent.

When Schulberg saw the test, he offered Archie a long-term contract at $450 a week, with provisions for option renewals and hefty raises during the five-year term of their agreement.

Archie said yes, and the contract went into effect on December 7. This was less than six weeks after *Nikki* had closed, and Archie had found himself once again "at liberty," that marvelous actor's euphemism for unemployment. (Ironically enough, Mrs. Gering was not offered a contract.)

The Paramount brass didn't like his name and told him to find a new one. Several weeks later he had made no progress at all. He was having dinner that night with Fay Wray and her writer husband, John Monk Saunders. Maybe Saunders could think of something. After all that's what writers were for, right?

What they both suggested was that Archie use the name of his character in *Nikki*: Cary Lockwood. But Archie had doubts about the name. So did the Paramount executives. There was already an actor named Harold Lockwood, and everyone knows there's no point in going out of your way to confuse an audience. The first name was fine. Cary had warmth, dignity, and style. But what could he use for a last name? It should be ethnically neutral and probably should only have one syllable. Stars needed names that were both glamourous and easy to remember. Too many syllables interfered with memory, especially at the box office. Thus Julius Garfinkle became John Garfield, Frances Gumm became Judy Garland, and Marion Michael Morrison became John Wayne.

But who would Archibald Alexander Leach become? Archie and the Paramount executives pooled their ideas, and a secretary typed the list. They tried out each of the names with Cary. Nothing seemed to work. Finally they came to *Grant*. They tried it out.

"Cary...Grant." "It works." "Yeah, it's okay." "Whadya think?"

Archie Leach thought about it. He liked it. And so a few weeks before his twenty-eighth birthday, Archie Leach had a new job, a new residence in a sunny climate, a whole new set of possibilities in his life and a new name.

When Cary Grant left that meeting, he was feeling pretty good about himself.

3

The Early Years at Paramount

A WEEK LATER CARY GRANT was hard at work filming *This Is the Night*, the first of the seven feature films he would make for Paramount in 1932. The schedule was grueling. On the set at 5:30 A.M. every morning, he would not get home until 6:00 or 7:00 P.M. Exhausted, he would often still have lines to learn for the next day's shooting.

This was vastly different from what Cary now realized was the relaxed pace on Broadway. After the frantic rehearsal period was over, life for a performer on the Great White Way settled into a comfortable routine of performing in the evening, having a late supper and animated conversation with friends until 3:00 or 4:00 A.M., then home to sleep until noon.

All that was over. In 1932 Cary Grant worked fifty-two weeks. He never had more than two consecutive days off at a time. Often he didn't even get that.

Cary Grant referred, in later years, to his stint at Paramount as the era of his "charming idiot"roles. It's an apt description of the second- and third-rate films he made in those years. Paramount obviously did not know what they had in Grant. No one took the trouble to question whether the best of his talents was being made.

In his first film, *This Is the Night*, Grant got fifth billing behind Lili Damita, Thelma Todd, Roland Young, and Charlie Ruggles. He played an Olympic javeline thrower in a protracted marital mix-up comedy. Directed by Frank Tuttle, the sets got better reviews than the movie.

But Cary was noticed. The New York Herald Tribune critic wrote:

"As the jealous husband, an undistinguished straight role, Cary Grant...plays with amiable assurance."

Often working on two pictures at the same time, Cary, in 1932, also appeared in *Sinners in the Sun*, with Carole Lombard and Chester Morris; *Merrily We Go to Hell*, Fredric March and Sylvia Sidney; *Devil and the Deep*, Tallulah Bankhead, Charles Laughton and Gary Cooper; *Blonde Venus*, directed by Josef von Sternberg and starring Marlene Dietrich and Herbert Marshall; *Hot Saturday*, Nancy Carroll and Randolph Scott; *Madame Butterfly*, Sylvia Sidney and Charles Ruggles.

Cary Grant later remembered *Blond Venus* as "my first good part," a statement that proves how memory is distorted by time. Grant's role as the rich playboy who keeps Marlene Dietrich as his mistress so she can pay her husband's (Herbert Marshall) medical bills, provides him with little to do except act as a good-looking foil for Dietrich. Sternberg has admitted that he made up the scenario on a day-to-day basis as filming progressed, because he didn't like the script provided by Paramount.

And it shows. Dietrich is required to play, by turns, a loving wife, reluctant prostitute, self-sacrificing mother, and cabaret singer by the time *Blonde Venus* mercifully ends.

The New York Times reviewer, however, noted that:

"Cary Grant is worthy of a much better role. . ."

Hot Saturday was a milestone for Grant: his first starring role. He got top billing over Nancy Carroll, for whom the film was a comeback effort, and Randolph Scott, also a new contract player in the Paramount stable. The two men went on to become good friends and shared, through most of the Thirties, a beach house in Santa Monica.

Grant's role in *Madame Butterfly* as the heartless sailor who loves Cho-Cho San (Sylvia Sidney) and then leaves her would be completely forgotten except for a chance meeting that occurred when the movie was being filmed. Grant was on his way back from a quick lunch in the Paramount commissary, still dressed in the dazzling dress whites his role required.

Just as he walked by a limousine was pulling up to the main

Paramount office. Inside was Paramount executive Emmanuel Cohen and Paramount's new star, Mae West. She had just had a smash hit on Broadway in *Diamond Lil*. Now Paramount wanted her to do it for the screen, but a leading man hadn't yet been found. Paramount's leading male star at the time was Gary Cooper, but somehow he just didn't seem right for the part. His pokerfaced seriousness didn't strike any sparks off the famous Mae West bawdiness.

Mae West stopped in mid-sentence as she alighted from the limo and gazed in wonder at the deeply tanned and handsome man walking toward one of the sound stages in a white Naval officer's uniform.

She turned to Cohen. "Who is that?"

"Oh, that's Cary Grant," Cohen said. "He's making *Butterfly* right now with Sylvia Sidney."

Mae West was still looking at Grant's receding figure.

"I don't care if he's making Little Nell. If he can talk, I'll take him."

"For what part?" Cohen asked.

"The lead, of course," she said.

The studio had doubts. They'd sunk a huge investment in Mae West, having outbid every other studio in Hollywood to win her. They didn't care to take any chances. They wanted her leading man to be much further along in his career than Cary Grant was, and they offered to borrow a bigger name from one of the other studios. But Mae West was adamant. She wanted Cary Grant. When they told him he was going to star opposite Mae West, Grant hadn't even met her yet.

Mae West's immediate reaction to Cary Grant provides a good illustration of the kind of instincts that make a star. She knew Grant would be good for her, and he was. He provided the right balance of innocence and sophistication, charm and naivete that were an ideal setting for the sexual innuendoes that were Ms. West's stock-in-trade.

New Yorker critic Pauline Kael has written that Cary Grant "was Mae West's classiest and best leading man, but he did more for her. . .than she did for him. She brought out his passivity, and a quality of refinement in him which made her physical aggression seem a playful gambit. With tough men opposite her, she was less charming, more crude."

There would be two Cary Grant-Mae West films: *She Done Him Wrong*, the screen version of *Diamond Lil*, and *I'm No Angel*, a bit of fluff with Ms. West as a circus entertainer and Grant as the socialite she falls in love with.

In speaking of these two films, Cary Grant has said of his co-star:

"I learned everything from her. Well, not everything but almost everything. She knows so much. Her instinct is so true, her timing so perfect, her grasp of the situation so right."

She Done Him Wrong remains the best film Mae West ever made. She plays the mistress of Noah Beery, Sr., the owner of a lively Bowery saloon in the Manhattan of the 1890's. She is an entertainer in the saloon and unaware of most of Beery's nefarious doings. Then Grant enters her life as the captain of the next-door Salvation Army post.

When Grant comes to see if she can lessen the noise emanating from the saloon, he makes his request and then apologizes:

"I'm sorry to be taking your time."

Mae doesn't mind.

"What do you think my time is for?"

On another occasion, as he is leaving the saloon, she deliciously sizes him up and murmurs, "You can be had."

This is also the movie in which Mae West delivers her famous and much-quoted invitation. Hoping to get better acquainted with the handsome young Salvation Army officer, she suggests:

"Why don't you come up and see me sometime?"

Grant hesitates.

"Come on up. I'll tell your fortune."

In addition to breaking box office records, *She Done Him Wrong* was also credited with the establishment of the National Legion of Decency as well as the cause of a major censorship drive within the movie industry.

The movie left Cary Grant solidly established as a star, but it didn't appreciably improve the roles Paramount was offering him. He was still getting lots of "charming idiot" parts as well as low-budget remakes of Gary Cooper hits or worse yet, roles that Gary Cooper had turned down. And to top it all off, he was still working at an almost impossible pace: seven films in 1932, six in 1933.

In addition to all these pressures, a bomb intended for safe detonation during one of the combat scenes in *The Eagle and The*

Hawk exploded prematurely on the set where Cary Grant was at work, filming a segment of this story of World War I flying aces. It left several severe cuts on his face. Grant's co-workers in the film, Fredric March and Jack Oakie, narrowly escaped injury in the March 16, 1933 mishap.

No wonder Cary Grant fell in love. The studio would surely give him time off for a honeymoon, and it seemed the only way he'd get a vacation and some much-needed rest.

* * * * * *

Virginia Cherrill was born on a farm in Carthage, Illinois and spent most of her life trying to get as far away from it as possible. After her father gave up farming, her mother got a job as a cook at Kemper Hall, a Kenosha, Wisconsin, boarding school for rich Chicago girls. Part of her pay was room, board, and tuition for her daughter.

At eighteen Virginia was named queen of Chicago's Arts Ball. At nineteen she married a young Chicago attorney named Irving Adler. At twenty she divorced him and headed for Hollywood to visit her Kemper Hall classmate, Sue Carol, who was working as an actress. (Later, Sue Carol would become an agent and the wife of Alan Ladd.)

In 1928 boxing had become a fashionable way to spend a Hollywood evening, and when Sue discovered her friend was coming to town, she got a pair of ringside tickets. Also attending the fights that night was Charlie Chaplin, who came over and introduced himself. (This was a totally unnecessary nicety. They *knew* who he was.) He asked Virginia if she would take a screen test. She had come to Hollywood hoping that Sue could arrange just such a request from one of the studios. And now it was all happening so easily.

When Chaplin saw Virginia's test he offered her the female lead in the new movie he was planning. *City Lights* was released in 1931, and Cherrill, who had never acted or performed in her life, surprised the critics with her poignant and touching performance as the blind flower girl in the silent film.

Overnight she had become a star. But the experience, though heady, was short-lived. Chaplin had no immediate plans to use her again but that was the least of her troubles. Unfortunately, her voice was pitched too high and with its flat, Midwestern nasal tones, it effectively ended her career as a movie star before it had hardly begun.

None of this, however, was immediately apparent. After the filming of *City Lights* was completed, Virginia was briefly engaged to Broadway musical comedy star Buster West. With his father, West had appeared in a dancing act in George White's *Scandals*.

Then after her triumph when the film was finally released in 1931, Virginia had a much-publicized romance with New York society figure, William Rhinelander Stewart. There was an engagement announcement. Then wedding plans were set: the pair would be married on William Astor's yacht, the Nourmahal. In his capacity as ship's captain, Astor would perform the ceremony. Then a leisurely honeymoon cruise to the South Pacific was planned.

The yacht actually put out to sea from Honolulu, but returned several hours later. There had been no wedding. Stewart said nothing. Virginia tersely announced that their engagement had been "broken by mutual consent."

She then appeared in an eminently forgettable movie called *The Nuisance* with Lee Tracy and Madge Evans at MGM and was "at liberty" when she showed up at a party at the Malibu beachhouse that Randolph Scott and Cary Grant shared. There was a heavy fog that night, and Cary always remembered the way her hair curled into ringlets from the dampness.

"I fell in love with her almost the minute she walked in," he said later.

Virginia was 5'4", a flaxen blonde with blue eyes. Cary was exactly as Mae West had described him: "tall, dark, and handsome." They were a striking pair and soon were seeing each other as often as Cary's schedule would allow.

The romance blossomed throughout the summer, and, by fall, Cary had asked her to marry him, and she had accepted. But Cary wanted to avoid the circus atmosphere of a typical Hollywood wedding, and he carefully planned their separate getaways from California. He convinced Paramount that after nearly two straight years of work, he needed a two-month vacation.

Virginia left for New York by train several days before Cary made the same trip by plane on November 9, 1933. After a week in

New York, they sailed for England on the *Paris*. They had planned to be married immediately, but Cary was struck with a severe respiratory illness within days after they had landed. It was probably pneumonia. In any case Cary Grant spent Christmas in the hospital. In those days before antibiotics it took him nearly a month to shake off the infection, and it was late January before he and Virginia boarded a train for Bristol. It was a grand homecoming. Cary threw a party at the Grand Hotel and introduced his pretty and famous fiancee to his relatives and friends.

On February 9 the handsome pair were finally wed in London at the Caxton Hall Registry office. The wedding had overtones of the screwball comedies that were making their debut that year on American movie screens.

They made their appearance at the Registry in relays. First Grant arrived. While he grew noticeably irritated, more and more reporters arrived on the scene. Finally he made a phone call. Twenty mintes later Virginia finally showed up. Maybe she wanted to be sure he wouldn't end up in the hospital again leaving her stranded in full view of an international contingent of reporters.

Neither was dressed in what London considered proper attire for exchanging wedding vows. Grant wore a beige tweed suit with a dark brown wool scarf around his neck. Virginia had on a slim-skirted suit of yellow and black checks, a matching cloche stylishly dipped over one eye, a bright yellow scarf, and a sable coat. In news photos taken on that day, Virginia looks like a dozen other blonde starlets from that period. Her husband looks proud, hesitant, vulnerable, and very young.

They were due to catch the boat train to Plymouth where they were booked to return to the States on the *Paris* once again. Virginia's tardiness had put them badly behind schedule, and the crowds outside Caxton Hall were now enormous.

Cary and Virginia dashed out the front door, intent on getting a taxi, but were soon separated by the crowd. Each jumped into a taxi and looked around for the other. Neither spouse could see the other. They had hopped into separate taxis. Grant had to brave the crowd once again and make his way to Virginia's taxi.

They made the boat train with minutes to spare, and, although from the outside it may have looked like a screwball comedy, neither Cary nor Virginia thought it very funny. It was Cary

Grant's first personal experience of the unpleasantness of large unruly crowds of movie fans. It was an experience he always tried to avoid in the future.

* * * * * *

No one knows exactly when trouble began, but as it turned out, Cary and Virginia's courtship lasted longer than their marriage.

They returned to Hollywood and settled into a small beachhouse not far from the one Cary had shared with Randolph Scott before his wedding. Cary began work on *Thirty Day Princess* with Sylvia Sidney, the first of five films he would make for Paramount in 1934.

At first they were seen everywhere, at premieres, dinners, and parties. The gossip columnists described Cary and Virginia as "blissfully happy." Everyone agreed they were one of "the most strikingly attractive couples in movieland."

But by summer their close friends knew something was wrong. And in September Virginia moved out of their house. By the end of the month, when she hadn't come back, each of them made statements to the press.

"I'm still in love with Cary and I hope and feel certain that we will be able to patch things up and continue with our marriage," Virginia said.

Cary, too, sounded hopeful when he talked to reporters.

"It is silly to say Virginia and I have separated. We have just had a quarrel, such as any married couple might have. I hope when I get home tonight Virginia will be waiting for me."

But she wasn't, and several days later, Grant's houseboy discovered him unconscious in his bedroom at 2:28 P.M. and called the police and a doctor. The servant said there were "poison tablets" on a bedside table.

By the time two physicians arrived, the servants had partially revived him, and when Cary said that he had taken poison, the doctors pumped his stomach. Later, he said that he had only been drunk. And whatever was in the bottle of pills, the police said that it had never been opened.

When Cary had been revived he said there hadn't been any poison pills, that he'd merely been drunk. He admitted that after he'd gotten drunk, he made a number of phone calls and did not clearly remember what he had said. The next day, without ever identifying the unopened bottle of pills, Cary told reporters he was glad he hadn't taken any poison.

"You know what whiskey does when you drink it all by yourself," he said. "It makes you very, very sad. I began calling people up. I know I called Virginia. I don't remember what I said to her, but things got hazier and hazier.

"I'd sure hate to leave this world," he said. "It would be a much better one if Virginia would come back, though. See if you guys can fix it up so she'll forgive me.

"I'm ashamed of getting drunk," he added. "In Hollywood, a comedian can get drunk, but a 'straight' man can't. I'm a 'straight' man and people won't like it."

Virginia, who had been staying at her mother's place in Beverly Hills, rushed to their house and went in to see him as soon as the doctors had finished pumping his stomach. Cary explained that he had been drunk. Virginia seemed in complete control of any sympathy she may have felt.

"You know where to find me," she said tartly and drove back to her mother's house.

In December Virginia filed a separate maintenance suit, asking for $1,000 dollars a month support and division of their community property which she estimated at $50,000. She said that Cary Grant was so stingy she had been forced to pawn her engagement ring.

Superior Court Judge Dudley Valentine ordered Grant to pay Virginia $167.50 a week pending trial of her separate maintenance suit.

Later, after a property settlement had been effected out of court, she dropped the separate maintenance suit and filed a divorce action. She said that Cary Grant drank too much, and that when he was drunk, he beat and choked her, and threatened her life. She said that he spent most of his free time reading his press clippings. She said that he sarcastically told her she had no talent as an actress. She said that he nagged her without cause, would not accompany her to "places of amusement," and wouldn't pay her bills.

Cary Grant said nothing, did not contest the divorce, and did not appear in court the day it was granted: March 26, 1935.

The Cary Grant-Virginia Cherrill marriage appears to be an almost classic tale of a love affair breaking up on the shoals of youth, inexperience, and the fishbowl atmosphere of Hollywood. Cary Grant was thirty years old when he married for the first time, but in many ways his emotions were those of a much younger man. Instinctively shy he had spent over half his life in the world of show business, a calling that tends to magnify one's normal insecurities rather than easing them. Much of that time had been spent on the road. He had had virtually no experience in the emotional tactics necessary for sucess in a permanent, long-term relationship.

Added to these unfortunate realities was the fact that Cary Grant still carried the emotional scars left by his mother's mysterious disappearance when he was nine years old. Underneath the handsome and debonair exterior was a man who deeply doubted his own worth. In the depths of his unconscious mind, the child reasoned that if he had been truly worthwhile, his mother would not have left him.

A curious footnote to Cary Grant's first marriage can be read in a brief item that United Press printed on September 6, 1934. This was just after Virginia had walked out of Hollywood and gone to stay with her mother in Beverly Hills. Their close friends knew about the breakup, but the public remained unaware of the troubled marriage until stories appeared in the papers early in October.

Here is the United Press story in its entirety:

> *Hollywood, Sept. 6, (U.P.)—Mysterious telephone calls to the home of Mrs. W.B. Cherrill, mother of Virginia Cherrill, film actress, today brought an investigation by Hollywood police on suspicion the screen player was marked as victim of a possible kidnaping plot. Mrs. Cherrill summoned detectives when the caller kept breaking the connection.*
>
> *Miss Cherrill, who played opposite Charlie Chaplin in "City Lights," is the wife of Cary Grant, screen player.*

Cary admitted to making a number of phone calls the night his houseboy found him drunk. It is difficult not to suspect that his marital troubles had reduced leading man Cary Grant to the childish stunt of dialing his mother-in-law's number, and then, out of either confusion over what to say or what was perhaps a desire to harass his estranged wife, hanging up as soon as either of them answered the phone.

Later that year, Virginia married England's Earl of Jersey. She later divorced him after thirteen years of marriage and returned to southern California where, in 1948, she married engineer Florian Martini, a former RAF pilot whom she had met during the war. When Newsweek wanted to photograph her in the mid-Sixties for their "Where Are They Now?" feature, Virginia refused to have her picture taken.

"My life is so different now," she explained, "that the Hollywood period might never have existed."

* * * * * *

The collapse of his first marriage left Cary Grant tinged with a bitterness that he was usually, but not always, able to hide. He moved back into the beachhouse he had shared with Randolph Scott before his marriage. He told Scott he had made up his mind never to get married again.

Cary's domestic unhappiness was not eased by fulfillment in his work. Paramount continued to use him in inferior vehicles, and he was becoming more and more impatient with their shortsightedness.

Using whatever obstructionist tactics he could think of, Cary Grant made only two films for Paramount in 1935. *Wings in the Dark*, with Myrna Loy, is an improbable story of a blinded flier (Grant) who is miraculously able to take his plane up in the fog and rescue his love (Loy) when the plane she is piloting is lost over Newfoundland as she is returning from a flight to Moscow. He is able to perform this feat via special instruments he had cleverly invented.

The Last Outpost, with Claude Rains and Gertrude Michael, was another of the Gary Cooper rejects. Rains plays a Lawrence of Arabia figure responsible for leading an Armenian tribe away from a band of Turks intent on an Armenian massacre. Grant is a British officer captured by the Kurds. Rains has to rescue him, too. Inexplicably Rains develops a fierce hatred for the man whom he has rescued, a hatred that generates enough plot complications to keep the movie going until its closing scene in which Rains dies in Grant's arms.

Grant's five-year contract was coming up for renewal late in 1936. The Paramount brass, showing the same lack of foresight that had characterized their handling of Cary Grant from the beginning, now made what was by far their worst mistake. They decided to punish him, to teach him a lesson by humiliating him.

Paramount loaned leading man Cary Grant to RKO for a mere supporting role in a film that would star Katharine Hepburn, who had a reputation of being temperamental and difficult to work with. The director would be George Cukor, who had a reputation of being a "woman's director," and a man who was either unable or unwilling to bring out the best in the male actors appearing in his films.

Cary Grant was intended to emerge from this experience chastened and ready to cooperate with the men who ran Paramount.

But that's not quite the way it worked out.

George Cukor and the Breakthrough

IN 1918 SCOTTISH WRITER COMPTON MACKENZIE published a novel called *The Early Life and Adventures of Sylvia Scarlett.* It is an offbeat tale of larceny, sex disguise, and two-bit swindles.

George Cukor read the novel years later and was totally charmed by it. He immediately wanted to make it into a movie. No one was interested.

Cukor, the grandson of Hungarian immigrants, was born in New York in 1899. Like Cary Grant he spent most of his adolescence in theatres, but as a spectator rather than as a performer. His parents hoped that their son would become a lawyer like his uncle, but Cukor's heart was captured early by another love.

"I was fascinated by the theatre from the time I was twelve," he has said.

From that time on he went to the theatre every chance he got which meant two or three times a week.

"I saw everything—from the second balcony. How the hell I got away from school I don't know, but I seem to remember my family being very easygoing about it. And I saw New York theatre at a marvelous period. I was right at the hub of it.

"I saw all the Barrymores in their heyday and Laurette Taylor and Yvette Guilbert and Isadora Duncan and the Diaghilev Ballet.

All these things left their mark on me. I saw everything, good and bad, and it educated me."

After high school Cukor got a series of jobs as a stage manager for various productions. He began directing while working as the manager of a stock company in Rochester, New York. He was on his way. Throughout the Twenties Cukor worked as a Broadway director, slowly and steadily rising to the first ranks.

And in 1929, in the great raids by Hollywood on the New York theatre world, Cukor was signed by Paramount. It was a brief and not entirely happy relationship. Cukor ended up suing the studio over his name as director being removed from a film's credits.

The lawsuit was eventually settled out of court. Cukor wanted to leave Paramount to work with David Selznick at RKO, and part of the settlement was a release from his Paramount contract. In 1932 Selznick and Cukor made three films: *What Price Hollywood?*, *A Bill of Divorcement*, and *Rockabye*.

It was in the second of these three movies that Cukor took a chance on a young actress to play the role of Sydney Fairfield, an unhappy English society girl in Clemence Dane's play. Her name was Katharine Hepburn.

She was asked to test for the part at a special studio that RKO sometimes rented in Manhattan when they needed to run a screen test on a Broadway actor. Her test was a disaster. She was much too aware of the camera and spoke her lines with a terrible earnestness, frequently emphasizing the wrong words. Selznick and Cukor, viewing the test in Hollywood, hardly knew what to make of it.

"There was this odd creature," Cukor recalls, "she wasn't strictly speaking 'pretty'. She was unlike anybody I'd ever heard."

His immediate reaction was that Katharine Hepburn was simply too odd and wouldn't work in the part. But then, toward the end of the test, she had to pick up a glass in a very emotional scene. She wasn't even facing the camera; it was focused on her back. But it was that brief moment that got her the job.

"There was an enormous feeling, a weight about the manner in which she picked up the glass. I thought she was very talented in that action. David Selznick agreed. We hired her," Cukor says.

A Bill of Divorcement got rave reviews from the New York critics and established Katharine Hepburn as a major star. It also fed the legend that George Cukor was a "woman's director," a legend that irritated Cukor from the beginning.

"As far as I'm concerned, acting is acting, great acting is great acting, it excites me and I respond to it," he has said.

Cukor and Hepburn next worked together on *Little Women*. And it was during the filming of Louisa May Alcott's charming story of a New England family that Hepburn and Cukor discovered they had both read and loved Compton Mackenzie's novel, *The Early Life and Adventures of Sylvia Scarlett*.

Cukor knew that Katharine Hepburn would be perfect in the title role. Hepburn's faith in Cukor as a director was complete. They both knew *Sylvia Scarlett* could be a magnificent movie. Now all they had to do was convince a producer.

Over the years Cukor had approached Louis B. Mayer on several occasions trying to get backing for *Sylvia*. Mayer wanted no part of it.

But after Katharine's success in *Alice Adams*, RKO producer Pandro Berman recklessly gave her *carte blanche* to do whatever she wanted as her next project. She couldn't wait to give Cukor the news. They immediately financed a script out of their own pockets. Then they went back to Berman and presented their plan.

Berman never wanted to make *Sylvia Scarlett*.

"I despised everything about it," he recalls. "It was a private promotional deal of Hepburn and Cukor; they conned me into it . . . I said to them, 'Jesus, this is awful, terrible, I don't understand a thing that's going on.' I tried to stop them, but they wouldn't be stopped; they were hell-bent, claiming that this was the greatest thing they had ever found."

In spite of Berman's misgivings he honored his promise to Katharine Hepburn and switched on the green light for the project. Cukor started assembling a cast. He knew right away the actor he wanted to play the part of Jimmy Monkley, a Cockney con man with a ruse in every port. He wanted Cary Grant, and he told the RKO lawyers to begin negotiations with Paramount. Cukor tried not to get his hopes up. After all Grant had been playing leading roles at Paramount for several years now, ever since Mae West had tapped him to play opposite her in *She Done Him Wrong*. They might be quite unwilling to lend him to RKO for a supporting role, no matter how perfect Grant was for the part.

But there were no problems. Paramount quickly agreed to lend Cary Grant to George Cukor. And Cary Grant, who had never before worked with a really top-notch director, also thought it a good idea. Besides, the character of Jimmy Monkley spoke to something deep in his own raffish, music hall soul. It gave him a chance to expand traits that had lain dormant during most of his professional career. Playing Jimmy Monkley was truly like a breath of fresh air after all those "charming idiot" roles.

"For once," Grant said later, "they didn't see me as a nice young man with regular features and a heart of gold."

The other members of the cast included Edmund Gwenn as Henry Scarlett, Sylvia's father; Brian Aherne as Michael Fane, the artist that Sylvia (Kate) falls in love with, and Natalie Paley, Dennie Moore, and Lennox Pawle in minor roles.

The script by Gladys Unger, John Collier, and Mortimer Offner tells the story of Henry Scarlett who is forced to leave France because one of his larcenies is discovered. His daughter, Sylvia, leaves with him disguised as a boy. In London they join up with Jimmy Monkley who is eager to get his hands on some smuggled diamonds he's heard about. The three of them pull a number of swindles and then go on the road with a band of travelling actors. Sylvia drops her boy's disguise when she meets the artist, Fane. After her competition runs away, she wins him in the end. The father goes mad, and Jimmy Monkley seems set for a lifetime of petty crime.

Most of the exteriors were shot on the California coast above Malibu. Brian Aherne remembers the filming of *Scarlett* as a kind of paid vacation.

"We had a lovely time! We swam and sunbathed and shouted with laughter. We were all young—very young. Both George Cukor and Kate had cooks who used to vie with each other to prepare the lunches. The meals were equally delicious—served on benches on the cliffs above the sea."

Howard Hughes occasionally joined them for lunch, landing his biplane on a nearby landing strip. He and Katharine Hepburn were seeing a great deal of each other at this time, and Hughes was also soon to become one of Cary Grant's best friends.

Aherne recalls a scene that called for Cary Grant to rescue a drowning girl. The Pacific surf was very cold that day, and Grant refused to do it. The actress, Natalie Paley, was "out there bobbing up and down. It was *freezing*, and she was really almost drowning, and occasionally you'd hear 'glug, glug, glug!' And George said, 'Oh, go in, Cary, she's *drowning*!' and Cary said, 'I won't, it's too cold!'

"So finally George said, 'Oh, Christ!' And he sent in Kate instead, and she rescued Natalie. You should have heard what Natalie said after that."

Unfortunately *Sylvia Scarlett*'s audience did not enjoy seeing the movie nearly as much as its cast had enjoyed making it. The film was neither a critical nor a box office success. Producer Berman was furious. The night the movie was previewed half the audience walked out, and the rest frequently burst into spontaneous booing.

The whole evening was a debacle. Katharine Hepburn usually did not go to previews of her films. But she loved this picture so much and was so sure it would be a success that she attended the preview with Cukor. They, too, left early. Watching the audience reaction was too painful to endure.

Kate was terribly depressed and drove back to Cukor's house with him. Berman was already there.

"You got me into this crap," he shouted. "That plot! And not one person in the audience understood a word of those English accents!"

Kate said that she and Cukor felt terrible.

"We'll make it up to you," she said. "We'll do another picture for you free of charge."

"Oh, God, no!" Berman shouted on his way out. "I never want to see either of you again."

Berman eventually calmed down but he never changed his opinion about *Sylvia Scarlett*. He called it "by far the worst picture I ever made, and the greatest catastrophe of Kate's Thirties career."

In fact there was only one person who emerged from *Sylvia Scarlett* smelling like a rose and that was Cary Grant. In reviews that ranged from lukewarm to hostile, he was invariably singled out for virtually the only critical praise the movie got.

Variety's critic said that "Cary Grant practically steals the picture."

Time magazine said, "The film is made memorable by Cary

Grant's superb depiction of the cockney."

Director Cukor also found it hard to write off.

"The picture (*Sylvia Scarlett*) did something to me. It slowed me up. I wasn't going to be so goddamned daring after that."

Katharine Hepburn freely admits that "he (Grant) was the only thing that really made a hit in *Sylvia Scarlett*."

And Cukor seems to relish the role he played in releasing the unique talents of Cary Grant:

"Up to then, he had been a rather handsome, rather wooden leading man. But suddenly, during the shooting, he felt all his talents coming into being—maybe because it was the first part which really suited his background. He suddenly burst into bloom. It produced a wonderful performance."

On another occasion, Cukor said:

"You see, up to then Cary Grant had been a conventional leading man. This part was extremely well written, and he knew this kind of raffish life; he'd been a stilt-walker in the circus. And he'd had enough experience by this time to know what he was up to, and suddenly this part hit him, and he felt the ground under his feet."

He felt the ground under his feet. And having felt it, Cary Grant wanted to walk around on that ground and become totally at home there. He got a chance to do just that when MGM wanted to borrow him for a supporting role in *Mutiny on the Bounty*. He literally begged Paramount to let him play the part of the idealistic young aristocrat whose illusions are shattered by his tour of duty on Captain Bly's *Bounty*. But Paramount refused to let him play a lesser role to Clark Gable's Mr. Christian. Grant's part went, instead, to Franchot Tone who got an Oscar nomination for his efforts.

But then, almost inexplicably, Paramount let MGM use him in a second-rate movie called *Suzy* starring Jean Harlow. It was back to the "charming idiot" roles with a vengeance.

Several months later, when it was time to renegotiate his contract, Grant told Paramount that he would not sign any contract, no matter what the terms. He would sell his services to the highest bidder. More importantly he would be free to take the good parts and turn down the bad ones based on his own assessment of his abilities. He would not have to depend on the Paramount front office to look out for his best interests as an actor. From now on, thank you, he'd look after his own interests without the dubious help of Paramount.

"It takes a good deal of courage to overcome obstacles in this business," Grant has said. "If you're willing to go on for years being the sappy juvenile or ingenue, you're out before you know it. Only when you rebel do things really come your way."

He knew he was taking a big step, but working conditions had become literally intolerable.

"Only Mae West and Marlene Dietrich were permitted to choose their parts at Paramount, and I was fed up with what I was doing," Cary later recalled. "It didn't turn out too badly. Without a contract, I pushed my money up to three hundred thousand a picture in no time.

And that is how Cary Grant, early in 1937, became Hollywood's first and most successful freelance actor.

5

The Peak Years I: 1937-1941

THE SCREWBALL COMEDY, like the Broadway musical, is a distinctly American genre. Both forms utilize the tremendous sense of possibility and energy that have always been an integral part of the American character.

When faced with the Great Depression of the Thirties, Europe turned to fascism. Americans had a better solution. We elected Franklin Roosevelt to the presidency and invented the screwball comedy to keep our spirits up while wating for the New Deal to cure the temporary (who could doubt it?) collapse of our economy.

Film historians generally agree that *It Happened One Night* with Clark Gable and Claudette Colbert, is the first recognizable screwball comedy. The 1934 movie casts Gable as the newspaper reporter who, by chance, finds runaway heiress Colbert. The film is thoroughly enjoyable, but Gable is a trifle too wooden, and Colbert is a trifle too fragile to engage in the no-holds-barred sexual repartee that was to characterize this genre at its best. This was sexual repartee in the widest possible sense: the leading men in these movies weren't primarily interested in seduction, and the women had lots on their minds besides snaring a husband.

In the screwball comedy the sexes, for possibly the first time in American mass entertainment, approached equality. The Great Depression had put many women to work and had taught many men that there are worse things in life than your wife having to take a job: there was the spectre of no jobs at all for anyone.

And once large numbers of American women had tasted the rough autonomy involved in supporting themselves and frequently their families as well, there was no going back to a clinging vine role. The heroines of the screwball comedies reflect this new spirit. Think of them: Carole Lombard, Jean Arthur, Rosalind Russell, and Katharine Hepburn come immediately to mind. These were bright, breezy, fast-talking, wisecracking ladies. If they stumbled and fell, whether it was over a job or a man, they did not sit there and stew in self-pity. They picked themselves up and went blithely on their way.

It takes a special kind of man to relate to such a woman, and nobody ever did it as well as Cary Grant. He was not the leading man in the first screwball comedy; Gable was. But for all intents and purposes, once he made *The Awful Truth* with Irene Dunne, and *Topper* with Constance Bennett (both in 1937), the genre appeared to have been invented just for him.

Between 1937 and 1941, Cary Grant made fifteen films. None of them were really bad, although *The Howards of Virginia* (1940) comes close. Grant does not belong in costume dramas. He seems ill at ease and not quite in control of his enormous energies.

These same energies, however, served him brilliantly in most of the movies he made during this period. Seven of the fifteen have become enduring classics of the American cinema; most of them are prime examples of the screwball comedy at its very best: *Topper*, with Constance Bennett; *The Awful Truth*, with Irene Dunne; *Bringing Up Baby*, with Katharine Hepburn; *Holiday*, with Katharine Hepburn; *Gunga Din*, with Victor McLaglen and Douglas Fairbanks, Jr.; *His Girl Friday*, with Rosalind Russell and *The Philadelphia Story*, with Katharine Hepburn and James Stewart.

In *Topper*, Cary Grant and Constance Bennett play a lighthearted young couple who are killed in an auto accident and come back to earth as ghosts. Their self-appointed mission is to rescue Roland Young, playing a henpecked banker, from his dreadful, silly wife, played by Billie Burke.

The Awful Truth is more directly a romantic comedy and the best of his three movies opposite Irene Dunne. After a trivial marital spat they have decided on divorce. During the period of interlocutory decree, Grant has visiting rights to their dog. This gives him a chance to see her, although he is somehow never quite able to say that the divorce was a mistake, and he wants her back. In the end it is Dunne who must make the definitive move toward reconciliation.

Gunga Din is a special case. In addition to its frequent moments of farce and low comedy, this film also contains several splendid battle sequences, and what can only be called the love story between Grant and the adoring Gunga Din, played by Sam Jaffe. Filmed in the foothills of California's Mount Whitney with searing summer temperatures often reaching 110 degrees, the location was perfect in rendering the steaming Indian landscape. In other ways, however, the movie lacks cohesion. Primarily a colonial adventure story in the mold of *Lives of a Bengal Lancer*, there are also vaudeville and soap opera segments. Ann Evers and Joan Fontaine play wives to Grant and Fairbanks, but the women's roles are obviously an afterthought. The stream of energy in the movie runs between the men. It is the sheer physical exuberance of Grant, Fairbanks, and McLaglen that raises *Gunga Din* to the level of a classic. Even the tricked-up ending, with the slain Gunga Din shown in Heaven wearing a British uniform, cannot destroy its ebullient integrity.

The movie works for Grant and ultimately for everyone, because he is playing opposite actors who can match, at least in this film under director George Stevens, Grant's awesome energy level.

In this first peak period of Cary Grant's career, however, there were only two actresses with whom he could let out all the stops, secure in the knowledge that Katharine Hepburn and Rosalind Russell could give just as good as they got.

Grant made three films with Katharine Hepburn in these years, films that brought both of them to their peaks as comic actors: *Bringing Up Baby*, *Holiday* and *The Philadelphia Story*. Probably because of her long offscreen love affair with Spencer Tracy, conventional wisdom has it that Kate Hepburn was at her best in the series of comedies she made with Tracy for MGM.

The problem, so often the case with conventional wisdom, is that it simply isn't true. Hepburn and Tracy made some delightful movies, but part of their appeal to the inevitably sexist audiences of the period is the unstated feeling that Tracy is going to bring Kate down a notch, teach her a lesson, knock her off her high horse. His seriousness is shown to be good and just what the flighty, wrapped-up-in-herself Hepburn needs.

This basic rationale to their screen relationship is best illustrated by the interchange reputed to have taken place between them when they first met on the set of *Woman of the Year*.

"I'm afraid I'm a little tall for you, Mr. Tracy," Kate said.

"Don't worry, Miss Hepburn," Tracy replied, "I'll cut you down to my size."

But in all the movies Katharine Hepburn made with Cary Grant, she never had to worry abut being cut down to size, never had to rein herself in, never had to subdue her coltish high spirits. Grant liked her fine just the way she was.

RKO producer Pan Berman, with the *Sylvia Scarlett* disaster and several other mediocre Hepburn films fading from memory due to Kate's success in *Stage Door*, ordered his writers to come up with a comic vehicle for Hepburn's talents. Hager Wilde finally devised a wacky story about a bubble-headed Connecticut heiress named Susan Vance who drags a naive and unworldly paleontologist through a series of farcical adventures that revolve around Ms. Vance's pet leopard, Baby. After being turned down by Ray Milland, Ronald Colman, and Robert Montgomery, Howard Hawks was signed as director. He approached Cary Grant for the part of the shy scientist.

"I wouldn't know how to tackle it," Cary said. "I'm not an intellectual type."

"You've seen Harold Lloyd, haven't you?" Hawks asked.

Then Cary understood what the part was all about: the innocent abroad. That's the way he played it, and it worked beautifully.

Years later Cary Grant recalled with pleasure, his first comedy collaboration with Katharine Hepburn.

"Working with her was incredible. You never saw such timing! She had a mind like a computer—every detail worked out! Yet computers don't have instincts, and her instincts were infallible. She taught me just about everything I know abut comedy—how to time my lines, the solemn way to say something comic, and if there was anything she didn't know, which I doubt, then Howard Hawks could fill in the rest."

Saying that Hepburn taught him "everything I know" about comedy is almost exactly what he said about Mae West. Grant has always been willing to give generous credit for his achievements to others. It is not clear whether this has been due to an extraordinary emotional generosity, a need to gain approval that was instilled in him as a child, or simply, that as the best romantic comedian Hollywood has ever produced, he always knew he could spread the credit around without seriously diminishing his own position. Or most likely, a combination of all these factors.

It was in this movie that Grant, under Howard Hawks' direction, first developed his famous whinny.

"We had a scene in *Bringing Up Baby* where he's angry," Hawks explained. "I said, 'pretty dull. You get angry like Joe Doakes next door. Can't you think of somebody who gets angry and it's funny?' And then I remembered a man who practically whinnies like a horse when he's angry—so he did it."

In *Holiday* and *The Philadelphia Story*, Grant and Hepburn were working once again with George Cukor, the director who brought them together on the ill-fated *Sylvia Scarlett*.

Both movies were adapted from Philip Barry plays, a writer whose style Cukor describes as "very witty, sometimes high-flown, sometimes sentimental. Barry had a rather 'in' view of the rich, of the really grand people."

Holiday tells the story of a young man (Grant) who falls in love with a rich girl (Doris Nolan). But when she learns that he's not interested in making money and would rather just enjoy life for awhile, she fears she's made a bad mistake. Grant's philosophy seems eminently sensible to Nolan's younger sister (Hepburn), but Grant doesn't have time for her throughout most of the film. Finally in the movie's closing moments, the two kindred spirits get together.

This is also the basic plot of *The Philadelphia Story* with the roles reversed. Now it's Hepburn who won't recognize that her ex-husband Grant is her true love and has been all along.

It is almost inconceivable that the boisterous Cary Grant of *Sylvia Scarlett* and *Gunga Din*, the wacked-out Cary Grant of *Bringing Up Baby*, could play his roles in these two movies to such polished, urbane perfection. He has enough physical presence to steal every scene. He never does. And yet that same physical presence contributes enormously to the success these two films so rightly enjoyed. This sense of great physical energy is something he shares with Hepburn; it's what makes Grant and Hepburn seem so *right* for each other. The audience sees this before they do, and their finally getting together at the end of the three Grant-Hepburn comedies goes way beyond the traditionally sentimental happy ending and fade to black. These two people *belonged* together.

The same thing happens in *His Girl Friday*. Rosalind Russell comes across as a totally grown-up and adult woman who knows exactly what she wants and is determined to get it. Unfortunately we can see right away that what she thinks she wants (Ralph Bellamy) isn't what she really needs: her ex-husband and former boss, managing editor Walter Burns, played by Cary Grant.

As reporter Hildy Johnson, Roz Russell has bought the feminine mystique right down to a sappy dream of marrying insurance man Bellamy and living with him in a house complete with white picket fence.

She wants to be "respectable." She's the best reporter in town: that's one of the reasons Grant loves her, but early in the movie she's just too dumb to see what an exciting life she had before she left the paper and divorced him.

She stops in to say hello as she and Bellamy are on their way to Albany where they're to be married. They'll live with his mother.

"Albany? Mother?" Grant says, in unbelieving tones.

Clearly, Roz must be out of her mind, but what can he do to make her see that? Throughout the movie he cooks up one scheme after another to trick Hildy into covering just one more big story. It's the biggest compliment he can pay her: she's the best there is and if she doesn't enjoy using her considerable journalistic prowess, he knows its hopeless anyway. If she can't see her own worth, how will she ever see his?

The one thing he won't do is pander to her nitwit dream of "respectability." He won't light her cigarettes, won't hold open doors for her, won't treat her like a dependent creature who needs to be shielded. He loves her because she's tough, brave, and witty. And, of course, it doesn't hurt anything that she's the best reporter he's ever worked with: he wants her back on his staff.

Finally in the closing moments of *His Girl Friday*, Russell finally gets it through her otherwise bright head that reporting is more fun than tending a white picketed cottage, and that Grant may not light her cigarettes, but he respects her for the same reasons he loves her. He's met his match and knows it.

Recently *His Girl Friday* was shown at a small Greenwich Village revival movie house. The young audience, composed primarily of New York University students, stood up and spontaneously cheered when all Grant's machinations paid off, and Russell let Bellamy take the train to Albany without her.

Time gives the proper perspective on what's important and what isn't. When the movie was released in 1940, a number of newsmen and editors objected strenuously to the "callous and unscrupulous" Walter Burns, as played by Grant. They thought the movie showed most reporters as people who would sell their grandmothers for a good story.

Aside from the fact that then and now, many reporters *would* sell their grandmothers for a good story, Cary Grant was vastly amused by their discomfort for other reasons.

"It's a funny thing about newspapermen," he said in an interview while working on a later film with Irene Dunne, *Penny Serenade* (in which he again plays a newsman). "They can dish it out, but they can't take it. They're forever exaggerating what movie people are like. It makes their stories better. But let movie people, for the sake of better stories, exaggerate what newspapermen are like, and they don't like it. Doctors object to movies about doctors. Truck drivers object to movies about truck drivers. They all say, 'We aren't like that.' We know they aren't like that. We know movie actors aren't like that, too, when we go in for broad gestures and ham a yard wide in every picture about Hollywood. If we showed any profession as it actually is, movies would be as dull as dishwater. Entertainment consists of exaggerating everything except human nature."

The journalists' criticism had obviously touched a raw nerve. Grant was never to feud openly with the press as Katharine Hepburn did, but his marriage to Virginia Cherrill and their subsequent divorce had taught him the bitter lessons that not all reporters could be trusted to be accurate, and that none of them could be trusted to respect your privacy. After all their very livelihoods depended on how effectively they *abused* your privacy.

He had become very wary of giving interviews and pointedly told reporters on numerous occasions that his private life was nobody's business but his own.

In addition to his bitter memories of the way in which the painful experience of his first divorce had been dragged through the daily papers, the only other jarring note in Cary Grant's public life during these years was in December, 1938, when he and several other Hollywood figures were subpoenaed by the Justice Department to testify as to what they knew about a $1 million bond fraud engineered by William P. Buckner, Jr., heir to an insurance fortune and, at the time of the government inquiry, fiance to Loretta Young.

Buckner had allegedly inflated the bonds of the Philippine Railway Company in a complicated scheme that involved using movie stars' names to impress potential investors and employing call girls to entertain Washington legislators.

Grant's name was one of those used to create an aura of legitimacy around the scheme. He was the first actor to answer the summons and was questioned for fifteen minutes in the United State's Attorney's office in New York. Grant told U.S. Attorney William P. Maloney that he knew nothing of the scheme, hadn't bought any bonds, and hadn't ever met Buckner.

But the story made the front page of newspapers all over the country, that stories linked Cary Grant to a $1 million fraud. His screen image was that of a nice guy. Why should it be tarnished through the most spurious guilt-by-association mix-up?

Most of his publicity, however, was openly and unashamedly adoring. This was the heyday of the fan magazine. Boasting millions of readers, the fan magazines tried hard to give the illusion they were imparting inside information about what the stars thought, what they felt, how they lived. No detail of life's minutiae escaped their scrutiny. One of them solemnly told its readers that Grant preferred a bath to a shower, often had kippers for breakfast (preferred tripe and onions but couldn't get them in southern California) that he never drank coffee, never used sugar, and had his suits tailored in London. The story ended on the titillating note that Grant wore only his pajama tops to bed, never the bottoms.

Cary continued to share the Malibu beachhouse with Randolph

Scott throughout the Thirties. Grant enjoyed a brief swim in the Pacific in the mornings before he left for the studio. The two men gave occasional small parties. Carole Lombard once described the way they handled their household accounts:

"Cary opened the bills, Randy wrote the checks, and if Cary could talk someone out of a stamp, he mailed them."

Fan magazine stories carefully explained that Cary and Randy didn't get married because they couldn't afford to.

"Here we are," *Modern Screen* quoted Cary, "living as we want to as bachelors with a nice home at a comparatively small cost. If we got married, we would have to put up a front. Women—particularly Hollywood women—expect it."

Cary Grant worked most often for RKO and Columbia after he left Paramount in 1937. The Scott-Grant living arrangement made stufio executives uneasy. Almost from the beginning of their careers, Grant had been a bigger star than Scott, but each man could certainly afford his own house. What would people think? Stories began appearing in the fan magazines about what a he-man Cary Grant was. Randolph Scott never made the money that Cary Grant did, so the studio bosses didn't worry quite as much about the invincibility of Scott's masculine image. But Cary Grant was another matter.

"Randy says the guy's regular," says one fan mag story. Randolph Scott is then quoted as telling a story meant to illustrate that Cary Grant is a regular fellow:

"We went on a fishing trip recently in Shasta National Forest. We left the hotel at dawn and packed in to the McCloud River.

"Well, the country was plenty wild and, like a dope, Cary had worn tennis shoes. He kept slipping and falling all over the boulders. Finally, in disgust he took the shoes off, tied them to his belt and continued on in his bare feet. Naturally, by the time we got back his dogs were plenty sore and bruised. But not once was there one yap or complaint out of him."

The story in *Movie Mirror* also quotes Scott as saying that Cary Grant "is easy to live with, considerate of others, doesn't interfere or try to give advice however well meant, has the courage to fight for his convictions, is a graceful winner and a good loser, never outfumbles in doing his share, and has a punchy sense of humor."

Grant was obviously wasting his time walking on rocks. He was much better suited to walking on water.

* * * * * *

After his divorce from Cherrill, Grant dated a succession of starlets, although his relationship with some of the women he was linked with was a total fabrication. Those were the days when Hollywood columnists were churning out stories about the stars in an endless stream. They couldn't always verify each item themselves, and press agents for rising young actresses knew a good thing when they saw it. Even a fictitious date with Cary Grant acquired a certain reality when it appeared in a column. It might be just what his client needed to get noticed by the right producer, the one who would make her a star—and the agent rich.

Grant seemed to understand this was an occupational hazard:

"I don't go out nearly as much as the columnists claim. I never did. The only reason I get in the papers so often is because I'm a so-called eligible bachelor. There are only a few of the species left, so the columnists have to use the names over and over, whether you were actually out nightclubbing or not. There's no fun in reporting married couples out with each other. There's no scandal in that."

Grant did, however, have bonafide romances with actresses Mary Brian and Ginger Rogers. Finally, in the late Thirties, he began seeing actress Phyllis Brooks exclusively. The columnists began predicting marriage. There were rumors of engagement rings and a possible secret wedding. This went on for months.

Finally, in an anticlimactic announcement from Lake Tahoe, Grant and Ms. Brooks announced that they were, indeed, engaged. The marriage, however, never took place. There were no public scenes or recriminations. Their engagement seemed to dwindle away.

* * * * * *

The war had begun, and it changed lives in Hollywood just as it did elsewhere. Grant, like many other stars, went on long tours to sell U.S. Savings Bonds. Before America entered the conflict, Grant, without publicity, had donated his after-tax salary of

$62,500 from *The Philadelphia Story* to the American Red Cross for British war relief. A number of other English actors, directors, and writers working in Hollywood had also made hefty contributions.

But after the fall of France in the summer of 1940, England was left to face the fierce Nazi war-machine alone. In their native land a surge of public opinion rose against Hollywood's British contingent. They were described, in the British tabloid press, as "slackers," "deserters," and worse.

Eventually the furor died down. England survived the saturation German bombing of the Battle of Britain. And the public criticism more or less came to a halt when America finally entered the war in December, 1941, after the surprise Japanese attack on Pearl Harbor.

The movie colony's English population, who had given privately in the war's early years, thought it wise to make their contributions known even after the storm of criticism had died down. When Cary Grant was signed by Warner Brothers to appear in *Arsenic and Old Lace*, he announced he was giving his entire salary to the American Red Cross and other charities connected with the Allied war effort: the United Service Organizations (USO) and British War Relief.

Grnat, along with virtually every major Hollywood actor who did not serve in the Armed Forces, also entertained servicemen as part of various USO troupes. Cary and his old friend from Pender and vaudeville days, Don Barclay, refurbished their vaudeville routines for the USO stages.

Cary's link with the war in Europe was quite real. There was more to it than the simple fact of his being a British subject. On January 26, 1941, Cary Grant got the news that his aunt and uncle, Mr. and Mrs. John H. Leach, had been killed in an air raid. Also dead were the Leach's daughter (Grant's first cousin), son-in-law and grandson, all of them crushed in the rubble when a German bomb scored a direct hit on their Bristol home.

By this time Cary Grant had made several trips back to England. He'd been reunited with his mother who was no longer institutionalized. He liked being able to provide her with a comfortable life, free of the economic worry that had preyed on her mind during his boyhood. The years when "the whole world knew who

Cary Grant was, but my own mother didn't know me" were, at last, over. His father had died in 1935. The official hospital report said Elias Leach had died of "extreme toxicity," a term that is probably a euphemism for liver failure due to acute alcoholism. No matter what the official reports say, however, Cary Grant believes that his father died of a broken heart, of grief that he was never able to make his life any better than it was.

Transatlantic flights were not the commonplace then that they are now. There was only one way to travel to Europe: on one of the great liners. Their passenger lists read like directories of the rich, the famous, and the people who serve the important function of introducing the rich and famous to each other. The rich like the famous because they are frequently talented, therefore amusing. The famous like the rich because their company testifies to the fact that they have, indeed, made it. If the rich want to spend time with them, their fame must be deserved.

Countess Dorothy di Grasso was one of these intermediaries. She took to Cary Grant right away. He was not only famous, he knew how to enjoy fame. He had begun to consciously play at being Cary Grant. You could invite him to dinner and rest assured that he would be urbane and witty, possibly even scintillating.

Countess di Grasso also had a rich friend. Her name was Barbara Hutton and, in spite of being the richest woman in the world, she'd had *such* a dreadful life. A forlorn childhood and a couple of very bad marriages.

Wouldn't it be amusing if Barbara and Cary Grant hit it off? So the Countess invited them both to dinner.

Barbara Hutton

Wife #2

BARBARA HUTTON'S LIFE gives eloquent testimony to the truism that money won't buy happiness. She was the only child of Edna Woolworth and Franklyn L. Hutton. Edna was one of F.W. Woolworth's three daughters. He had built a financial empire based on the same idea that Henry Ford used to create his fortune: cheap, but sturdy, mass-produced, easily available goods for American workers. Ford took this idea and built the Model A, inventing the modern assembly line along the way. F.W. Woolworth invented the dimestore.

Edna Woolworth thought her father had a good thing going; she wanted her husband to become part of it. Frank Hutton, however, did not think that working for one's father-in-law the most advantageous of positions. If he had to work for a family firm, best that it be *his* family. He weathered the storm of his wife's recriminations and joined the Wall St. brokerage firm founded by his brother, E.F. Hutton.

Barbara Hutton was born on November 14, 1912. Five years later her mother committed suicide by leaping out a window of the Plaza Hotel. For many years the truth of her death was not publicly known. Official reports of the incident reflected the influence of the Woolworth name and the Woolworth fortune. They said that Edna Woolworth had died in her Plaza hotel room of suffocation resulting from an ear infection.

"I never knew my mother," Barbara said in later years. "I

hardly remembered her. But I have missed her all my life. I think any girl's life takes on a different pattern when she is brought up without a mother."

The pattern of Barbara's childhood was erratic. The idea of "home" became an abstraction. Most of her young life was spent in various boarding schools or with relatives. Her father appears to have been unaware that his daughter needed his company and a permanent home with him.

"My father was young and very busy," she said later. "He loved me, of course, but I was only an ordinary, rather stupid, little girl, and I couldn't be a real companion to a gay, brilliant young man, could I?"

Barbara Hutton frequently made such self-abasing statements. It is not clear whether her childhood experiences destroyed her self-respect or whether she had learned early in life that self-abnegation is a splendid way to underline the shortcomings of others. After all if both her mother and father had abandoned her as a child, it was to be expected that she would often do silly, stupid things. Who could expect more? (This psychological strategy was first given a name by psychiatrist Eric Berne in his 1964 bestseller, *Games People Play.* The game is called "Wooden Leg.")

Barbara's grandfather died in 1919 without a will. It wasn't until 1924 that Barbara's senile grandmother also died, leaving the way clear for Barbara and her two aunts to divvy up $78,317,938 between them. Barbara's father, who had done very well on Wall St., invested her share so shrewdly that by the time she was twenty-one, it had increased another $13 million. When Barbara Hutton reached her majority, she was worth $42,077,328. That's about the time she started touting herself as a "poor little rich girl."

When Barbara was fifteen she met a fortune hunter named Alexis Mdivani. He claimed to be a Georgian prince, but it hardly mattered. His alleged princedom was securely in the hands of the U.S.S.R. whose communist leaders showed no signs of restoring his title. Alec carefully nurtured his relationship with Barbara as best he could from a distance.

When Barbara was eighteen, her coming out party in New York at the Ritz-Carlton cost sixty thousand dollars. Her father, with whom she had been quarelling for years, gave her, in addition to the thirteen million dollar increase in her fortune, a private Pullman railway car. She named it the "Curly Hut." She'd been getting a five thousand dollar a month allowance from the estate from the time she was sixteen. Her father hoped that she would learn how to handle money.

After her debut he took her to Europe, hoping to escape the swarms of fortune hunters who materialized wherever Barbara settled in the States.

When Barbara was twenty, she married Alec Mdivani. He'd acquired credentials since their first meeting, having recently been divorced by an Astor heiress. He was ready to move up.

On their wedding night, he showed how much he was interested in her.

"You're too fat," he said.

A spunkier girl could have made any number of appropriate replies ranging from "Drop dead!" to "You're fired!" Barbara Hutton, however, consumed nothing but black coffee until she had lost forty-six pounds. Her weight dropped from 148 to 102. She also, as it happens, destroyed her health.

"I had got the idea I wanted to get married," Barbara said after their divorce two years later. "I was always so lonesome. I wanted a companion. Besides, I thought I would have more freedom if I got married. Unfortunately, the money did something to Alec. He began throwing it around like confetti."

Mdivani walked away from the marriage with the income from a two million dollar trust fund. The day after her Reno divorce on May 13, 1935, she married another titled foreigner, Danish Count Kurt Haugwitz-Reventlow. That union lasted six years and produced her only child, Lance, born Feb. 24, 1936. Barbara Hutton gave up her American citizenship to marry Haugwitz-Reventlow. When World War II began, she returned to the U.S.A. and announced that she had changed her mind. She wanted to be an American citizen, after all. Movie audiences heard her say this on the old Movietone newsreels. They booed and hissed. The "poor little rich girl" routine was wearing very thin.

Haugwitz-Reventlow walked away from marriage to Barbara with \$1½ million. In spite of this he threatened to kidnap their son and take him to Canada. Barbara wanted to get as far away from him as she could and still be in the United States. She chose Los Angeles.

She stayed with Countess Dorothy di Grasso until she could find a place of her own. Cary Grant called one day, and Barbara answered the phone. Dorothy was out. Barbara remembered Cary Grant. He was Hollywood nobility, after all, and they had once met on a transatlantic crossing; had, in fact, once shared a table at

dinner on the *Normandie*. She gave Dorothy the message.
And Dorothy promptly invited Cary Grant to dinner.

* * * * * *

Cary Grant was different from the men Barbara Hutton had known before: he worked for a living. In addition he had money of his own. His personal fortune did not approach hers, of course, but it was enough to make him quite comfortable for the rest of his life if he never made another movie. Besides he'd make lots more movies. He was at the top of the Hollywood heap. Only a few other stars: Clark Gable, Spencer Tracy, John Wayne, and Gary Cooper were in his league.

Barbara Hutton was also different from the women Cary Grant had known before: she was independently wealthy. If she loved him, it would be for himself and not for what he could do for her. In addition Barbara Hutton was something of an innocent, a psychological luxury the rich often choose to indulge. It appealed to him. He had met just as many fortune hunters as she had.

Even before her divorce from Haugwitz-Reventlow came through on August 31, 1941, they were together constantly. On June 26, 1942, Cary Grant officially became an American citizen, and on July 8, Grant and Barbara Hutton were married at the Lake Arrowhead home of Cary's manager, Frank Vincent. Only a handful of guests were present at Vincent's retreat in the San Bernardino Mountains east of Hollywood.

They moved into a beachhouse not far from the one that Cary had shared with Randolph Scott. Barbara quickly made it clear this simply wouldn't do. She rented a huge house in Pacific Palisades from Douglas Fairbanks, Jr. Cary tried to feel comfortable, but a house that requires eleven servants in order to function often lacks a certain intimacy and coziness. In addition to the servants, there was Barbara's son, Lance; his nurse, Barbara's former governess; Barbara's secretary, and Cary's valet.

Then there was the problem of the newspapers. Barbara Hutton often tried to behave in the egalitarian way that she imagined the barely rich to behave, people who were worth only $3 or $4 million. She ordered a copy of the daily paper for everyone in the house.

"I'd come from the studio at night, park my car in the garage, and on the patio I'd wade through eleven copies of the evening *Herald and Express*," Cary said. "I'd say to Barbara, 'Now, why does *each* servant have to have his own special copy of the paper?' She thought they wouldn't like sharing."

Still, for someone in Barbara's position, it wasn't always easy to figure out who was a servant and who wasn't. Especially when Hollywood show people were involved.

One night the house was jammed with people, mostly friends of Cary's. It was a big, lively party, the kind of affair you'd expect to be given by a reigning movie star and his wife, the richest woman in the world. Composer-songwriter Hoagy Carmichael wandered over to the huge grand piano and began to amuse himself by playing a series of odd, quirky little melodies. Suddenly the lady of the house materialized.

"Could you play something a bit more lively?"

"Look, lady," Carmichael said, cigarette dangling from his mouth. "I'm a guest here . . . same as you. I'll play what I please."

Barbara had a word of her own for anything she felt lacked taste: "ig." That's all. Just "ig." The word itself has no taste but no matter. Barbara obviously felt it contained worlds of meaning. Once she and Cary were at a party held in an overdone Hollywood house, a not-uncommon phenomenon, expecially in the early Forties. It had a huge apricot-colored bar that stretched along one entire wall in the living room. The hostess was very proud of it.

"Don't you just love the bar?"

Cary Grant hesitated for a moment, shot a quick look at his wife and then said enthusiastically, "Oh, yes, it's so wonderfully ig."

It was supposed to be a private joke, but Barbara began shrieking with laughter and was, according to Grant, "still doubled up when we got to the car."

What the proud owner of the apricot-colored bar thought, no one knows.

But eventually the clash of their totally different backgrounds made itself felt. Cary continued to work as hard as ever. Barbara didn't understand that. When things began to get really bad, Cary insisted they move out of the Doug Fairbanks mansion. He bought a smaller house in Bel-Air and fired most of the servants. By that time it was too late.

On August 15, 1944, Barbara Hutton announced that she and Cary Grant had separated, and that there was "no chance for a reconcilation." She said that Cary "isn't happy."

"There is no thought of divorce at the present time," she told reporters. "Cary and I are remaining the fondest of friends."

It was a most unusual separation. Due to the wartime housing shortage, they both continued to live in the same house.

In announcing the separation, Barbara made a curious admission. She said that she and Cary had planned to part in June, but had postponed their separation after her former husband, Haugwitz-Reventlow, took their son, Lance, then nine years old, to Canada.

Haugwitz-Reventlow had continued to try to win custody of the boy and in April had filed suit in Hollywood in an effort to have U.S. courts honor and enforce an order he had won from the High Court of Justice in England. The decree gave him control of the boy's upbringing on the ground that Barbara and persons in her household "used coarse and vulgar language" in the child's presence.

Barbara countered with a lawsuit of her own in July seeking permanent custody. She said that during their marriage her former husband had exercised "an almost hypnotic influence"over her in a scenario designed to acquire her fortune.

"Cary decided to stand by me," she told reporters in August when she announced they were separating in spite of her continuing legal battles with Haugwitz-Reventlow. "But I think it's best we part now. Besides it's dishonest and unfair to take advantage of his name and protection, because I am fighting to hold my child."

In October there was a reconciliation. It lasted about four months. On February 25, Cary and Barbara parted once again, issuing a joint announcement:

"We have decided we can be happier living apart."

Finally on July 13, 1945, Barbara filed for divorce: her third. She charged "extreme cruelty," asserting that Grant had caused her "grievous mental distress, suffering and anguish without any fault on my part." She did not ask for alimony. The divorce was granted at the end of a four-minute appearance in Los Angeles Superior Court. Reporters attending said she was wearing a black moire suit, a jaunty black straw hat, and no nail polish. They also said her slip was showing.

Barbara told Judge Thurmond Clarke:

"Cary didn't like my friends and I didn't like his friends. When I had my friends to dinner, he would stay in bed. On the few occasions that he joined us, he just didn't seem amused. He was too bored, and it was all very embarrassing to me."

"Did it affect your health?" the judge asked.

"Oh, yes," Barbara said brightly. "Yes, my health was badly affected. It made me so nervous I couldn't eat or sleep."

"Divorce granted."

Cary Grant did not show up in court, although his manager, Frank Vincent put in an appearance. Barbara saw him as she was leaving the courtroom. She threw her arms around him.

"Hello, darling," she said.

Cary Grant walked away from his marriage to the richest woman in the world with nothing but experience. It turns out that he had signed a waiver to any part of her fortune before they were married.

Barbara announced plans to buy a seventy-five thousand dollar castle in Tangier. She said she wanted to "live like an Arab."

Evaluating his marriage to Barbara Hutton, Grant noted later that he had frequently been away from home on wartime bond-selling tours.

"We really saw very little of each other," he said. "You know, I'm not sure that either of us really wanted to marry the other by the time we got around to it. But I'm sure that I would have been a better husband to her today.

"My hope was to get affection. I didn't know I had to give it, too. Our interests were not the same. I was more interested in my work than I should have been, I suppose. I still have a great feeling for her. We are great and good friends."

He gives her credit for teaching him to appreciate art. During their marriage she gave him several paintings by Utrillo and Boudin.

"I remain deeply obliged to her for a welcome education in gracious living."

Once, on a Mexican vacation, they were exploring a magnificent cathedral.

"I noticed so many obviously poor people slowly walking around with enthralled faces, and I remarked how sad it was that those peons were so poor and the church was so rich. I couldn't understand the need for such a costly edifice," Cary Grant recalled later.

"Each one of these people alone could never afford such splendor," Barbara Hutton replied, "but together all of them contribute to make it possible and they can walk in it, sit in it, enjoy its beauty and rest. This is their church. It belongs to them."

"And she was right," Grant said.

After their divorce Barbara frequently phoned Cary for advice, but wouldn't take it when he urged her in 1953 to reconsider her plan to marry Dominican adventurer Porfirio Rubirosa. Grant warned her that Rubirosa was as unsavory as they come. Cary said the fact that she and Doris Duke were the two richest women in the world didn't mean they had to repeat each other's mistakes. Rubirosa had already been married to Doris Duke. His primary vocation in life was marrying rich women. His primary avocation was being named co-respondent in divorce suits that charged adultery.

Barbara Hutton did not take her third husband's advice. She married Rubirosa anyway. It lasted seventy-three days. Rubirosa was her fifth husband. Immediately after Cary, had been another "prince": Igor Troubetzky, a French-born Russian aristocrat. They met while skiing in Switzerland. When she was ready to call it quits, he wanted her to pay three million dollars for the privilege of divorcing him. After Rubirosa and Troubetzkoy there were two others: German Baron Gottfried Von Cramm, a former international tennis star, and Vietnamese Prince Doan Vinh. She married Mr. Vinh with her feet painted red. In Vietnam this symbolizes a woman's deference to her husband. But red-painted feet didn't help that marriage last, either.

As she approached her sixties Barbara Hutton began to make philosophical pronouncements:

"All the unhappiness in my life has been caused by men, including my father, and I think I'm pretty timid about marriage. But also I'm too timid to live alone and life doesn't make any sense without men."

Lance Reventlow always spoke of Cary Grant as his favorite stepfather.

"I was only seven years old when my mother and Cary were married, but I remember that he was a marvelous father to me. He was so warm and charming, and I loved going to the studio with him. He was very good with children," young Reventlow recalled later.

Even after the Grant-Hutton divorce, Lance would often spend his boarding school vacations with Cary Grant whom he came to regard as both an older brother and a father. When Lance was twenty-one, his mother bestowed $25 million on him. He took up auto racing and began to do rather well at it. On Dec. 5, 1958, shortly before his 23rd birthday, the blond six-footer won the Governor's Cup Race in Nassau. His custom-made racing car sported a Chevrolet engine. This event marked the first time in twenty-four years that an American car and driver had won.

Grant watched Lance drive once in Palm Springs. When the race was over, Reventlow couldn't wait to see what Cary thought of his style.

"Well, how did I do?" he asked.

"You're out of your head," Grant replied.

Cary Grant attended both of Lance's weddings, the first to actress Jill St. John, and the second to former Walt Disney mousketeer Cheryl Holdridge.

He also attended Lance Reventlow's funeral. The thirty-six year old heir to the Woolworth fortune died on July 24, 1972, when the small private plane from which he was surveying a possible land purchase crashed in the Colorado Rockies near Aspen. A thunderstorm was blamed for the mishap which left three other persons dead.

* * * * * *

During the years that Cary Grant was married to Barbara Hutton, he did not make a single movie that approached the string of hits he'd had between 1937 and 1941. In fact 1941 is included, not because the two movies he made that year were hits, but for other reasons. *Penny Serenade*, his third and last collaboration with Irene Dunne, won him his first Oscar nomination. The movie, which made no bones about being a straightforward tearjerker, cast Grant as a quite ordinary man overwhelmed with personal sorrows. He performed admirably but the script simply wasn't Cary Grant material.

His other 1941 movie, *Suspicion*, was important because it marked the beginning of his working relationship with director Alfred Hitchcock, an association that would eventually play a large role in reviving Grant's career which floundered badly in the 1940's.

7

Holding His Own, the 1940's

CARY GRANT HAD BECOME one of the top ten box office stars in the late Thirties, and he did not relinquish that position for many years. That elusive star quality we call charisma kept moviegoers lining up to see his films. Grant is so attractive on so many levels that spending a few hours with him in a darkened theatre is enjoyable, even when he is appearing in movies far below his level of accomplishment.

The screwball comedy needed a light touch. The actors and directors working on such films needed an inner awareness and perception of the comic rationale that gives meaning to the wacky goings-on. Otherwise things become tiresome rather than hilarious. This light, intelligent touch is easy to recognize, but hard to define. It meant, among other things, noticing that the social milieu no longer provided a backdrop of hard times on which to bounce off the wackiness. As times got better, people weren't content to lose themselves in nuttiness. They wanted a piece of the action for themselves. The war meant rationing, the draft, bombs, rubble, and grief. But, here in the States, it also meant jobs. Nobody had time for the sheer irrelevance of the screwball comedy anymore. Life had suddenly turned serious.

A movie that beautifully illustrates the collapse of the screwball comedy is *Arsenic and Old Lace*, a film that Cary Grant made in 1941. It was finally released in 1944, after the Broadway stage version had closed.

Frank Capra, who had directed Clark Gable and Claudette Colbert in *It Happened One Night*, had fallen in love with *Arsenic and Old Lace* when he saw it on Broadway. He thought it a "wholesome black comedy." Capra considered Cary Grant "Hollywood's greatest farceur," and he persuaded Warner Bros. to meet Grant's fee of one hundred thousand dollars. So far, so good. Then Capra proceeded to have the Cary Grant part of Mortimer Brewster substantially rewritten.

That was not good. Cary Grant's performance, as directed by Frank Capra, was a sad case of "more is less." Capra, perhaps sensing that screwball comedies were losing their audience, thought he could regain their loyalty, so to speak, by turning up the volume full blast. *Arsenic and Old Lace* is the story of two dear little spinsters whose idea of charity is to send lonely old men on a one-way trip to the Great Beyond. Their macabre travel service is fueled by their elderberry wine, liberally laced with arsenic. A few slugs and the lonely old gentlemen are lonely no more. Also living in the house is their brother, Teddy, who imagines that he is actually Teddy Roosevelt. Raymond Massey plays a sinister and long-lost brother who suddenly shows up, seeking refuge from the police. The only sane person in this strange family is Mortimer Brewster, the youngest brother, played by Grant.

The movie would have worked much better, had Capra kept Cary Grant as a fragile and beleaguered island of sanity in a totally mad household. Instead Capra apparently encouraged Grant to play his scenes at a level of intensity approaching hysteria. After awhile it simply isn't funny anymore.

The movie had to be shot in four weeks. Josephine Hull and Jean Adair, playing the two nutty sisters, were allowed to leave the Broadway version to do the movie only if it could be accomplished during their scheduled vacation time. On the first day of shooting, there was an interesting reunion.

Capra introduced character actress Jean Adair to leading man Cary Grant. Jean smiled and shook his hand.

"You don't remember me, do you?" Grant asked.

"I've seen you on the screen many times," Jean said, "but I don't recall having met you personally."

Then Cary Grant told her that he was Archie Leach, the boy acrobat who had been struck down by rheumatic fever and confined to bed in a Rochester boardinghouse. Actress Jean Adair had visited him everyday, with small gifts of fruit and candy and conversation.

The light of recognition dawned on Jean Adair's face. "Oh, my word . . . it *is* you," she said, studying the now-famous face carefully. "I didn't recognize the name, but I remember you. You were a very nice boy . . . and so grateful."

Cary Grant leaned over and kissed Jean Adair, who had become a sprightly old lady since he'd last seen her twenty-two years ago.

"He's still grateful, Miss Adair."

In 1941, fresh from his triumph in *The Philadelphia Story,* Cary Grant still had faith in the Hollywood comedy, the genre that had allowed his own immense talents to burst into magnificent bloom. He had no doubts that the primary purpose of movies was entertainment.

"When I go to the movies, I want to forget the dirty dishes in *my* sink, and what's on *my* mind. I want to forget my troubles, get out of myself. I want to laugh a little. I don't always want to see comedy. I want to see love stories, too, and murder mysteries and adventure yarns," Grant said in a 1941 interview. "And I figure I'm human. Other people must be the same way.

"Most people go to the movies for the same reason that many financiers read detective stories at night—to get completely away from the pressing problems of the day," he continued. "We should make films with that in mind. We shouldn't give people their own lives on the screen. People can find enough misery and hardship in the world without going to the movies to find it. That thought influences me more than anything else in picking a script. I read fifteen to twenty scripts for every picture I actually do. And the question I keep asking myself is: 'Would this make people forget their own worries—at least for an hour or so?"

We shouldn't give people their own lives on the screen. But that is just what Cary Grant did when he agreed to play the role of Cockney drifter Ernie Mott in *None But the Lonely Heart,* a film based on Richard Llewellyn's novel. The story of how Cary Grant was approached for the Ernie Mott part may be apocryphal, but it's so illustrative of the way Hollywood works that it's worth telling anyway.

RKO general manager Charlie Koerner was supposedly looking for a story that would be suitable for Cary Grant. Cary was becoming more selective these days. He could afford to be. Since practically anything Grant appeared in turned out to be a hit, he had far more offers than time.

Then Koerner got a tip via the Hollywood grapevine. Cary Grant had read a novel called *None But the Lonely Heart. He liked it*. Koerner went into action and quickly acquired the movie rights to Llewellyn's novel. Now he was ready for the next step. He called producer David Hempstead.

"I want you to get set to make a picture, Dave," Koerner said.

"What is this picture I'm to make?" Hempstead inquired.

Koerner had that nice feeling you get on those rare occasions when you look at the hand Fate has dealt you and discover that it is a royal flush.

"*None But the Lonely Heart*. Grant likes it. I've just paid sixty thousand dollars for it," Koerner said.

"I don't want to seem the prying type, but just what is the story all about?" Hempstead asked.

Koerner had not the foggiest notion. "C'mon over to my office," he said. "We'll call Grant up and ask him."

Hempstead arrived minutes later, and Koerner had his secretary put through a call to Cary Grant. (Like U.S. Presidents and five-star generals, studio heads in those days remained unfamiliar with the workings of the telephone.) When Grant was on the line, Koerner told him the good news.

"Well, Cary, we've bought that story for you, but I'm a little vague about the story line, and I want you to give Dave here a brief rundown on it."

"What story?"

"*None But the Lonely Heart*." Koerner prompted him.

"I haven't read it," Grant said. "A friend of mine told me he thought it was very good. That's all I know about it."

Whether Cary Grant read *None But the Lonely Heart* before or after Koerner's phone call seems unimportant. After reading it, he agreed to take the part of Ernie Mott.

In the meantime Koerner and Hempstead asked New York playwright Clifford Odets to write the screenplay. Before his death in 1963, Odets reminisced about his first Hollywood experience.

"Early in 1943 I was just about to go into the Army. I was doing plays on Broadway at the time, but I asked my agent if he could find a property for me to write in Hollywood so I could earn some extra money to give to my family while I was in the service. The agent came up with a book called *None But the Lonely Heart*, which a studio wanted adapted for the screen. I read the book, liked it, said I'd do it and took a train to Hollywood. When I arrived at the studio, I asked the producer whom he had in mind for the lead. 'Cary Grant,' he told me. There was a stunned silence on my part, and then I asked, 'Has anyone read this book?' It seemed that no one had. 'Well,' I said, 'it's about a 19-year old boy with pimples whose two desires in life are to have a girl and get a new suit of clothes. This is Cary Grant?' Anyway, I changed the concept of the book considerably. When I met Cary Grant—for the first time—he said to me, 'I'd like you to direct me in this movie.' I explained that I had never directed anyone, let alone Cary Grant, but he told me if I could write the words, I should certainly be able to direct their use. So, maybe Cary doesn't own a string of race horses, but if he believes in you, he's willing to gamble his whole career on you."

Unfortunately the bet didn't pay off. It had far worse results for Odets. It was fifteen years before he got another chance to direct.

None But the Lonely Heart tells the story of Ernie Mott, an embittered Cockney whose father was killed in World War I. His mother, played by Ethel Barrymore, has barely survived over the years running a junk shop. Mott flirts with a life of crime, is almost caught, and returns home only to discover that his mother is in jail. She had been caught with stolen goods, serving as a fence for another band of East End thieves. She did it in order to get a bit of money together for Ernie. She's recently learned she's dying of cancer.

This is a story that would obviously strike deep chords in Cary Grant. Ernie Mott's troubled and painful love for his mother is an emotion with which Cary Grant was deeply familiar. And the sordid life of the poor in rigidly class-conscious, prewar England was another theme that he knew from bitter experience. So for the first time in his career, Cary Grant chose to do a film that was a direct expression of his own experience and values. If the movie had succeeded, it might have given a whole new impetus to his career the way the screwball comedies had done in the late Thirties.

Ernie Mott is supposed to be a troubled adolescent. When Cary Grant made *None But the Lonely Heart*, he was forty years old, a full-bodied, handsome man, obviously in his prime. Ernie Mott should have been played by the young Tom Courtenay, who could have shown Ernie as the scrawny, hungry, confused, and anguished slum boy that Llewellyn intended to portray in his novel.

But by 1944 audiences simply couldn't forget that Cary Grant was—well, Cary Grant. Odets' direction didn't help matters. He creates a sense of foggy gloom that almost brings the movie to a standstill. In a series of painterly setups, he self-consciously manages to leave us with a sense of nostalgia for a simpler time, rather than with a sense of dirt, noise, pain and confusion of slum life.

In spite of these handicaps Cary Grant was nominated for an Oscar, his second. (Bing Crosby won it, however, for his fatherly priest in *Going My Way*.) It seems absurdly ironic that the two movies for which Grant received Academy Award nominations cast him in roles so far from what he did the best. *Penny Serenade* was a soap opera. *None But the Lonely Heart*, a kind of proletarian melodrama. Chalk it up to the madness of the world which seems to be heightened in Hollywood.

The reviews were lukewarm to negative, and the box-office response was disappointing. *None But the Lonely Heart* is now often revived in college film series. It was a noble failure and remains worth seeing simply for the talents present: Grant, Ethel Barrymore, and Clifford Odets—even if, in this vehicle, those talents mostly went awry.

Very early on Cary Grant made a conscious decision to "never complain, never explain." It's impossible to know how deeply the failure of *None But the Lonely Heart* struck him. One can only note that over a year passed before he went back to work.

* * * * * *

Alfred Hitchcock was destined to play an important role in Cary Grant's career, but that role took a long time to come to fruition. Hitchcock and Grant first worked together in 1941 on *Suspicion*, a film that won Joan Fontaine an Oscar for her portrayal of Grant's shy and fearful wife.

Fontaine's Oscar for Best Actress may well have been a delayed reaction to her 1940 performance as the naive and ultimately terrified wife in another Hitchcock film, *Rebecca*. If Cary Grant could have played the husband in *Suspicion*, as the author and as

Hitchcock intended, he might well have walked off with his first Oscar. The movie script was adapted from a novel by Frances Iles called *Before the Fact* and tells the story of an innocent young Englishwoman who slowly and almost unbelievingly comes to the realization that her husband is a murderer and plans to kill her, too. In the book that's just what he does, and that's the way Hitchcock planned to end the movie. But RKO wouldn't let good guy Cary Grant be an on-screen murderer. So Hitchcock had to rewrite and reshoot the final moments of *Suspicion.* Turns out that Joan Fontaine was simply letting her imagination run away with her. Her husband is really a nice guy. Hitchcock has always said that he bitterly regretted the compromise ending forced on him and his actors by RKO.

By 1946, however, after the success of *Spellbound* and other money-making movies, Hitchcock had acquired a much larger measure of control over his work. And it shows. That year he put *Spellbound*'s star Ingrid Bergman and Cary Grant opposite each other in *Notorious*, a film that was both a World War II spy thriller and a love story. It succeeds splendidly on both levels.

Ben Hecht's screenplay tells the story of Alicia Huberman (Ingrid Bergman) whose father, an American citizen, has been convicted of treason. Alicia, however, is completely loyal to the United States. American agent Devlin (Cary Grant) recruits her to infiltrate a ring of German spies in South America. Obviously they will be sympathetic to her because of her father. Bergman falls in love with Grant almost immediately, but he still has doubts about her background. After her father's conviction and subsequent death in prison, Alicia had begun to drink too much and was developing a rather messy life before Devlin rescued her for intelligence work. Thinking her love for Devlin isn't returned, Alicia marries a top German spy, Alexander Sebastian, head of a worldwide German chemical cartel, for the express purpose of spying on him.

She learns that everything the cartel is doing revolves around Sebastian's wine cellar which is always locked. At a big reception in the huge house where Alicia lives with Alex and his dominating mother, Alicia manages to get the key to the wine cellar. In scenes that build to almost unbearable intensity, Alicia and Devlin finally make their way into the wine cellar. Devlin then discovers that numerous bottles contain uranium ore. Alicia's German husband is deeply involved in the German effort to build an atomic bomb.

They hear footsteps, and, in their haste, Alicia and Devlin break one of the bottles. They escape detection then, but Alex later finds the broken bottle, hastily swept out of sight, and comes to the shattering realization that he is married to an American spy. Alex and his mother proceed to slowly poison Alicia. But, of course, Devlin rescues her in the end. There are now no doubts in his mind either: he loves Alicia all the more having nearly lost her.

In *Notorious* and in their 1958 film, *Indiscreet*, Ingrid Bergman was right for Cary Grant in the way that Katherine Hepburn was in an earlier stage of his career. Bergman still had a touch of the girl about her when she played opposite Humphrey Bogart in *Casablanca*, but in *Notorious* she is a deliciously grown-up woman clearly in her prime. She radiates a mature and exquisitely sensuous eroticism that is all the more exciting for its having to be subdued and restrained before the demands of her work as a spy.

Hitchcock claims that Grant later accused him of slanting both *Suspicion* and *Notorious* in favor of leading ladies Fontaine and Bergman.

"That, of course, is ridiculous," Hitchcock says. "Joan Fontaine won an Academy Award for her performance, but not because I slanted the picture. She was just very good. So was Ingrid Bergman in *Notorious.*" Hitchcock said Grant didn't lose his temper. "He only becomes petulant."

After Cary Grant made *Notorious* for Hitchcock in 1946, he was not to make a really first-rate picture until he again worked with Hitchcock in 1955. After *Notorious* came a string of mediocre movies. There are only a few Grant films from this period that have not become an embarrassment to watch. *Crisis*, with Jose Ferrer, casts Grant as surgeon who is forced to perform a delicate brain operation on a South American dictator. *People Will Talk*, an oddly courageous movie written and directed by Joseph L. Mankiewicz, concerns a college professor (played by Grant) who stands up under an investigation by a fellow professor reminiscent of that period's McCarthyism (a political disease that took a heavy toll among Hollywood writers, actors, and directors). Many of them, suspected of Communist sympathies, were blacklisted and unable to find work for many years. *People Will Talk* was released in 1951, the year that McCarthyism was at its worst. There were not many movies that stood up, even indirectly, to the fledging fascist from Wisconsin. Cary Grant and Joe Mankiewicz took that risk.

Most of the films Cary Grant made in those years do not begin to provide an outlet for either his comic talents or his abilities as a romantic leading man. No one can figure out what Cary Grant was *doing* in abominations like *The Bachelor and the Bobby-Soxer*, with Myrna Loy and Shirley Temple; *Every Girl Should Be Married*, with Betsy Drake (who would become his third wife); *Room for One More*, again with Ms. Drake; *Monkey Business*, with Charles Coburn, Ginger Rogers, and Marilyn Monroe in a small part.

In the years just after his divorce from Barbara Hutton, Grant's friends noticed that he was frequently gloomy and sometimes depressed. He wore a scowl more often. The basic insecurity in his character had always been there, of course, but his successes in the screwball comedies of the Thirties had done much to send it underground. Now, with another failed marriage, the critical and box office hostility to *None But the Lonely Heart*, and a string of so-so parts in mediocre movies, Grant's insecurities surfaced with a vengeance.

It is evidence of the basic healthiness of his character that he sublimated his doubts through a microscopic attention to every detail in the making of his movies. Nothing was too minute to escape his notice. In 1947 he made *The Bishop's Wife*, a gentle and totally inoffensive piece of fluff based on a Robert Nathan fantasy. Co-star Loretta Young remembers Grant's obsessive concern with details that most people would not notice.

"There was one scene in which Cary and I were to enter a house. It was a snow scene, and as we started to stamp the snow from our boots before entering, Cary suddenly stopped short."

"Just a minute," he said. "If it's cold outside and the house is nice and warm inside, why isn't there any frost on the windows?"

"Production came to a complete halt while the frustrated set dressers scurried about putting fake frost on the windows. Then and only then did we complete the scene," Ms. Young recalled.

One Hollywood director, however, did not take such a benign view of Cary's fussiness.

"Of the sixteen hours a day that he's awake, I don't think there are twenty minutes when he's not complaining. I've never seen a man more constantly in turmoil," he said.

Leo McCarey, who directed Grant in *The Awful Truth, Once Upon a Honeymoon* and *Affair to Remember*, said:

"I call him the Lovable Irritant because he wants to have his say about everything in the whole picture. Every so often I have to remind him I've won three Academy Awards."

A rumor wound its way through the Hollywood grapevine that one director was so unhinged after making a picture with Grant that he had to be hospitalized.

Grant's old friend and former vaudeville partner Don Barclay believed that Grant took roles in a number of comedies during that period with the barely suppressed subconscious hope that they'd take him back to his big-shoes and baggy-pants days with the Pender troupe.

Barclay remembers watching Grant shooting one of the picnic scenes from *The Bachelor and the Bobby-Soxer*. A woman standing next to him was getting upset over the rather undignified goings-on.

"Why do they do these things to Mr. Grant," she asked Barclay. "Making him carry a potato on a spoon, and doing those dreadful falls in the mud!"

"Madam," Barclay said, "if you will watch the expression on Mr. Grant's face, you will see that it is little short of beatific."

* * * * * *

One of Cary Grant's closest friends during these years was Howard Hughes, who was still leading an active and vigorous life, piloting his own plane and squiring numerous starlets to various Hollywood night clubs.

"Every time I'm a bachelor again," Cary said, "Hughes calls up and suggests that we "go and see what the world's made of."

In 1947 reporters asked why the two men didn't collaborate professionally, with Hughes producing and Grant, then one of the top two or three male box-office stars, as the male lead.

Grant said that he was committed to other producers for the next two years but that after that, he wanted to do a series of pictures based on a $25 million "flying boat" that Hughes was in the process of building at Long Beach.

"The movies would be laid ten years or so in the future," Grant said. "The hero would belong to the world police. The plot would concern his adventures as he flies from one country to another battling intrigues against the peace of the world. A different picture would be made about each country, weaving its customs into the story."

Grant's instinct for hits seems way ahead of its time on this project. What he described to reporters in 1947 sounds like a brief scenario for the James Bond movies which starred Sean Connery and didn't surface until the early Sixties.

The miraculous "flying boat" by which the hero would get from one country to another prefigures the fantastic technological devices that were to become such an important element in the Bond movies.

In January, 1947 Hughes and Grant caused a national manhunt when they did not show up as scheduled at the Amarillo, Texas airport. With Hughes at the controls the two men had taken off from the Wright Field in Dayton in a twin-engined, B-23 converted bomber early on a Friday evening. They were expected in Amarillo before midnight. There were also two crewmen on board. Hughes radioed the Indianapolis airport at 6:49 P.M. Then there was silence.

The hunt began on Saturday morning, with both airline personnel, Civilian Aeronautics Board (CAB) investigators, and reporters conducting an airport-to-airport phone search of every landing strip between Dayton and Amarillo.

Late in the afternoon the El Paso airport reported that Hughes had landed his big plane there during the night. He and Grant intended to clear customs and then proceed to Mexico City. When Hughes was told that customs officials would not be available until 8:00 A.M., he flew to Nogales, Arizona. Without ever notifying the Amarillo airport of their change of plans, Hughes and Grant slept for a few hours in Nogales and took off, shortly after 8:30 A.M. on Saturday morning.

Their trip had originated in New York. Grant had spent a few days resting there while Hughes spent his time on a reorganization plan for the Transcontinental and Western Airline, in which he had recently become a major shareholder.

Newspaper switchboards all over the country were besieged with phone calls from Cary Grant's fans, most of them women. According to published reports few of the callers inquired about Hughes' safety.

The lives of Howard Hughes and Cary Grant diverged dramatically after the 1940's. Hughes began his slow but inexorable withdrawal from reality, and Cary Grant continued to perfect what was becoming his major role: Cary Grant.

Cary Grant and Howard Hughes, at the time of their friendship, were both bachelors and both multimillionaires. They shared another trait. They hated crowds. Grant had begun to go on record about his aversion to autograph seekers, an admission of less-than-total love for one's fans that was not often tendered by the Hollywood stars. Grant said that he could see nothing less important in life than an actor's autograph. Unfortunately an uncommon number of movie fans didn't agree with him. The battle had to be fought over and over again.

"Autograph collecting is just a racket," Grant told a reporter. "Those kids will beat hell out of you just to get some scribbling on a scrap of paper. They climb all over you. They jump on your car. They follow you to your hotel."

Grant said that if you refuse, you let yourself in for a barrage of four-letter words—the ones that he'd prefer to believe kids that age hadn't heard yet.

"But if you stop and sign, you feel like a silly fool," Grant continued. "There you are—in the middle of the sidewalk—surrounded by rude, yelling, wriggling kids and writing away like crazy."

Cary Grant would occasionally give an autograph if the request was politely phrased and came at a convenient moment. But he hated people to interrupt him when he was dining out. Especially if a stranger came up to his table in a restaurant and said, "I know I'm bothering you, but . . ."

"In that case," Grant would ask icily, "why do you bother me?"

The response to Cary's irritated question might well be, "Just who the hell do you think you are?"

To which Cary would reply, "Obviously you know who I am—but I don't know who you are. Now please go away."

By the time he was telling this story, Cary Grant had become very skilled at turning away autograph seekers. That wasn't always the case. Once, early in his career, he finally, in exasperation, broke a catsup bottle over a persistent fan's head.

On another occasion descending many floors in a Manhattan

skyscraper's elevator with an awed lady who couldn't quite place him, he steeled himself for the inevitable question. Finally they reached the ground floor. The doors slid back. The woman nervously adjusted her hat, started to leave the elevator, then turned to him and blurted, "Look, are you a movie star or something?"

"Yes, madam, indeed I am," Cary said and stalked out onto the crowded Fifth Avenue sidewalks.

* * * * * *

In the 1940's Cary Grant also began to meditate on the nature of fame, the unique qualities of Hollywood, and the vagaries of time. His contemplation of these more or less eternal verities produced a wonderful monologue that he delivered to whomever would listen.

He likened Hollywood to a streetcar, the kind where you get on in the rear and slowly make your way forward—where the exit is located. The trouble was that the closer you got to the front of the streetcar, the closer you were to being shoved off entirely.

Cary also believed that the Hollywood street car ran on a circular track, starting nowhere and arriving nowhere. The whole point of the game is just to keep moving, "doesn't matter where." There's only one car on the line, and only a couple of hundred lucky souls can manage to squeeze themselves inside. Hundreds more try to claw their way aboard at each stop. Hundreds are trampled in the rush, but a few actually make it.

As soon as the doors are closed and the car begins to move, the conductor begins to chant, "Move up front! Plenty of room up front!" And at the next stop, when a new group of hopefuls tries to clamber on board, a handful of bruised, battered, and bedraggled actors get pushed off and land with a heart-wrenching thud on Oblivion Street.

"It's a terrifyingly hard job to get aboard in the first place," Cary said. "And once you have bucked and line-plunged your way to a handhold on the back platform you have to fight with fang and claw to keep from getting jarred loose at the first turn.

"You see," he continued, "chivalry has no place on the streetcar marked Fame. There's just no room for it. Your fellow passengers are intent on gouging out your eyes and busting your ribs and stamping on your feet. If a woman gets in your way, correct

Hollywood etiquette is to slug her before she slugs you. Any display of good manners marks you for a sap and a sissy, therefore ineligible for the long ride.

"Some easy-going chumps, too soft-hearted to play the Fame game according to the Hollywood rule book, have been bounced off the back of the car before they had a chance to pay their fare. Others have been knocked through a window as they paused to apologize to somebody for inadvertently breaking an arm."

Cary Grant obviously loved this subject. It was hard to get him to stop talking.

"If you're strong, ruthless, and lucky enough to get a seat the trick is to glue yourself to it and sit tight until some tougher mug shoves you up toward the front, which is the first certain step toward landing out on the pavement."

Cary said that one day when he was just walking along on his stilts, minding his own business, he chanced to see a streetcar transfer lying on the sidewalk.

"I climbed down, parked my stilts and got on the car. I've been riding ever since."

Continuing his amusing analogy, Grant said that when he looked around that streetcar after he boarded it, he discovered the two best seats were taken by Clark Gable and Spencer Tracy.

"Nobody could budge them," he confided. "They just sat there, about as vulnerable as two tons of fresh-quarried granite. Nobody could shove them up or down or out of the window.

"I've been watching those two ever since, wondering how they managed to stay aboard the car all these years with never a sign of cracking. I'm thoroughly convinced they'll last as long as the car itself.

"Recently I've had a feeling that I'm due to get nudged up to the front. My ride has some distance still to go, but, unlike Gable and Tracy, I'm not as rugged as Stone Mountain.

"The newcomers that fight their way aboard are getting tougher at every stop. Some of the big shots who were enjoying a lovely ride when I came aboard have fallen by the wayside and been forgotten. I've relished every minute of my ride, but I'm not kidding myself that it will last forever. There are some new fellows aboard who need space to expand. Down at the rear end, just inside the door, is a young chap named Tyrone Power. He'll be moving up pretty soon into the neighborhood of Gable and Tracy. If he's lucky and can stand the pummeling he may last as long as they have.

"Out on the back platform is a husky young gent named Vic Mature. I think he has his eye on my seat, and for all I know he may be sitting in it this time next year.

"Meanwhile, I'm getting a kick out of my ride, even though I get a nervous chill whenever the conductor, a realistic old cuss named Time, calls out: 'Kindly move to the front of the car.' "

Cary Grant first delivered this spiel in the early Forties. He refined it from time to time but continued to use the streetcar analogy in talking about Hollywood until well into the Fifties. Looking back, it's seems incredible that either Tyrone Power or Victor Mature were ever thought to be serious competition by anybody. Who would go see one of their movies today?

Years later, writer-director Richard Brooks, recalls that Cary once said to him:

"I can see all these young, good-looking guys getting on the trolley and crowding me forward. One of these days they're going to push me off the front end."

Brooks couldn't believe that Grant really worried about such things. Brooks laughed and slapped Cary on the back, "They can't push you off, Cary. Everybody knows you're the motorman."

But Brooks doubts whether Cary believed him.

* * * * * *

After Cary Grant finished filming *The Bachelor and the Bobby-Soxer* in 1947, he sailed for England and his first real vacation in two years. Grant had a long visit with his mother, now living in her own house in Bristol. Cary also enjoyed seeing his cousin, Eric Leach and Eric's wife, Margaret.

His vacation over, Cary returned to the States on the Queen Elizabeth. The passengers included an extraordinary number of Hollywood "royalty" as well as a small society contingent. Among others on board were Merle Oberon, John Hay Whitney, then Ambassador to England; playwright Freddie Lonsdale, and Elizabeth Taylor and her mother.

Also on board was a twenty-three-year old American actress named Betsy Drake. She was on her way home after appearing in a London production of *Deep Are the Roots,* an American play about the modern South and its racial unrest.

8

Betsy Drake, Wife #3

BETSY DRAKE'S GRANDFATHER was the architect for Chicago's Drake and Blackstone Hotels and put together a sizable fortune during his life. His son, Carlos, moved to Europe after he was married. Carlos and his wife had a daughter, Betsy, born in Paris on September 11, 1923.

Most of the family fortune disappeared in the stockmarket crash of 1929, and Carlos Drake moved his family back to the United States in 1929. They settled in the Washington, D.C. area. Betsy attended high school in Virginia. She won a college scholarship and studied theatre for two years, then dropped out to work as a model. After a few non-acting jobs on Broadway, Betsy began working in summer stock. Then she heard that an American company was planning to take *Deep Are the Roots* to London. She auditioned.

She was incredibly pretty: dark blond hair and a face that was both gentle and intelligent. Possibly because of the financial turmoil her parents lived through, Betsy Drake grew up into an introspective and rather shy young woman. She loved the theatre and decided to be an actress because the characters you played gave you a kind of platform from which you could be involved in life. Her part in *Deep Are the Roots* had been her first major role. Now she was planning to return to New York. She had a cold-water flat in Greenwich Village waiting for her, and she hoped her stage experience in London's West End would open doors for her on Broadway.

Cary Grant had seen Betsy Drake perform in *Deep Are the Roots*. She had a fresh and unspoiled quality that few Hollywood actresses could boast. Grant asked his theatre companion, film producer Alexander Korda, if he knew anything about Betsy Drake. Korda told him he thought Betsy had recently signed a contract with Warner Brothers producer Hal B. Wallis. Grant filed away the information. He would make a courtesy call when Betsy Drake got to Hollywood.

* * * * * *

Betsy Drake first saw Cary Grant at the customs shed in Southampton. After a long run her play had closed, and she would be alone on the trip back to the States. She had taken the boat train down to Southampton and stared gloomily out the window during the whole trip. It was a typically dreary English day, damp and dismal.

While she was waiting to have her passport stamped by English immigration officials, two Rolls-Royces suddenly roared into the shed. The doors of the first one opened and out stepped movie star Cary Grant and a man whom she recognized from the London newspapers as Freddie Lonsdale, a playwright who specialized in quietly humorous drawing room comedies. She'd read that when Freddie wasn't working on the production of one of his plays, he could most likely be found on one of the great liners plying the North Atlantic.

Then Betsy noticed the second Rolls. It was stacked to its ceiling with luggage and—good heavens! hampers of wine. She also noticed that both Cary Grant and Freddie Lonsdale were in exceptionally high spirits.

The next scene in the meeting of Betsy Drake and Cary Grant depends on whose version you care to believe. Cary Grant swears that Betsy Drake flirted with him their first day at sea.

"As I crossed the lobby," he told her "you opened the telephone booth and took an elegant pose."

Betsy, however, doesn't remember noticing Cary Grant from a

phone booth. What she remembers is sitting on the top deck and feeling rather lonely. She looked up and saw Merle Oberon, who introduced herself.

"I have a friend, Cary Grant, who would like to meet you. Will you lunch with us?"

Cary Grant gallantly admits that after he realized Betsy Drake was on board, he recruited Ms. Oberon to act as intermediary.

"I told Merle to go tell her she had to have lunch with a lonely man."

The lunch was obviously a success. Cary Grant reported that "except for that night, when she had a previous date, I snagged her for every meal of the crossing."

They were together constantly in a shipboard romance that was a kind of preview of a movie that Cary Grant would make ten years later with Deborah Kerr. In *Affair to Remember* Cary Grant and Ms. Kerr also meet on a great liner and fall hopelessly in love.

Betsy's fresh beauty and candid openness of spirit also attracted playwright Lonsdale. Cary, who considered Freddie "probably my closest friend," says that if Lonsdale had been twenty years younger, Cary would "certainly" have lost Betsy to him.

After their arrival in New York, Cary tried to convince Betsy to come to Hollywood right away. But she still had her heart set on the Broadway stage. Within a few weeks however, Betsy Drake was in Hollywood. Grant had convinced Dore Schary, then production chief for RKO to test her. The result was a part opposite Grant in a movie called, *Every Girl Should Be Married*. When Cary Grant wanted something as bad as he wanted Betsy Drake, he usually got it.

Not only did he put an unknown actress opposite him in *Every Girl Should Be Married*, he let her have most of the close-ups. Her scenes clearly predominated. Several critics noticed another oddity in the movie. Betsy Drake's acting style appeared to be a-not-very-effective attempt to combine the best of Margaret Sullavan and Katherine Hepburn. The critics also noticed Cary Grant, in several scenes, rather crassly and with deadly accuracy, mimicking Ms. Drake who was, of course, mimicking Sullavan and Hepburn.

If Betsy Drake was hurt by this apparently gratuitous cruelty, she never said so publicly. They were often seen together until

Grant left for Europe to work on his next film, *I Was a Male War Bride*, with Ann Sheridan.

The movie was plagued with problems right from the start. First Ann Sheridan was out of commission due to a severe bout of pneumonia. Shortly after she was back at work, Cary Grant was struck by illness. At first the doctors said it was influenza. When Grant didn't respond to treatment for the flu, more tests were run, and it was discovered that he had hepatitis.

Grant claims that he lost forty pounds in three days after the onset of the debilitating disease. Even after his release from the hospital, he was laid up for additional weeks in a London flat. When she got the news, Betsy Drake immediately booked a flight for London. She kept him company and nursed him through his long convalescence.

I Was a Male War Bride had an unusually long production time due to the serious illnesses of its two stars. The filming took ten months, with locations in Germany, France, and England. Finally, however, the picture was in the can, and Cary Grant and Betsy Drake arrived back in Los Angeles in April of 1949. Cary said that he had asked Betsy to marry him. As the weeks went by various Hollywood columnists began to wonder in print if Ms. Drake's engagement to Cary Grant would simply drift into oblivion in much the same manner as his former betrothal to Phyllis Brooks.

The speculations stopped months later when Cary Grant and Betsy Drake flew to Arizona in a Constellation piloted by Howard Hughes, who by then owned RKO. They were married on Christmas Day by the Rev. Stanley M. Smith in a desert home at Scottsdale, twenty miles from Phoenix. The next day they were back in Hollywood, each at work on a different movie.

Betsy officially moved into the six-room Beverly Hills ranch house that Cary had bought after his divorce from Barbara Hutton. He had, from time to time, thought about having it properly decorated, but when the time came to actually call contractors and interior designers and face the prospect of workmen disrupting his routine, he always found a good reason to put off the project to some vague future time.

Betsy was no different. The house was comfortable. She had her books, and her telescope, located above the L.A. smog, sometimes gave her dazzling views of the moon, Venus, and Mars. Betsy's books caused problems. She bought them by the dozen—twenty or thirty at a time. This not only seemed a waste to Cary, but a vast inconvenience. He could seldom—or so it seemed—sit down or go to bed without moving a stack of books out of the way.

Betsy has said that she eventually had to "smuggle" books into the house, "the way a lost weekender hides whisky."

When Cary wasn't working, they drove out to the house he'd bought in Palm Springs, an older Mexican-style structure with thick adobe walls to keep out the desert heat and a sloping tiled roof. Set away from the road on three acres of land, it was a place where life was calm, unhurried, and peaceful.

They had a huge table set outdoors under a large tamarisk tree. Betsy read and tried her hand at both writing and painting. Cary read movie scripts. There was, of course, a swimming pool, and they both spent long hours sunbathing. Cary had become famous for the year-round tan which he maintained partially because of his aversion to makeup. With a constant suntan he need never wear any.

But Betsy Drake seemed to enjoy the occasional rainy day, which had its own special rhythm.

"We get up in the morning, put on bluejeans or shorts, and sit around drinking coffee, discussing everything from God to the garment industry," she said.

Then Cary discovered horses. As usual there was no such thing as a casual interest for Cary Grant. His friend, fellow actor David Niven, remembered the onset of his new enthusiasm.

"He decided that riding horses wasn't enough—he had to be the best damn horseman in the district. So he took lessons. Next he invited my wife and myself to visit him in Palm Springs and go riding. I hadn't ridden with him for some time and at that point, I was, I remember, a little pompous about my Sandhurst riding school training."

David Niven was in for a big surprise.

"I was stunned at the new Grant. No tired old trail horse for him; no sleazy blue jeans and greasy saddle. He appeared beautifully outfitted in a dark blue Western outfit complete with silver buttons. He openly sneered at my jodphurs, leaped on to an immense, snarling stallion, jumped a five-barred gate out of the corral, and disappeared in a cloud of dust."

Menacing role opposite Joan Fontaine in "Suspicion" contrasted with Cary's sensitivity as shown with settlement house kids in 1940s and daughter Jennifer (see preceeding page) in 1966.

The screen crackled when hard-boiled editor Cary clashed with reporter Rosalind Russell in "His Girl Friday," based on the Hecht-MacArthur story of news reporting, "The Front Page."

On July 8, 1942, Cary married heiress Barbara Hutton at the Lake Arrowhead home of his manager, Frank Vincent. Three years later the marriage ended in a quite amicable divorce.

"An Affair to Remember," a remake of a Charles Boyer-Irene Dunne tear-jerker, presented Cary at the height of his mature popularity in 1957. His co-star was British-born actress Deborah Kerr.

But in his later years, there was no co-star who matched the Grant *savoir-faire* with a glamor of her own so successfully as Grace Kelly in the popular Paramount comedy-drama "To Catch a Thief."

With third wife, Betsy Drake. They married on Christmas day, 1949.

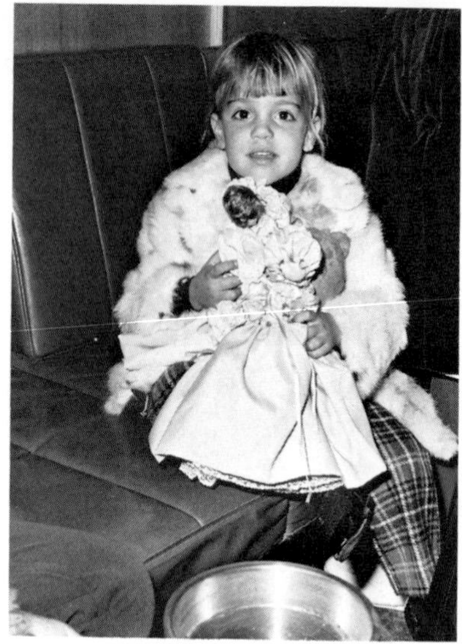

First fatherhood came to Cary at age 62. Here he is shown with his fourth wife Dyan Cannon and baby Jennifer. R: Jennifer age four.

"Father Goose" with Leslie Caron, made in 1964, was Cary's next to last picture. While making it, he was seriously courting Dyan Cannon.

One of Cary's most successful pictures, both at the box office and artistically, "Charade" co-starred Audrey Hepburn. "Make no mistake," wrote one critic. "Cary Grant is going to go on forever!"

He was not only Ingrid Bergman's co-star in "Indiscreet," he was also her very good and loyal friend. He helped her through her split with Roberto Rossellini and ignored gossip this caused.

Still remarkably young for his age, Cary is shown here prior to the 1976 Republican primaries with then first lady Betty Ford. The horn-rimmed glasses enhance the Grant charm.

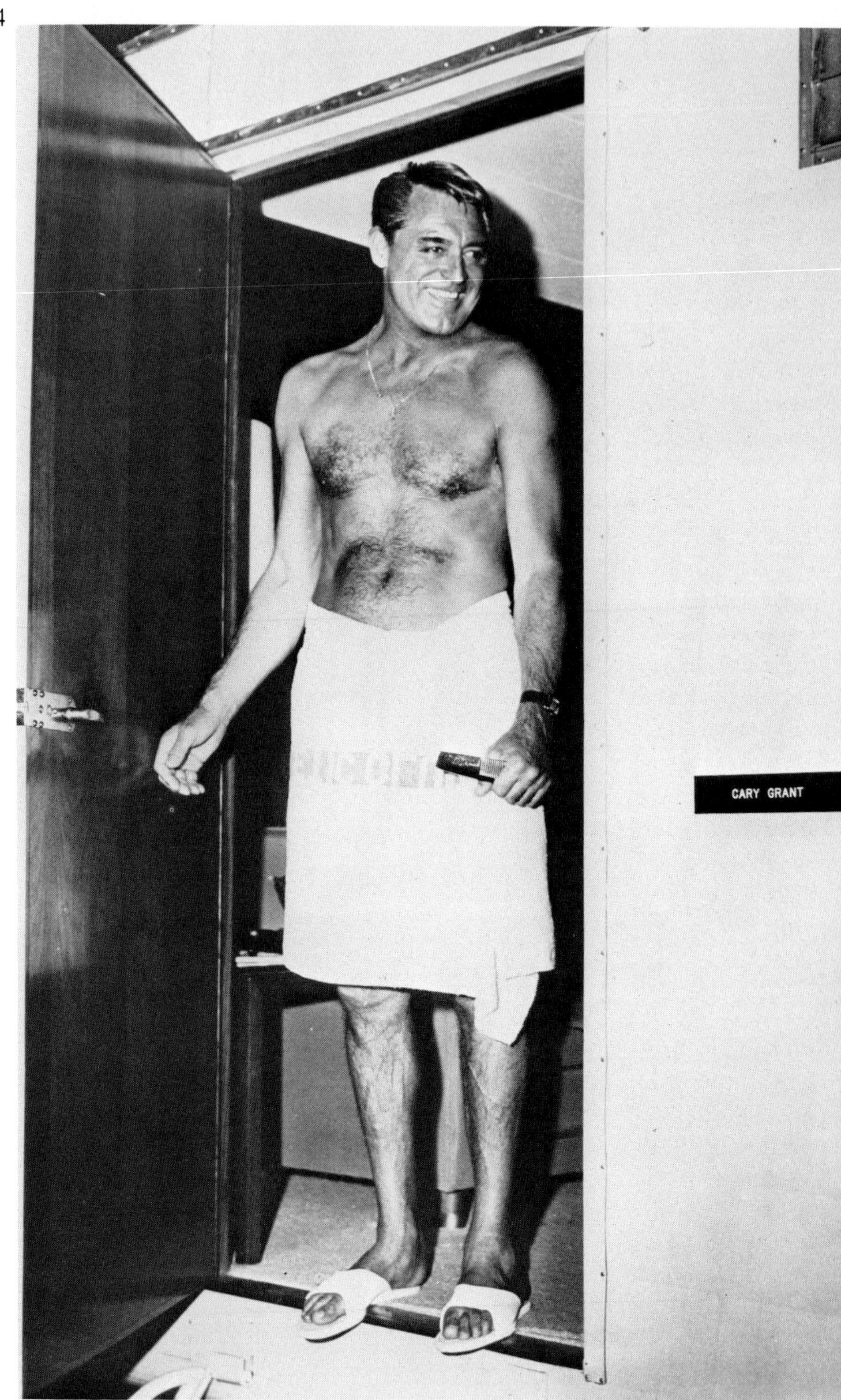
CARY GRANT

David Niven does not seem the type of person who would fabricate such a story. The next morning when Niven and his wife went downstairs for breakfast, they found Cary getting ready for his swimming lesson.

"But dammit," Niven said, "you've been swimming all your life."

"Yes," Cary said, "but I haven't been swimming *perfectly*.

Betsy enjoyed riding, too, even though she didn't feel motivated, as Cary did, to become the best horseman in Palm Springs. What she enjoyed the most was getting up very early, before dawn, and riding out into the desert to view the splendid desert sunrise. She and Cary did this often, cooking bacon, eggs, and coffee on a small portable camping stove.

Other times they would take the horses out for a slow canter at night and, when they found a good place, stop and cook steaks under the silver light of the desert moon. The addition of a bottle of Chateauneuf du Pape and the smell of sage made these meals unforgettable.

Betsy and Cary lived in the Beverly Hills house when he was filming in Hollywood. On workdays, they had breakfast brought in to them in bed at 7:00 A.M., and Cary skimmed the papers while he had orange juice, soya toast, and black coffee.

"He always wakes up in a fine humor," Betsy said. He would bound out of bed and do a dance around the room before taking a shower. The sight of Cary doing a jig clad only in his pajama top usually left Betsy "helpless with laughter."

Cary usually got home from the studio about 7:00 P.M. After a simple dinner of meat, vegetable, brown bread, and wine, they would watch television or read until it was time to go to bed. Their way of life was described as "monastic" by some Hollywood writers. Other writers, less understanding of the Grants' need for solitude and privacy, called it "bleak."

Director Billy Wilder said in the mid-Fifties that he didn't know anyone who had been inside Cary Grant's in ten years. Grant bristled at Wilder's statement.

"It's probably true that he (Wilder) didn't know anybody who had been inside my home, but then I don't know anyone who has been inside his."

Grant then proceeded to describe what "friendship" often means:

"I know men and women who have dozens of people around them constantly, and not a friend amongst them. They group together in fear and secret dislike of one another, and when not with one another openly gossip about one another."

Cary and Betsy virtually never showed up at Hollywood nightclubs and their appearances at any of the posh restaurants that lined La Cienaga in those days were rare. They both preferred plain food and were happy eating their dinner off a tray while watching television.

These simple tastes were endlessly written about, not only because of Cary's status as a top box office star, but because his unadorned home life was in such contrast to both his screen image and the conspicuous consumption that many Hollywood stars indulged in.

Deborah Kerr and her husband, Tony Bartley, spent several weekends with the Grants in Palm Springs in the months after Cary and Deborah completed the filming of *Affair to Remember*. Ms. Kerr described the Grant's Palm Springs house as "delightfully comfortable in a non-glamourous way."

"Betsy and Cary," she added, "have mastered the art of living in their simplicity."

Cary didn't mind if his friends and co-stars noticed that he wasn't addicted to life in the grand style. (Had his years with Barbara Hutton left him with a permanent aversion to ostentation?) Cary Grant often said that the living room in the Beverly Hills house looked like a "waiting room in a train station." And he frequently reiterated his belief throughout their marriage that the Beverly Hills house was "too small for two people."

Neither of them, however, could seem to make a decisive move to find something bigger. Cary was notorious for looking at houses. Los Angeles real estate agents knew he was "looking." They called Grant's secretary, Frank Horn, whenever they thought something suitable had turned up. Horn would go out and take a look and then report to Cary. From 1949 to 1958, Frank Horn looked at over three hundred houses. Some of them he touted to Cary, some he didn't. Cary, however, never found any of them to be what he was looking for.

In spite of his sudden enthusiasm for riding, Betsy Drake said her husband was a man of "no hobbies." It caused a certain amount of marital friction that, on the other hand, Betsy was a woman of "many hobbies."

The first thing she took up after they were married was photography. Making his way around, over and through piles of photographic paraphernalia was even more irritating to Cary than navigating his way through a sea of Betsy's books.

"Betsy, you should have hobbies that don't take up so much space," he said. "I suggest that you learn to write on the head of a pin."

Then, without giving up her photographic experiments, Betsy decided that she would learn how to cook.

"I couldn't even boil an egg without burning it when we first married," she said.

Betsy, after a number of culinary disasters, did learn how to find her way around a kitchen, but her first efforts produced one of Cary's favorite stories: how he walked into the kitchen one day and "found her studying a turkey, trying to decide which was the front and which was the back."

Betsy had always been interested in psychology, yoga, and related subjects, but this interest had lain dormant during the early years of her marriage. Then she discovered a book on hypnotism by clinical psychologist Leslie LeCron that again sparked her interest. She immersed herself in this fascinating subject over the next several years.

Her total absorption roused Cary's curiosity. He had been smoking two packs of cigarettes each day for many years now, and he hated it. He'd tried to stop again and again, but nothing seemed to work. After a few days or, at most, a few weeks, he'd light up and all his willpower would vanish in a puff of smoke.

Betsy wondered out loud on several occasions if hypnosis could help Cary kick the smoking habit.

Finally, he gave in.

"Merely to please you," Cary said, "I will let you use hypnosis on me to see if it will help me give up smoking."When it was time to go to sleep that night, Betsy sat on a chair next to their bed and put her husband into a hypnotic trance. Her soft voice was pitched into a soft drone as she told Cary, over and over, that he was getting sleepy, that he couldn't keep his eyes open. Finally he was under. Betsy was amazed. She hadn't been sure she could do it.

Betsy sat by their bed for a half hour, telling Cary again and again that he hated the taste of tobacco, that he hated the idea of drawing smoke into his lungs. Over and over, again and again.

The results were beyond anything that either of them could have imagined. The next day when there was a break in the shooting, Cary got Betsy on the phone.

"What happened last night as I slept?" he asked her. "I can't smoke anymore."

Betsy was delighted. From two packs a day to nothing—overnight. And it didn't even hurt. Using self-hypnosis, Betsy proceeded to kick her own cigarette habit in just four days.

A year after Betsy had cured Cary of his need for cigarettes, he asked her help once again. The doctors had told him after his bout with hepatitis that it would be best if he gave up hard liquor. But Cary had grown used to the occasional martini or Scotch. He knew that he was hardly a problem drinker, and there was probably no harm in the relatively small amount of alcohol that he drank. But the hepatitis had had a weakening effect on his liver. Why take chances?

Betsy put him under once again and told him this time that he had lost all desire for hard liquor. Again it worked. He simply lost his taste for anything alcoholic except a glass or two of white wine with dinner.

This convinced Cary that Betsy was onto something. He read all the books she'd already accumulated on hypnosis and then went out and bought everything else he could find on the subject. As with riding, swimming, and getting a tan, Cary Grant didn't get involved in anything halfway.

"A droning voice has a remarkably trance-like effect on the subconscious," Cary said, "that's why prayers, spoken aloud, are most effective at the tiring day's end."

"Hypnotism is really utter, complete relaxation, which is the secret of success in everything from golf to acting to love-making," he said. "We are all products of our thoughts. If you put in your mind the thought that a specific things will happen to you, if you permeate your being with this thought, then it *will* happen."

Grant claims that he learned to deaden the pain of the dentist's drill via self-hypnosis, thus eliminating the need for novocain.

"Since I can turn off pain in any part of my body, it isn't difficult to cut off feeling in one whole side of my face," Cary said. "My dentist and I have a signal. When I snap the fingers of my right hand, he starts drilling. But I'm not good enough yet to anesthetize a single tooth."

One of the most impressive feats of Cary's new skill came in 1957 when a lump suddenly appeared on his forhead and grew with frightening speed. By the time surgeons removed the non-malignant lipoma, it was the size of half a golfball. Cary says that each night before going to sleep, he would hypnotize himself and direct his subconscious mind to heal the incision immediately.

The doctors had told him that it would take at least a month for the incision to heal, and that there was no way to avoid a scar. Within a week, the incision, which had been made in a normal wrinkle on Cary's forehead, had not only healed, but had left no traces whatsoever. There simply wasn't a scar. Plastic surgeons called it "incredible."

A similar incident occurred when he was filming *The Pride and the Passion*. He was accidentally cut in several places on his back in a sword-fighting scene. The filming schedule called for him to be bare to the waist in a scene coming up in four days. Doctors said it was impossible for the cuts to heal in such a short time. Cary put his autohypnotic talents to work.

"Every morning and every night I said to myself, in effect, 'Pure oxygen, being breathed into my body, go directly to my wounds and cleanse them, while all poisons and disease leave as I exhale.' It worked," Cary said. "In four days there was no sign that I had ever been hurt."

* * * * * *

Unfortunately Cary Grant was rarely able to harness his hypnotic skills and insights when it came to the crucial business of deciding which direction his career should take. Ever since he had become Hollywood's first freelance actor back in 1937, Grant had always suffered doubts about parts that he'd accepted. After he had agreed to play opposite Irene Dunne in *The Awful Truth*, he went into a frenzy of indecision about his role as her estranged husband. After several days of filming had already been completed, he still wasn't sure. The more he thought about it, the worse it got. Finally,

Cary managed to convince himself that the entire project was doomed. *The Awful Truth*, as he saw it, was an awful mistake, and he wanted no part of it.

Grant sat down and wrote an eight-page memo to Columbia Studios chief Harry Cohn. The memo had a title: *What's Wrong With This Picture, by Cary Grant*. He offered Cohn five thousand dollars to be released from his contract. Cohn had the good sense to turn him down and *The Awful Truth* turned out to be a critical and box office success as well as an enduring classic of American film comedy.

But as Cary Grant became a bigger star, there were fewer and fewer people who could give him the advice he so obviously needed regarding which roles he should take and which he should pass up. He turned down offers to appear in *Roman Holiday* and *Sabrina Fair*, roles that later went to Gregory Peck and Humphrey Bogart. He could have starred olposite Judy Garland in *A Star Is Born*, a film that had the additional advantage of George Cukor's direction. Again he said no. Perhaps his biggest blunder in this area, however, was when he turned down a part in the Academy Award-winning, *The Bridge on the River Kwai*. The role of the British officer who must not only protect his men from the brutal Japanese guards but must shield them from their increasingly neurotic commander, as played by Alec Guinness would have been perfect for Cary Grant. It was the kind of meaty, three-dimensional character he should have been playing for years. William Holden took the part and ran with it.

Instead Grant made movies like *Room for One More*, *Monkey Business*, and *Dream Wife*.

Co-starring Betsy Drake in their second and final movie together, *Room for One More* is based on a true story by Anna Perrott Rose about a family who takes in stray children. Grant plays the usual fumbling American husband, Dagwood Bumstead style, to Betsy's unflappable wife and mother.

Monkey Business may be remembered for putting Marilyn Monroe on the screen in her first speaking part, but not for much else. Cary Grant plays a scientist who discovers a youth elixir and then, after inadvertently drinking some of it, begins to act like a teenager. Then everybody in the lab drinks the stuff, and total confusion breaks out. A totally *forced* confusion lacking the spontaneity that true comedy requires.

Director Howard Hawks put it this way:

"I don't believe the premise of *Monkey Business* was really believable, and for that reason the film was not as funny as it should have been. The laughs are born out of the inhibitions that restrict each of us and are here abruptly removed by rejuvenation. It was a good story. Perhaps we pushed the point a bit too far for the public."

After he finished filming the romantic comedy *Dream Wife*, with Deborah Kerr, Cary announced that he and Betsy were going to take a long and leisurely trip around the world on a tramp steamer. He made it clear that he was finished making movies for the simple reason that they were finished with him. Hollywood, for complicated reasons of its own, wasn't writing, producing, and directing Cary Grant movies anymore. After twenty-two years in the film colony, Cary Grant believed that his days there were over. Perhaps he had simply outgrown Hollywood. And it could well be that Hollywood had outgrown him. What difference, in the final analysis, did it really make?

"It was the period of the blue jeans, the dope addicts, the Method, and nobody cared about comedy at all," he said.

Bob Pender had taught his boys that you should always leave your audience wanting more. That's just what Cary Grant planned to do.

And that is exactly what might have happened if it hadn't been for Alfred Hitchcock.

The Peak Years II: 1955-1963

SOME DIRECTORS HATE ACTORS. Others fear actors. A few like George Cukor actually like and respect them. There are a few directors who seem to enjoy humiliating them. In a class by himself is Alfred Hitchcock.

Hitchcock has impressed many persons as cold and withdrawn, virtually unreachable. One of the few things in this life that can thaw Alfred Hitchcock is the truly professional actor. He does not give that accolade to very many. He gives it to Cary Grant.

Hitchcock simply didn't take seriously Grant's announcement that he was retiring. It was unthinkable that a pro like Cary Grant would retire. He didn't have to talk to Grant to know what the problem was. Cary Grant was a unique talent. What he needed, obviously, were unique parts in unique movies opposite unique leading ladies.

What could be simpler?

Alfred Hitchcock called Cary Grant in Palm Springs and asked if he could drive out for the day.

"Of course," Cary said, "we'd love to see you. But I should tell you that it won't do any good. I've made up my mind."

When Hitchcock arrived the next day, they had lunch by the pool. It reflected bright blue underneath the desert sky. They could see waves of heat rising in the distance. Cary went through all the reasons why it just didn't make sense for him to continue working in Hollywood. In his orderly, precise and, well-thought-out-manner, he ticked off all the factors in favor of his retirement from the screen.

Hitchcock patiently listened to all of it. Then when Cary had run out of things to say, Hitchcock took a sip of the Pouilly-Fuisse they'd had with lunch, leaned back in his chair, and folded his hands over his substantial paunch. In his slow and deliberate manner of speaking, he told Cary Grant about a movie he wanted to make if he could get the right actors.

The story concerned John Robie, a reformed jewel thief, who is once again under police suspicion due to a rash of burglaries that seem to fit his old *modus operandi*. Robie agrees to track down the real burglar for the insurance company that is having to make good on most of the stolen jewels. The romantic interest would be a rich American girl.

Hitchcock saw that he had aroused Grant's interest. Hitchcock went out to his car and came back with a script. He placed it on the table.

"There isn't a thing wrong with you, old man, that a first-rate script won't cure," Hitchcock said. "I'd appreciate if you'd read this as soon as possible."

Then Hitchcock, the great master of sereen suspense, took his leave.

Cary walked him out to the Rolls-Royce that was waiting in the drive.

"Alfred, me pal," Grant said, using a bit of Cockney dialect on his fellow Britisher, "I don't want ye to git yer hopes up."

Hitchcock waved away the apologies.

"Not at all, my good man," he said. "Just give it an honest reading and tell me what you think. *I* think you'd be perfectly splendid as John Robie."

He settled himself in the back seat. The driver started the quiet, but powerful, Rolls engine. Hitchcock leaned forward.

"One last thing. It might help you as you're reading. Grace Kelly has agreed to play the American girl. . .and the entire film, both exteriors and interiors, will be shot on the Riviera."

He leaned back and told his driver they could leave now.

Cary Grant went back to the pool-side table and picked up his copy of *To Catch a Thief*. He stretched out on a chaise, shaded by the tamarisk tree from the glare of the afternoon sun and started to read. By the time dinner was served, he had finished the script and made up his mind. He would tell Hitchcock "yes." After nearly two years away from the cameras, he was ending his retirement.

To Catch a Thief was released in August, 1955. The critics were glad to see Cary Grant back on the screen, but, otherwise, their reaction to the film was lukewarm. Movie fans, however, went wild over the sizzling on-screen love affair between Grant and Grace Kelly. At age fifty-one Cary Grant had reached his prime. The years had refined his facial features, rather than eroding them.

Grace Kelly, under Hitchcock's direction, managed to suggest that underneath her cool, blonde facade was a sensuous and passionate woman. Almost a third actor in the movie was the Riviera scenery which Hitchcock used to great advantage in several chase scenes along La Moyenne Corniche.

Even though Hitchcock demanded that Cary Grant put aside his longtime fear of heights and scamper over the steep-pitched roofs of Cannes in the movie's breathtaking finale, Grant had nothing but praise for the director.

"Hitch is great," Cary told reporters, "but he is the most unorthodox, unpredictable director I've known, always doing the unexpected. He knows what he's doing but he doesn't let his actors in on the secret."

"When Hitch tells us to do a scene in a certain way, he doesn't explain why," Cary said. "It's very confusing at first, but when I learned to do what he ordered and not ask questions, I felt as safe and secure as a baby in its mother's arms."

Cary also had high praise for Grace Kelly. He described her acting as "intelligent, direct, and unaffected."

"Would you like to make another picture with Grace Kelly?" a reporter asked.

Cary Grant smiled. "I can be ready in ten minutes," he said.

Grant's passion for meticulous detail was also exercised on the set of *To Catch a Thief*, in spite of Hitchcock's equally developed penchant for planning and tying up loose ends. When Grant learned that the set designers were planning to use reproductions of famous paintings, he was aghast. He insisted on using original paintings from his own collection.

Cary Grant enjoyed working with Grace Kelly so much that he later tried to put together a project in which the two of them would star: an updated production of *His Girl Friday*, in which Rosalind Russell had played opposite Grant in the 1940 version. Nothing, unfortunately, ever came of his plan.

* * * * * *

The rejuvenation of his career did nothing for his marriage to Betsy Drake. They had been drifting apart for a long time. When Cary started making movies that required his going to distant locations for months at a time, it didn't help matters. Sometimes he would ask Betsy to come with him, sometimes he didn't. Even when he was home, he would spend long hours by himself in his den. Betsy knew there was a "Do Not Disturb" sign on the door even if she couldn't see it.

Cary had an incredible amount of physical energy and when he wasn't working, he often didn't know what to do with it. His excess energy seemed to turn into a black sullenness that made life gloomy for everyone around him.

Grant did not find another script worth doing until nearly two years after he'd filmed *To Catch a Thief*. During that time Betsy and Cary endured a marriage that was beginning to disintegrate. Neither of them, however, wanted to admit it.

Then Fate forced their hand. Cary agreed to appear in Stanley Kramer's production of *The Pride and the Passion*. Grant played a British naval officer in the time of Napoleon sent into Spain to retrieve a huge cannon before the French can capture it. His accomplices and co-stars were Frank Sinatra and Sophia Loren. By the time the three of them hauled that monstrous cannon over the Spanish countryside, the Ancient Mariner's Albatross seemed like a pet canary.

A few weeks after shooting began, the reports emanating from the location site hinted very strongly that Cary Grant had developed a crush on Sophia Loren that was even harder for Kramer to handle than the unwieldy cannon. Then the reports stopped hinting. Grant said he wanted Sophia to come to Hollywood and make a movie with him.

Sophia Loren was not legally married to film producer Carlo Ponti under Italian law. He had no way of dissolving his union with his first wife: Italy had no divorce. But in every other way Loren and Ponti were married. And while Sophia Loren enjoyed the attentions of the handsome Hollywood film star, she knew very well who had rescued her from the slums of postwar Naples, who had created and guided her career. It was Carlo Ponti. Still, one couldn't be *rude*. The reports continued. Then Betsy Drake showed up.

Everyone, of course, behaved like ladies and gentlemen. There was no hint of anything except total affection between Cary Grant and Betsy. Sophia Loren had already told Cary Grant she couldn't make a film with him right away, because she had promised her husband she would star in one of his films: a World War II story to be called *Two Women.*

After several weeks on location Betsy was eager to return to the peace and stillness of Palm Springs. Since she and Cary had made *Room for One More* five years ago, Betsy had virtually given up acting. What she found taking more and more of her time was writing. She had almost completed the research and first draft of what she hoped would be her first published book. She wanted to get back to California and work on it.

She kissed Cary goodbye. He had ordered a car and driver to take her south to Gibraltar where she would board the Italian liner, the *Andrea Doria.*

It was a quiet crossing. Betsy soaked up the sun, enjoyed the northern Italian cuisine, and worked on her manuscript. On the evening of July 24, Betsy was in her stateroom and ready for bed by 10:30 P. M. She had noticed that the sun and the salt air made her sleepy earlier than usual. She read for awhile and then turned out the lights. She awoke when a terrible blow reverberated throughout the ship. Or did she imagine it? She sat up, all her senses alert. Minutes later the abandon ship signal was heard. She threw a dress on and went out into the corridor. Others were hastily leaving their staterooms. No one knew what had happened.

Only after they were rescued off the Andrea Doria by the Ile de France, did Betsy and her fellow passengers learn that the *Andrea Doria* had collided with a Swedish liner, the *Stockholm*, in a heavy fog off Nantucket. The *Stockholm* made it to a nearby port. The *Andrea Doria* sank to the bottom of the Atlantic, taking fifty-one persons with her.

Betsy and the others who were rescued lost everything. In Betsy's case this included two hundred thousand dollars worth of jewelry that Cary had given her and nineteen of the twenty intricately embroidered Indian saris that Barbara Hutton had presented to Betsy shortly after she and Cary were wed. The most heartbreaking loss of all, however, was her manuscript and all her research materials. This writing project had absorbed her for the last several years. Now it had entirely vanished.

Betsy lined up with everybody else outside the radio room of the *Ile de France* so she could let Cary know she was safe. Finally she got off her cable telling him she was among those rescued. She signed it: *your safe, sound, and rescued wife.*

As it happens the cable had reached him before a newspaper did. He knew there had been a close scrape of some sort but for several hours didn't know what kind of a scrape it had been.

Betsy's near tragedy brought them, for a few months, closer than they had been in years. Cary constantly mentioned her name to interviewers. He said to one reporter:

"I love her so much that, for once in my life, words fail me."

The truism says that "absence makes the heart grow fonder." Cary was perhaps ready with kind words and lavish praise for his wife, because he was so seldom home. He was working more than he had in years. Between 1957 and 1959, Cary Grant made seven movies. Among them were the immensely popular *Affair to Remember* with Deborah Kerr, an almost tragic love story that one critic called a four-Kleenex movie; *Indiscreet*, with Ingrid Bergman, a first-rate romantic comedy that displays both Grant and Bergman at their lighthearted best and *North by Northwest*, another Hitchcock thriller which many critics consider one of his finest films.

Cary Grant had kept in touch with Ingrid Bergman ever since they had worked together on *Notorious*. She was, in fact, one of his very favorite people. When the scandal of her affair with Roberto Rossellini had rocked Hollywood, Cary Grant was one of the few people who would publicly say a good word about Ingrid Bergman.

After seven years, however, Rossellini had decided that a younger, more exotic woman suited him more. The call from Grant to appear opposite him in a new movie came at the very moment when it became clear to Ingrid Bergman that she could no longer stay with Rossellini. The breakup of this marriage was in many ways worse than when she had left her first husband and their young daughter in 1950 in order to marry Rossellini. She was older now, and there were some who were eager to say that Rossellini's abandoning her for another woman was exactly what she deserved. News photos of her leaving the Rome airport for London show an exhausted-looking woman whose unhappiness and misery is etched in the lines on her face.

Waiting for her at Heathrow, in addition to over fifty reporters and photographers, was Cary Grant. He hugged her warmly when she left the plane and sat silently and patiently at her side as she answered reporter's questions in a thin voice that sounded as if it would crack at any moment.

She and Rossellini had been legally separated only a few days, since the previous Thursday. She would not answer questions about the separation, but said that she was "happy within myself," even though many questions concerning her relationship with Rossellini brought tears to her eyes. The questions might have gone on for hours if Cary Grant had not herded Ms. Bergman through the mostly sympathetic throng to the car he had waiting. He helped her settle into her hotel, he provided a sympathetic ear as they ate the excellent dinner that he had ordered sent to her suite, and he was at her side constantly for the next several days. He took her on sight-seeing tours of London. He took her shopping for antiques, one of her favorite pastimes.

By the time they were ready to start filming *Indiscreet*, Ingrid Bergman had begun to look like her old and quite exquisite self again.

Cary Grant might not be a very good husband, but there is surely no better friend one could have in all the world.

Less than a year after *Indiscreet* was released, Grant announced that he and Ms. Bergman were planning to make another film together. The original screenplay by Harry Kurnitz dealt with an Irish aristocrat, his son, and a woman they both fall in love with. Much to the disappointment of both Grant and Ms. Bergman's fans, the film was never made.

A few years later Cary Grant described Ingrid Bergman as:

"a fascinating, full-blooded yet temperate woman who has the courage to live in accord with her needs and strength enough to accept and benefit by the consequences of her beliefs in an inhibited, critical, and frightened society.

"Ingrid needs no uninvited busybody to proclaim her debts; she knows and pays them herself. I commend her highly to you."

After Ingrid Bergman had married Swedish theatrical producer Lars Schmidt, Cary visited them in their home outside Paris. The talk turned to antiques. Ingrid wanted a plain wooden cabinet for a certain corner. Cary filed the information away.

Two years later he saw just what Ingrid wanted in a Chelsea antique store. He immediately called Ingrid in Paris to see if she had yet found a similar piece on her own. She hadn't.

"Splendid!" Cary said. "You've got it now. I just found exactly what you said you were looking for."

The simple mechanics of phoning Paris had taken several hours, and when Cary got back to the antique shop he was dismayed to learn that the piece of furniture he had promised to send to Ingrid Bergman had been sold to someone else. It was months before he could bring himself to tell Ingrid what had happened.

* * * * * *

Ernest Lehman's original script, *North by Northwest*, is a perfect story for an age in which unknown, but implacable forces threaten and harass us for reasons not clearly discernible. The film's great popularity is at least partially due to the fact that it can be viewed not only as an exciting suspense story, but as a modern Greek tragedy. Our pity and terror for the bewildered and increasingly terrified hero helps us to deal with our own psychological demons of doubt, fear, and uncertainty.

Hitchcock recognized these elements when he was casting the film. He says he wanted no one but Cary Grant to play the part of the pursued and threatened hero, Roger Thornhill, who is mistaken for a secret agent and is subsequently pursued by other secret agents who are inexplicably trying to kill him. The more Thornhill attempts to clear up the confusion regarding his identity, the more intensely he is pursued. Hitchcock wanted Grant because "audiences can identify with him."

Two sequences in *North by Northwest* have become classic examples of screen terror at its best—or worst. The first is when a peaceful pastoral setting suddenly turns deadly as a small plane that we thought was dusting the fields of crops begins a relentless assassination attempt on Thornhill. The most tame of settings becomes, in the blink of an eye, a huge death chamber limited only by the horizon. It is another brilliant metaphor of modern life. We cannot escape the Bomb no matter where we live. Modern agribusiness has decreed that we cannot even escape ingesting poisons along with our daily bread. Strontium-90 from past nuclear tests sifts gently down to earth from the upper atmosphere and settles into our bone marrow. A certain percentage of us will develop cancer from these and other chemical pollutants of modern life. Yes, we know how Cary Grant feels as he stumbles over that now desolate field with literally no place to hide.

The final, surreal chase scene across the presidential images of Mount Rushmore is another example of the metamorphosis of the familiar into the menacing. We remember Mount Rushmore from our fourth grade history books. Now here it is again, only it's different. Hitchcock forces us through these two scenes to confront the destructive forces in everyday life that most of us would much rather ignore.

North by Northwest, especially in the two segments discussed above, gave Cary Grant a chance to combine talents that he had, up to then, exercised only separately. There were movies in which he was a suave romantic leading man, and there were movies, especially in *Gunga Din* and the screwball comedies, in which he is allowed to unleash his physical energies and display his considerable physical coordination. *North by Northwest* is the first movie Grant ever made in which he displays both skills at the same time, which was undoubtedly another factor in the movie's success.

Grant had been working for a long time to perfect the role he did best: Cary Grant. His portrayal of Roger Thornhill may well represent the pinnacle of his efforts.

Cary Grant's success in becoming Cary Grant can best be illustrated by one of Hitchcock's offhand remarks during the filming of *North by Northwest*. They were shooting a scene in New York's Plaza Hotel. The action required Cary to walk across the foyer of the famous hotel. Everything went smoothly. Only one take was required. One of the many bystanders turned to Hitchcock:

"But you didn't tell him how you wanted him to do it."

"Listen," said Hitchcock patiently, "Cary Grant's been walking across this foyer for over thirty years. What can I tell him he doesn't already know?"

Back during his days on Broadway, Cary, unsure of who he was, decided that Noel Coward would be a good model. Coward was then the reigning king of sophistication, and Cary quite consciously imitated his walk, his expression, and the way he kept his hands in his pockets when in public.

"I'd casually put my hand in my pocket," Cary recalled "and it would get stuck there with perspiration. My biggest gesture was raising an eyebrow."

Seeing himself bigger than life on the screen came as a shock.

"I don't think any non-actor can ever know how horrifying it is to hear your voice, see yourself, and see how you walk."

Years later he shuddered to think of it. Seeing himself from a distance made Grant realize that the Noel Coward image wasn't working. And slowly, very slowly, with many stops and starts, Cary Grant began to emerge.

The difficulties involved in completely becoming Cary Grant may be underlined this way: Grant had been among the top box office stars for many years, ever since the late Thirties. But it wasn't until 1958 that Cary Grant was named the Number One male box office star. Elizabeth Taylor was named the top female star. The poll was conducted by *Boxoffice Magazine*, an industry publication.

As so often happened in Cary Grant's life, the professional success was marred by unhappiness in his personal life. While publicly professing their love for each other, Cary and Betsy had been steadily going their separate ways. They agreed that if they lived apart for awhile it might improve things between them. In October, 1958, Cary Grant and Betsy Drake released a carefully worded statement to the press:

"After careful consideration and long discussion, we have decided to live apart. We have had and will always have a deep love and respect for each other, but, alas, our marriage has not brought us the happiness we fully expected and mutually desired.

"So since we have no children needful of our affection, it is consequently best that we separate for awhile.

"We have purposely issued this public statement in order to forestall the usual misinformed gossip and conjecture. There are no plans for divorce, and we ask only that the press respect our statement as complete and our friends to be patient with and understanding of our decision."

Then began one of the strangest separations in the history of marriage. Cary and Betsy were seen together frequently, more frequently, in fact, than when they were living together. They always spent her birthday together. She would frequently visit him for weeks at a time if he were filming on location.

Betsy began seeing other men. Cary openly squired a series of dazzling beauties to various parties, openings, and dinners. Once Cary and Betsy attended the theatre, each with different partners.

"Look," Cary said to his companion, pointing to Betsy several aisles away, "that's my wife. Isn't she beautiful?"

The young lady at Cary's side didn't know whether he was putting her on and decided not to ask.

Cary told a writer for a national publication:

"Betsy and I still love each other very much. We dine together two or three times a week. When I'm away from California, we telephone and write to each other all the time."

At about the same time that Betsy and Cary decided to live apart for awhile, Cary began psychotherapy with Dr. Mortimer Hartman. But this wasn't your garden-variety fifty-minutes-on-the-couch psychotherapy. Cary was one of 112 Californians who participated in a study of LSD (lysergic acid diethylamide). What is not generally known is that Betsy was one of the 112 guinea pigs along with her husband. In fact the project was probably her idea. Betsy was the one who was perennially fascinated by the study of the human mind and psyche.

It may have been the little tablets of LSD that made Betsy decide that they ought to separate. Up to then their marriage had been lived entirely on Cary's terms.

"It was terribly frustrating to be married to him because he's a very self-sufficient man. He has a secretary and a valet. When I learned to cook," Betsy said, "I felt wonderful, for at least I was useful. Cary wanted to be free, yet he wanted me always on tap. He'd go ahead on movie locations. I'd be dying to go, but I'd wait weeks for the call that said, 'Come at once.' "

As Betsy's LSD sessions progressed, she noticed herself becoming increasingly impatient with Cary.

"I used to be such a nice girl, everyone thought, so well-bred, so retiring. No more. Now I blow up," she said.

Betsy remembered a turning point in her therapy came one night when she and Cary were supposed to go to a party.

"Then Cary, as usual, got on the phone. I waited an hour."

Finally, she walked into the room where Cary's endless phone call was taking place and used a series of phrases that are usually heard only in locker rooms and in Marine boot camp. Cary Grant could hardly believe his ears.

"Why, Betsy," he said, covering the phone's mouthpiece, "I've never heard you use language like that!"

Betsy said that the LSD sessions also helped her come to terms with the traumatic memories she had from that terrible night of chaos and confusion when the Andrea Doria sank.

"You learn to die under LSD," Betsy said. And in her case, this psychic "death" left her with a marvelous equanimity. She believed she had attained "peace of mind." And it enabled her to face certain unpleasant facts about her marriage.

"I left Cary, but, psychically, he'd left me long ago. I was still in love with him," she said a year after they'd parted, "and I'm not ashamed to say so. But he's going through a tremendous change. Who knows? He may come back to me, or not marry at all, or marry somebody quite different from me."

Betsy had nothing but kind words for her estranged husband.

"He's dizzy! Enormously stimulating! Younger than many young men I know."

Cary's more than seventy LSD sessions usually took place on Saturday afternoons. They lasted four or five hours and left him either shaken to the core or in a state of almost rhapsodic euphoria.

Grant's psychotherapist, Dr. Mortimer Hartman, speaking in the late Fifties, described LSD as a "psychic energizer which empties the subconscious and intensifies emotion and memory a hundred times." This flood of information about his own mind and subconscious hit Cary Grant, age fifty-four, with the massive and unstoppable force of a tidal wave.

"I know that, all my life, I've been going around in a fog. You're just a bunch of molecules until you know who you are. You spend all your time getting to be a big Hollywood actor," Grant said. "But then what? You've reached a comfortable plateau, and you want to stay on it; you resist change. One day, after many weeks of LSD, my last defense crumbled. To my delight, I found I had a tough inner core of strength. In my youth, I was very dependent on older men and women. Now people come to me for help!"

"All my life I think I've been running from what I wanted most. I've shied, for example, from women who look like my mother," Grant noted.

And suddenly one remembers that Elsie Kingdom Leach was a dark-haired, brown-eyed, olive-skinned woman. And one also remembers that Cary Grant had married three fair-skinned, blue-eyed blondes.

"I always felt my mother rejected me," Grant explains. "Now I've developed a great compassion for my parents."

Cary Grant believes that the LSD sessions gave him insight into *all* women, not just his mother.

"I love women. They're the mothers of the earth, so often imposed on by men."

He also believes that during one of the sessions he relived, in every way but physically, his birth.

The biggest change that outsiders, especially reporters, noticed in Cary Grant was the way he had changed from a man who appeared to resent personal questions into a man who was willing to talk non-stop about his most intimate feelings and emotions with what appeared to be total candor.

"I feel now that I really understand myself. I didn't ever before. And because I never understood myself, how could I have hoped to understand anyone else? That's why I say that, now, I can truly give a woman love for the first time in my life. . .because I can understand her.

"I've just been born again. I have just been through a psychiatric experience that has completely changed me. It was horrendous. I had to face things about myself which I never admitted, which I didn't know were there. Now I know that I hurt every woman I loved. I was an utter fake, a self-opinionated boor, a know-all who knew very little.

"I was hiding behind all kinds of defenses, hypocrisies and vanities. I had to get rid of them layer by layer. That moment when your conscious meets with your subconscious is a helluva wrench. You feel the whole top of your head is lifting off.

"With me there came a day after weeks of treatment when I saw the light. Now for the first time in my life I am truly, deeply and honestly happy.

"Quite suddenly many things became clear.

"For example—children. I am now aware of the insecurities of children. I know that things are done to us when we are young that affect us all our lives. If they are bad things, we are constantly trying to hit back for our hurts.

"I have been married three times, but never had a child. Now I am fit for children. I hope I will beget some.

"I'd half messed around with yoga, hypnosis, and religion and made sporadic attempts at mysticism. Nothing seemed to really give me what I needed until this last treatment.

"Perhaps I became a success because of a compulsory need. But I found out that a successful man is not necessarily a happy one. When I woke up after this treatment, I knew exactly who and what I was. I saw myself exactly as I am for the first time.

"All the sadness and vanities were torn away. I was pleased with the hard core of the strength I found inside of me. I think I've always been a pretty fair actor. Now I know I'm going to be the best actor there is.

"I've had my ego stripped away. A man is a better actor

without ego, because he has truth in him. Now I cannot behave untruthfully toward anyone and certainly not to myself.

"I am no longer lonely and I am a happy man.

"They told me this happiness will get greater and greater. Already I feel I am too happy to stand any more.

"Betsy and I have been separated now for many months. When I went through it, we found we loved each other more than we'd ever done before. Whether or not we get back together again, we shall always feel the same way about each other.

"With each wife there were areas of happiness and contentment, but each was incomplete, and my wives discovered it as soon as I did. I tell you this, my next marriage will be complete. Or if this one to Betsy persists, this will be a full, happy, utterly satisfying union. I just don't know yet.

"Why my marriages failed? It was principally because I brought a cloud to happiness. I could not have been a good husband to any woman. Marriage should be the apex of mutual agreement; mine were not. Now I know that I hurt every woman I loved and they tried to hurt me, too, but the faults were mine, always mine.

"When I finished my psychiatric treatmant recently I had two immediate reactions. My first was, "Oh, those wasted years, why didn't I do this sooner?

"Now everything is changed. My attitude toward women is completely different. I do not intend to foul up any more lives. I could be a good husband now. I am aware of my faults and I am ready to accept responsibilities and exchange tolerances.

"Every day now is wonderful. I wish I could live another forty years. I am convinced I will live to a healthy old age, but if I drop dead within the next ten years I will have enjoyed more living in the latter part of my life than most people ever know.

"Once you realize," Cary said, "that you have all things inside you, love and hate alike, and learn to accept them, then you can use your love to exhaust your hate.

"That power is inside you but it can be assimilated into your power to live. Then you can relax. Then you can do more than you ever dreamed you could do."

But Cary Grant did not just talk about himself. He talked about the human condition, life in general, what-it's-all-about. You know—The Big Picture. In the late Fifties and early Sixties, Cary

Grant simply could not stop talking about all the fantasic things that he'd learned courtesy of LSD. Pithy little nuggets of wisdom. Sort of like what Benjamin Franklin would have written, if Ben Franklin had been a Hollywood leading man who had gained insight via a magical chemical.

Cary Grant called his collected hallucinogenic wisdom *The Devastating Facts of Life*:

"Never do anyone a favor. It will make him feel inferior to you. Do someone a favor and you've probably made an enemy for life.

"If you want to make a friend, let someone do you a favor. It will give him a pleasantly rosy glow of superiority. Besides—it builds his character and leaves your own comfortably flabby.

"Have the good manners to wait until you're asked before offering an opinion. Once you are asked, say exactly what you think. You'll be misunderstood anyway, so you might as well taste the pleasures of honesty.

"Honesty is the best policy, and life is much too short to lie. These are cliches. But all the old cliches are true—a fact you will suddenly learn one day when you are about forty years old.

"Don't expect to be rewarded if you do tell the truth. Hypocrisy no longer has any power to shock us. We encounter it every day. But we encounter the truth so seldom that it shocks and embarrasses us, and we run from it.

"Learn how to be unhappy. If you have never been unhappy, you cannot possibly know what happiness is.

"Don't expect to know when you are happy. The most unfortunate thing about happiness is that it is rarely recognizable at the time it is occurring. When I was a young man, I either lived in my memories of the past or my hope of the future. One of the consolations of middle age is the ability to recognize happiness as it happens.

"The only way to remain happy is to know nothing or everything. Unfortunately it is impossible to know nothing for very long.

"Respect women because they are wiser than men.

"Women have an innate wisdom we men try to despoil from the time we're sixteen years old.

"A man owes it to me—if I have to look at him—to keep his hair combed and his teeth cleaned.

"Deplore bad taste and bad manners. Honesty is sometimes mistaken for rudeness, but honesty is still the best manners.

"Deplore your mistakes. Regret them as much as you like. But don't really expect to learn by them.

"Suspect people. You can't rely on them. They either die or disappoint you; or you, them.

"Rely on yourself. I know some people who have gone to their graves at eighty, screaming that the world was unfair, that they had had bad luck. I don't believe in bad luck. People make their own luck.

"For myself—at the present time—I think that life is a paradox. I've learned not to believe any longer in either high emotions or deep depressions. I would like to live just a little below or above the line.

"Live—if you can—with a certain amount of grace. This is a thing that very few people do these days.

"Have integrity.

"A lie can only beget more lies, dishonesty more dishonesty. Have integrity. You can live with a little more respect for the world and for yourself if you do."

* * * * * *

In the late Fifties and early Sixties, as he approached his sixtieth birthday, Cary Grant came into full flower. Suddenly everyone seemed to realize all at once that he wasn't just an incredibly handsome and skilled actor, he was a veritable institution. Everything about him became endlessly interesting—his clothes, his youthful appearance, his reputed fortune. He had lasted longer than any other major male star. How had he done it? What was his secret?

Grant had been turning up for years on various best dressed lists, and Hollywood reporters had carefully noted that he did not wear garters (Cary Grant's socks wouldn't *dare* droop), and had his trousers made with a special waistband that eliminated the need for a belt. He never wore undershirts. He had also designed his own special dress shirt.

"I used to go crazy reaching up under my shirt to pull the studs through," Grant said. "So I developed a fly-front dress shirt. You put the studs in. Then you button it."

As legend had it from the heyday of the fan magazines; for fear of ruining the hang of his clothes, he carried only three items on his person: a very thin cigarette case, a fifty dollar bill, and his car keys.

The legend was embellished:

Producer Stanley Donen said that when Grant made *Indiscreet* with Ingrid Bergman in 1958, he wore a tuxedo that had been made for him at London's Howes and Curtis Tailors in 1934. Cary Grant allegedly owned more clothes than any other man in Hollywood.

"If this is true, it's because I buy clothes that last," he said. "I still wear suits made twenty years ago, and I have several topcoats that are thirty years old."

Cary always wore his own clothes when making a movie, usually using fourteen to sixteen suits per film. Grant had many of his suits made in Hong Kong at a shop on Queen's Road Central near the Queen's Theatre. A few things were bought from Brooks Brothers in New York, and the Hollywood tailor Quintino was a nearby source for whatever garments Grant felt he needed quickly.

Clothes were always important to Cary Grant, and he was always willing to play Pygmalion when it came to other people's wardrobes. Writer-director Richard Brooks, with whom Grant worked in *Crisis*, remembers:

"Cary once told me my clothes were awful and suggested we both go to Brooks Brothers and try on suits together. The salesman handed both of us identical suits; we put them on. I still looked like a bum and Cary looked magnificent."

After his LSD sessions Cary began to credit his father for instilling clothes-sense in him.

"I learned a lot from him," Cary said. "He first put into my mind the idea of buying one good superior suit rather than a number of inferior ones. Then, even when it's threadbare, people will know it was once good. He taught me the feel of good cloth and a liking for expensive shoes. I've paid $150 for a pair of shoes—they *look* better, even after years of wear. I've always believed that it's good sense to pay a lot. Cartier's will buy a jewel back at the same price or better," he added. "There is nothing really cheap in this world anyway."

Buying good clothes and jewels, however, was just about the only investment that Grant would talk about. It was known that he had extensive real estate holdings in Palm Springs and Beverly Hills, and he once bought twelve hundred acres of prime coffee-growing land in Brazil, but those are the only crumbs of information available on a question that intrigued columnists for years: What has Cary Grant done with his money?

The only thing they were sure of was that he didn't squander it. Stories about Cary Grant's alleged stinginess were a staple of the Hollywood grapevine. Richard Brooks, however, had a different explanation for Cary's careful attitude toward money:

"I don't know all the emotions which keep Cary from being frivolous with his money, but I do know that he is just as careful with *your* money as he is with his own. If he is in your home and he sees an electric light burning unnecessarily, he'll get up and turn it off. I certainly wouldn't call Cary penurious. I remember one Christmas when he and I exchanged expensive presents. We were both disturbed over that because I believe we both felt that this sort of thing is a favor-seeking device. We agreed not to exchange Christmas or birthday presents again. Two years went by. Cary had been away a great deal. Suddenly, in June, I received a package wrapped in old newspapers from Hong Kong. It was a paperweight made from an old opium pipe, rare and beautiful. The card was from Cary, and said he thought I would like this because I collect pipes. Later, when I had moved to another home, an appraiser from an insurance company told me that my old paperweight was solid silver and worth at least one thousand dollars."

Cary Grant was making good money for eight or nine years before there was an income tax. By the early Sixties his fortune was estimated at $10 to $12 million. The decline of the great Hollywood studio system contributed to a substantial increase in Grant's fortune. For his work in *To Catch a Thief*, Cary Grant made seven hundred thousand dollars before taxes. The movie was produced and distributed by Paramount. Four years later many movies were being produced by small independent companies. The role of the big studio had become that of distributor. So when Grant's own production company made *Operation Petticoat*, distributed by Universal, Grant's final take was an incredible three million dollars for a single project. *Operation Petticoat*, as it happens, is far from Grant's best film, but it has made more money than any of the others. Cary Grant obviously did not enjoy the frequent references to his alleged stinginess.

"A man who says he isn't interested in money is a liar," he said.

One magazine writer said, "Cary Grant has the first nickel he ever made."

Cary replied waspishly, "I do not have that particular coin. If I did, by this time, it would be qite valuable and I'd sell it."

On another occasion, Cary said, "I'm sure I have that reputation (of stinginess) because I don't gamble or go to night clubs or give huge parties. And I don't believe in giving gifts at Christmas. I give presents when I feel like it. Also, I'm the only one who won't take orders to give to charities; I give as I please."

Cary Grant is also a man who likes to get what he has paid for. He is famous for carefully totalling up restaurant bills.

"I think it's everyone's *duty* to demand good service from good restaurants," Cary said. "Too many people meekly eat a foul dish instead of sending it back to the kitchen, thus establishing bad habits both for themselves and for the chef."

Once when Cary was spending several days at the Plaza in Manhattan, he ordered breakfast in bed: bacon, eggs, and English muffins. When his tray arrived he noticed there were three English muffin halves. He got room service on the phone.

"Can you tell me why I am being charged for two English muffins when I have been sent only one and a half English muffins?" Cary asked.

The question was kicked upstairs until the manager of the Plaza was on the phone explaining that most people didn't eat all four halves so the hotel kitchen put aside the extra half for Eggs Benedict orders. Whether the Plaza changed its muffin policy for the rest of its clients is not known, but when Cary Grant checked into the Plaza after that incident, a plate of hot buttered English muffins was immediately sent to his room.

* * * * * *

The stories about Grant's stinginess seem more than balanced by stories of his generosity, especially to people who helped him when he was young and struggling in New York. When Cary Grant was scratching out a living in vaudeville, Almira Sessions was an established vaudeville star. She not only encouraged Grant, but was often instrumental in finding him jobs. He never forgot. When the vaudeville circuit breathed its last, Almira Sessions went to Hollywood and became a character actress. She was regularly offered work in Grant's films.

In addition to the estimated two hundred thousand dollars that

Grant gave to various British war relief funds when World War II broke out in Europe, there are many stories of his generosity to old and failing former vaudeville actors, stories he will neither confirm or deny.

Like all of us Cary Grant's attitude toward money was forged in childhood. In his case the most noticeable economic realities of his youth were his father's inability to bring home a paycheck that covered more than the bare necessities of life, and his mother's inability to quietly accept that unpleasant fact of life. Money squabbles, in fact, were nearly constant in the Leach household. Thus, at a very early age, Cary Grant learned that money is *important*. It is simply unthinkable to waste it or spend it foolishly, and he never has.

Nobody ever made life easy for Cary Grant. He has worked very hard all his life, and he quite understandably feels that no one should profit from Cary Grant, the institutuion, except Cary Grant himself and those he chooses to work with. Like all rich and famous persons, he is a prime target for the get-rich schemes of others, less talented than himself. It enrages him to feel he has been used, not that he allowed it to happen very often.

Producer Robert Arthur, who worked with Grant on *Operation Petticoat* and *That Touch of Mink*, said, "Cary's anger becomes almost a phobia when he thinks he is being taken advantage of because he *is* Cary Grant."

Maggie Leach, wife of Cary's Bristol cousin, Eric, said that both Cary and his mother "have more difficulty taking things than giving them."

Director Richard Brooks corroborated Maggie's observation.

"Cary finds it difficult to accept anything from anyone—gifts, compliments, or even love—because he feels the moment you accept something, you are obligated," Brooks said. "Cary has a compulsion to feel free. Even when it comes to something as simple as having dinner with me, he will never say 'How about dinner a week from Tuesday?' That's already a commitment. If I'm free some night and Cary happens to be free that same night, then we have dinner together."

At one point, Brooks recalled, he and Cary hadn't seen each other for over a year. When they finally happened to meet, Brooks said, "Hi, Cary, how are you?"

"Dick, I love you very much," Cary said.

"Well, I love you, too but why do you say that?" Brooks asked.

"Thanks for not asking me why I didn't call or write in all this time," Cary replied.

And then Brooks understood for the first time how very much Cary Grant hates to feel guilty.

* * * * * *

Cary Grant was clearly getting annoyed by the endless stream of reporter's questions about his clothes and his money. What he really wanted to talk about was something he *didn't* have: children. He had suddenly discovered a whole new facet of existence, one he had been too busy to notice before.

Within months after Cary and Betsy had announced their separation, Cary said: "For the first time in my life, I feel I'm the sort of man who would make a good father. I'd like to have children—lots of them.

"I'd like to see them sitting around a great family table," he continued, "chattering away to each other. Up to now I've never felt ready for the responsibility of raising a family. I was still finding my true self—so how could I guide my kids?

"Now I'm happy and at peace with myself," Cary declared, "so I feel I could be a good father. And as I'm lucky enough to be very comfortable financially, I could give them material things as well.

"I can only hope the future will bring me a happy marriage and lots of happy children," he said. "Perhaps with Betsy again, perhaps not. Who knows?"

On another occasion he ascribed his failure to become a father and the failure of his marriages to his own emotional shortcomings.

"In each instance, the woman deserved my love, but, honestly, I had none to give. I didn't know how to love for the simple reason that I didn't know myself. I was racked with doubts, fears, and skepticism. I was unhappy with my past, dissatisfied with the present and fearful of the future. No man in my shape should have had children," Cary said. "Now it's different. I not only want to have children; I need them. If I had known all my life what I know now, I would have had a hundred children and built a ranch to keep them on."

Cary Grant apparently did not discuss his yearnings toward fatherhood with his estranged wife, Betsy.

"I suppose if Cary wants to have children with me, he'll tell me," she said mildly to a mutual friend.

Cary Grant gave so many interviews in the months follwing his LSD sessions, you wonder how he found time to make movies. But he worked steadily during that period. *Operation Petticoat* was released shortly after *North by Northwest* in 1959, followed by *The Grass is Greener*, with Deborah Kerr and Robert Mitchum in 1960, and *That Touch of Mink*, with Doris Day and Gig Young, in 1962. The latter places second in the list of Cary Grant's top money-making films, just behind *Operation Petticoat*.

Grant's co-stars on *Operation Petticoat* included Tony Curtis who had adored Grant from afar for many years.

"I first became a Grant fan while I was serving aboard a submarine in World War II. One of the few movies on the sub was *Gunga Din*, and they showed it so often that the entire crew knew by heart all the dialogue and sound effects," Curtis recalled. "After awhile, we would play the film without the sound and assign roles to different sailors. I always played Grant."

Tony Curtis got to be so good at playing Cary Grant that his brilliant impersonation of Grant is one of high points of Billy Wilder's outrageous comedy, *Some Like It Hot*.

Curtis had never tried to keep it a secret that he idolized Grant, and the first days on the set of *Operation Petticoat* were a bit awkward.

"It's difficult to be an idol—and overwhelming to be near your idol," Curtis admitted. The mutual embarrassment "quickly vanished," Curtis said, "because Cary's charm and humor kept him from taking my idolization seriously. We established a rapport almost immediately."

In *Operation Petticoat* Grant plays a submarine captain determined to get his damaged ship to safe harbor, and Curtis plays his larcenous procurement officer, able to get, by hook or crook, what the crippled ship needs to get even limpingly afloat.

It must have been a very nice moment for Tony Curtis when the reviews started coming in, and he was singled out for praise along with Grant.

Daily Variety said, "Tony Curtis is a splendid foil, one of two or three best young comedians around, and his own style meshes easily with Grant's."

In spite of the success of *Operation Petticoat* and *That Touch of Mink* and the vigorous resurgence of his career in the late Fifties, Cary Grant wondered how long he could continue making the sophisticated comedies on which his career had been built. The writers just weren't writing them anymore. They preferred to produce acid-tinged satires instead.

"I may appear old-fashioned," Grant said, "but I don't think it's necessary for me to go along with this new style."

His musings on comedy were perhaps prompted by the fact that he was on the third team of writers for a script that he hoped to put into production the following year. Somehow, mysteriously, Hollywood writers had lost the ability to do a Cary Grant comedy, no matter how much money was at stake.

"Comedy," Grant asserted, "is undoubtedly the biggest gamble in the movie business."

* * * * * *

The following year, Betsy Drake decided that her marriage to Cary Grant, in limbo now for four years, wasn't very funny either. Marriage, like comedy, is a gamble and hers wasn't giving the returns it should have.

In August, 1962, Betsy Drake asked the California Supreme Court branch in Santa Monica to dissolve her thirteen-year-old marriage to Grant. She charged "mental cruelty." Betsy said:

"He preferred watching TV to talking to me. He appeared to be bored with me. I became lonely, unhappy, miserable and went into psychoanalysis. He once told me he didn't want to be married. He showed no interest in any of my friends."

Cary, as usual, did not show up in court. After the divorce was granted, an interlocutory decree that would not become final for one year, Betsy told reporters, "I was always in love with him—and still am."

Betsy Drake's acting career went steadily downhill after her separation and divorce from Cary Grant.

"I gave up my career when I got married," she said. "I couldn't be an actress and a housewife, too, and if I were married now, I wouldn't be acting." (She was due to appear in a movie called *Clarence, the Cross-Eyed Lion.*)

The divorce had apparently been Cary's idea even though Betsy was allowed the face-saving courtesy of being the one to ask the court to dissolve their marriage. Nearly two years after the final decree, she still spoke wistfully about her years with Grant. They were, she said, "a valuable experience."

"I learned to be a wife," Betsy said. "Because of Cary, I was inspired to become a good cook, and I think I'll be a marvelous wife for someone else now. He encouraged me to learn all kinds of things, and I think my references are very good.

"But I also give him the best of references as husband material. He enjoyed home life—for a time. He was such a good sport when I first started to cook: some of my early efforts were dreadful. He'd eat burnt steak without flinching. Once when I was preparing my first fancy dinner, he kept coming to the kitchen to see if it was ready. I'd say no and he waited patiently. As I recall, I got it on the table around midnight," she added.

For his own part Cary Grant said something about Betsy Drake that he has never said about any of his other wives:

"Betsy was good for me. I've never clearly resolved why Betsy and I parted," Cary added. "We lived together, not as easily and contentedly as some, perhaps; yet, it seemed to me, as far as one marriage can be compared with any other, compatibly happier than most. I owe a lot to Betsy."

* * * * * *

As Cary Grant rapidly approached his sixtieth birthday, reporters and interviewers were interested in finding out the secret of Cary's apparently immortal good looks. Here he was in his late fifties, looking and acting like a man in his early forties. The jet-black hair was by now nearly gray, but there was nothing ordinary about Cary's gray hair. It was a beautiful silver gray, sleek and shiny and, of course, immaculately groomed.

A studio executive whose middle had begun to spread to all points of the compass, looked at Cary Grant's flat belly and said angrily, "It's ugly and unnatural for a man to stay that thin for that long."

How did he do it?

Astrologers would say that he was within the established pattern for Capricorns, who tend to bloom relatively late in life. Of Capricorns, it can truly be said, "You're not getting older, you're getting better."

Clifford Odets had a more down-to-earth explanation.

"Cary takes care of himself," Odets said. "He no longer smokes, he drinks wine very sparingly, he's in bed before midnight nearly seven nights out of seven, and no matter what's bothering him, he can turn it off and sleep well."

Director Stanley Donen agreed with Odet's "clean living" theory.

"Times are changing. Fifty-eight is not as old today as it was during our fathers' day. The weather is good in California, and Cary is a man of moderation. People live longer these days. Cary doesn't drink or stay up late. Sure he looks good, but why shouldn't he?" Donen asked.

Alfred Hitchcock thought it had something to do with clothes.

"When you look back to the Victorian era, both men and women were sartorially aged. Today everybody dresses alike, no matter how old they are. Cary looks young because he dresses young."

Cary had told numerous reporters that it was possible to "think yourself thin." He was back to his use of hypnosis.

"If you want to stay thin, you have to convince yourself that it's the most important thing in the world. You have to say it over and over again. 'I want to be thin.' You've got to get yourself so used to the idea that pretty soon you don't have to think about it at all. It just goes off repeating by itself," Cary added.

"The subconscious, I believe, holds all knowledge. If you really think thin, you'll get there," he continued. "You won't need a diet or a medical plan. The subconcious will tell you what to pass up or eat. You won't even want the rich desserts, and your subconscious will steer you to something equally nutritive and just as pleasant."

The reporter wryly noted that Cary's subconscious got a big boost from the masseur he always traveled with.

Hollywood make-up man Joe O'Gorman also gave short shrift to the "think thin" philosophy.

"He forgets that as an ex-acrobat, his body was disciplined right from the start. And he's a fantastic disciplinarian in all things—that helps."

After awhile Cary began to grow weary of questions about his looks, just as he had gotten bored with questions about his money and his clothes.

"I'm so sick and tired of being questioned about why I look young for my age and why I keep trim. Why do some idiots make so much of it—and why don't they go out and try to emulate it?" he asked.

"Everyone wants to keep fit, but what do they do?" Cary asked rhetorically. "They poison themselves with the wrong foods; contaminate their lungs with smoking; clog their pores with make-up; poison their bodies with alcohol."

By the time Grant's sixtieth birthday rolled around on January 18, 1964, he had discovered other reasons for his youthful appearance and manner. In a birthday interview, he said:

"I try to keep my mind youthful in ideas. I learn something new each year. In fact, I learn something new each day, if only not to behave the way I did the day before.

"I'm old enough to admit that I'm ignorant about a lot of things," Cary continued. "Very few young people will admit to any ignorance."

Ever since Cary's separation from Betsy Drake in 1958, he had been seen with a succession of young women, mostly actresses. His infatuation with Sophia Loren during the filming of *The Pride and the Passion* had, in fact, taken place while he and Betsy were still married and more or less living together.

He had described Ms. Loren as "a child with the wisdom of the ages" and had brushed off questions about their liaison by saying, "Who wouldn't fall in love with her? She's an adorable flirt."

He had given actress Kim Novak an intense whirl at the Cannes Film Festival in 1959. They were seen and photographed everywhere—and constantly. For awhile he was involved with Yugoslav women's basketball star, Luba Otasevic, who had once worked as a double for Sophia Loren. The was an airline stewardess named Debbie Lee and a dancer named Sheila Mosier.

Finally, there was Dyan Cannon.

Dyan Cannon and Fatherhood

DYAN CANNON WAS BORN Camille Diane Friesen in Tacoma, Washington, on January 4, 1937. For many years her official publicity biographies put her birthdate as 1939, but the Bureau of Vital Statistics in Tacoma says it was 1937.

Her father was Ben Friesen, a life insurance salesman and a Baptist. Dyan's mother, Clara, was Jewish, a bowling champion and a frustrated actress. Dyan Cannon has said that her parents:

"wanted me to be a good girl, what they thought was a good girl, and they wanted me to be Jewish and Baptist, like they were, and they wanted it to be 'here's fifty cents, eat that liver, it's good for you' and I'd go be sick from it afterwards."

Dyan also has a younger brother, David.

She attended the Universtiy of Washington for two years. The closest she got to things theatrical was a course in the history of the theatre. She thought it "a bloody bore." She went to Los Angeles and spent a year studying creative writing at UCLA. She didn't like that either.

"Nothing happened," Dyan said. "I got tired of school and went to work, running a showroom in the schmata industry. ("Schmata" is Yiddish slang for the garment industry.) There was a little modeling on the side.

According to Dyan Cannon, here's how she was discovered:

She was having lunch one day in a restaurant near the showroom. A man came over to her table and introduced himself. He was Mike Garrison, assistant to producer Jerry Wald. He wanted to know if she was an actress. Dyan figured an opportunity like this would not soon happen again. She reeled off the name of every play she could think of and said she had been in all of them.

She was tested for a part in *Harlow*. She didn't get the part, but she and several other young women were hired to travel around the country and promote the MGM film, *Les Girls*. Dyan and her co-workers on the tour were billed as "the coming stars."

"And we weren't even in *Les Girls*, Dyan said. "A real crazy business. But it was an enlightening experience. I made one movie in Portugal that was never released. I hope it never is."

Then she appeared in various minor television roles and for eight months was in a soap opera, *Full Circle*.

Dyan Cannon says that she had no childhood ambition to be an actress. When she was "discovered," she went ahead with it because her mother had once wanted to be an actress.

"Before she married my father, she spent some time in Hollywood with a director, trying to be an actress. She didn't make it and I guess I really did it for her."

Still, very soon after she arrived in Hollywood, Dyan began studying at Sanford Meisner's drama school. Meisner thought she had potential and touted her to publicist Frank McFadden who said he could make her a star by skillful publicity, a promise he was not able to keep.

"I think it was primarily my fault that he didn't succeed," Dyan said, "I didn't want to pose for pictures on dates, go to premieres, or do any of the things starlets are supposed to do. My values have changed, however. I realize now that publicity is important for an actress."

There are two versions of how, in 1961, Cary Grant first noticed Dyan Cannon.

According to the first version Cary was attracted, for professional reasons, to a cheesecake shot of Dyan that appeared in *The Hollywood Reporter*. She appeared in a full-page ad for *The Aquanauts*, a TV series that had a briefer life than a deep-sea diver without an oxygen supply. Dyan had a small role in the series.

"Dyan's part was so good—and she was so good in it," said

Ann McCall, one of McFadden's press agents, "that we decided to take full page ads in the Hollywood trade papers.

"Dyan, with that fabulous figure, posed for a cheesecake shot to go with the ad. It had hardly appeared before we got a call from Cary Grant. He was casting a young girl for an upcoming movie. At first we told him to watch the show again, which he did. Then he called again, several times, in the next few days," Ms. McCall said.

"Dyan didn't know what to do. I advised, 'With Cary Grant, how can you lose?'"

"Cary finally decided that Dyan wasn't young enough for the part—he wanted a sixteen-year old. But she wasn't too young for Cary—he asked her for a date."

The second version has it that Grant first saw Dyan when he was watching television. She was appearing in another forgettable series called *Malibu Run*. He quickly found out who the green-eyed blonde was and summoned her agent, Addie Fiddler, to appear at his office. When Ms. Fiddler appeared, Grant spent two hours asking her questions about Dyan Cannon—her background, her education, her hometown, her parents, her acting credits, and her philosophy of life. Ms. Fiddler knew the answers to some, but not all, of Grant's questions. She suggested that Cary Grant talk to her client in person. He thought that would be a fine idea. Dyan Cannon seemed right, he said, for a movie he was planning. When could Ms. Fiddler bring her around?

Addie Fiddler drove back to her office and immediately placed a phone call to Rome, where Dyan was vacationing with a girlfriend.

"Cary Grant wants to see you about a picture. Can you come back?"

"Is he paying my way?" Dyan asked.

"No, this is just an audition," Addie said.

"Then I'll talk to him when I get back in two weeks," Dyan said.

Or so the legend has it. Actresses with ten times more experience and exposure than Dyan Cannon, would have paid their way back from the moon for a chance to work with Cary Grant. Maybe Dyan Cannon really liked Rome.

The twenty-five-year old Dyan Cannon didn't seem right for the part of the sixteen-year old that Grant was casting, but after her audition was over, they had a long talk.

"I wasn't hypnotized—but I *was* enchanted by Cary," Dyan later recalled. "I was charmed, in the true sense of the word. We talked for a couple of hours. It was a marvelous conversation. I was completely smitten with him, and with his ideas. We talked about the movie he had wanted me for, about our theories and philosophies. We talked about me and my family. About the essence of perfume oils. About everything."

They began seeing each other. Frequently. Soon exclusively. An odd thing about this period is the extent to which Cary allowed Dyan's outspokenness to the press, once the Hollywood columnists finally got around to noticing that Cary Grant and Dyan Cannon were very definitely an "item."

Cary had traditionally been very reticent about discussing his relationships with women and, obviously, he must have exacted a promise of discretion from the women in his life, because none of them had provided reporters or Hollywood columnists with meaningful quotes. Dyan was different—which means, of course, that Cary had become different, too.

"I think," Dyan said, "that I'm his sister, his girlfriend, his mother, his everything. And I think he is the same way to me."

They spent a lot of time at his place in the evening, watching television.

"And I'll tell you there's not a thing wrong with that," Dyan said. "There's everything good with that, because for Cary to go out in public can be very tiring. There's so little privacy."

"I kind of enjoy just sharing the evening with him," Dyan added. "We talk quite a bit. And we read. It's very simple. We read his scripts, or my scripts, or he reads his books, or I read my books. It's just a very quiet, companionable evening. Nothing frantic. That's the beauty of it. I can't think of a nicer way to spend an evening."

The year after they met, Dyan got a part in a Broadway play called, *The Fun Couple.* Also in the cast were Jane Fonda and Bradford Dillman. Cary managed to spend a lot of time in New York during Dyan's rehearsal period. Out-of-town previews for *The Fun Couple* were held in Philadelphia. Cary spent several days there with Dyan before leaving for Paris where he was about to play opposite Audrey Hepburn in *Charade.*

"We were with a terrible show," Dyan said. (*The Fun Couple* lasted for three performances once it got to Broadway.) "I loved everyone I worked with in the show—they were all such hard workers, but we had such a terrible show. We weren't getting many laughs."

At dinner after the show one night, Cary Grant went through some bits of the play, delivering the lines in his consummate comic style until, Dyan says, "he had me on the floor with laughter." She was mock-furious.

"Why can't I do that?" Dyan asked. "I've been acting for three years. You've only been acting for thirty. Why can't I do that?"

They tried to ignore the difference in their ages, although the subject of age was usually the first to come up in an interview.

"I don't know how he keeps up the pace he does," Dyan said in wonder. "I'll be worn out, and he's still going. This is a man who's very young in many ways. Young in spirit. Young in mind. Younger in mind than he's ever been before."

"I'm only conscious of it when he reminds me," Dyan said, referring to the difference in their ages. "There *is* an age difference, of course, and not to discuss it would be as unreal as to dwell on it every minute. To say that neither of us pays attention to the age difference wouldn't be realistic, either. The age difference is there, but it certainly is not a barrier."

* * * * * *

Nor was Cary Grant's age a barrier when it came to his career. He was being offered, as usual, plum roles. Warner Bros. courted Grant for weeks, trying to get him to play Henry Higgins in *My Fair Lady*.

He thought it was absurd.

"Good heavens, man," he said to Jack Warner, "the way I talk *now* is the way Eliza talked at the beginning."

Besides, he had seen Rex Harrison and Julie Andrews in the Broadway version several times and thought they were both superb.

"They were shocked when I turned them down," Grant said of the Warner Bros. offer. "I told them it was ridiculous for them to ask me when they've got the man who lived the role. His educational background is better then mine, and his experience for the part was obviously better. Of course," he continued, "you don't turn down a $1 million-plus role without some thought, but that was my decision."

And in spite of his admiration for Audrey Hepburn, with whom he would soon make *Charade*, he felt it more appropriate for Julie Andrews to play Eliza Doolittle in the movie version of *My Fair Lady*, just as she had on Broadway. She created the role. She should be allowed to continue her success in Hollywood.

Charade is the last splendid movie that Cary Grant made. Two more films would follow before his retirement from the screen, but *Charade* is the more appropriate swan song. It's the last movie in which Cary Grant plays—Cary Grant, the urbane and polished romantic lover who doesn't need to take himself seriously because the girl most certainly will.

The girl in *Charade* was Audrey Hepburn, and her beautiful doe eyes light up like the Eiffel Tower whenever she looks at Grant. She plays a recently widowed woman whose husband may or may not have been a crook. In any case, he leaves $250,000 unaccounted for. Everyone, it seems, wants to find it; the French police; a passle of unsavory characters led by James Coburn and George Kennedy; Walter Mathau, who says he's an American agent; and Cary Grant, who keeps changing his story.

In the same way that Hitchcock so effectively used the Riviera landscape in *To Catch a Thief*, Stanley Donen lovingly shoots as many scenes as possible on the streets of Paris.

The love story between Grant and Ms. Hepburn is underplayed throughout. There is only one passionate kiss, but it takes place in one of the floating restaurants that ply the Seine, and it is more truly erotic than any X-rated movie ever made.

"Do you know what's wrong with you?" Ms. Hepburn asks Grant earlier in the film.

"Nothing," she answers for him.

New Yorker movie critic Pauline Kael beautifully sums up Cary Grant's final achievements:

"It's a peerless creation, the 'Cary Grant' of the later triumphs—*Notorious, To Catch a Thief, North by Northwest*, and *Charade*. Without a trace of narcissism, he appears as a man women are drawn to—a worldly, sophisticated man who has become more attractive with the years. And Grant really had got better-looking. The sensual lusciousness was burned off: age purified him (as it has purified Paul Newman). His acting was purified, too; it became more economical. When he was young, he had been able to do lovely fluff like *Topper* without being too elfin, or getting smirky, like Ray Milland, or becoming a brittle, too bright gentleman like Franchot Tone. But he'd done more than his share of arch mugging—lowering his eyebrows and pulling his head back as if something funny were going on in front of him when nothing was. Now the excess energy was pared away; his performances were simple, understated, and seamlessly smooth. In *Charade*, he gives an amazingly calm performance; he knows how much his presence does for him, and how little he needs to do. His romantic glamour, which had reached a high peak in 1939 in *Only Angels Have Wings*, wasn't lost; his glamour was now a matter of his resonances from the past, and he wore it like a mantle."

* * * * * *

While Grant was in Paris making *Charade*, Dyan Cannon landed the dancing and singing part of Rosemary in the road company production, *How to Succeed in Business Without Really Trying*. It kept her away from Hollywood for eighteen months. Cary flew into whatever city she was playing for as long as he could between his own professional commitments. He was then making *Father Goose*, with Leslie Caron, his second-to-last film.

The course of true love didn't, indeed, run smoothly. According to Dyan there were quarrels, break-ups, severings, and partings—none of them permanent. Cary complained about the perfume she'd brought back from Paris.

"Why do you wear so much perfume?" he asked crossly. "Are you trying to keep men away from you?"

Dyan claims that Cary's criticism didn't bother her in the least.

"Right away it broke me up, just broke me up," she said. "I just fell apart, it struck me so funny. After that it was all so lovely. I can remember walking away feeling very elated. I went home and I had this bottle of perfume which up to that time I'd loved. I diluted it, filled it half with water."

Cary Grant also began to exercise his famous perfectionism on Dyan's wardrobe, just as he had always done with his celluloid leading ladies.

"I don't think he mentioned my clothes until I'd known him for about eight months," Dyan recalled. "Then, in the middle of a date one evening, he said, 'You know, I saw a little dress down the street that would look very cute on you.' He described it to me, and I realized at once it was something entirely different from what I was wearing—completely different."

Dyan remembered that she was wearing "a little cotton dress, kind of fluffy and frilly."

"You don't dress like you are," Cary said. "You dress too old, or too young. Why don't you look for the middle road? Why don't you dress the way you look, the way you are?"

Dyan was a willing pupil.

"He felt I had been going from one extreme to the other," she said earnestly. "The dress he'd seen had a Smith College look—a sleeveless dress with a little jacket and a pleated skirt. Well, I found that he was right, and that that's best for me . . ."

Cary Grant may have turned down the role of Professor Higgins in *My Fair Lady*, but he was perfectly willing to play Pygmalion in his private life. And Dyan discovered she liked the role of Galatea.

"Cary has helped me in every area," she said. "You know, this is a man who's lived a great many years, and I listen to him. Much of what he says works for me. Some doesn't, but for the most part I go along. But Cary doesn't preach—that would probably annoy me. He'll go on at great length about things that have happened in his own life.

"I haven't lived that long," Dyan added, "but long enough to know that there's a great deal to learn from anyone who's lived and learned that much."

Cary was obviously instructing Dyan in more than simply grooming, perfume, and clothing. He wanted her to have the same kind of emotional breakthrough that he believed he had experienced via his LSD sessions.

"He's helped me find out what I'm all about," Dyan said. "I've always been a little high strung and impulsive, and he's kind of instilled in me the importance of people accepting their faults, their idiosyncrasies, and relaxing in the face of that, whether it be good or bad. Like having the courage of your convictions."

Eventually, Dyan bristled at the implications in all the stories about what Cary was supposedly teaching her about life and love.

"I like to think that if Cary's been of any help to me, I've also been of some help to him," Dyan said tartly. "Let's put it this way: he's a very organized man—in mind and body. I'm not all that organized. What the heck, so I've been helping him to *disorganize*. I don't think it's that important to be organized all the time. I've been pointing that out to him, and he's coming along just fine."

If Cary Grant was learning how to be more disorganized, however, there could be other reasons besides Dyan's influence. He was filming *Father Goose* at the time, an offbeat movie in which Grant plays an unshaven, grizzled, semialcoholic South Pacific beachcomber, pressed into World War II service as a lookout.

It was the first time he had departed from a "Cary Grant role" since *None But the Lonely Heart* back in 1944. Grant declared, when *Father Goose* opened at New York's Radio City Music Hall in December, 1964, that he felt a "great affinity" with his role as beachcomber Walter Eckland. Grant described Walter as his "alter ego."

"I'm closer to Walter than to any man I've ever played," Grant declared. "As precise as I've always been about my attire and appearance, there has been that hidden desire, a subconscious urge, to go around like Walter, unshaven, untidy.

"I'm not a lover, really," Grant added. "I don't drink, but I'm sometimes grumpy, and have that hard shell of defense, seemingly impenetrable, but which can be softened at the right time by the right person."

Dyan Cannon had obviously learned how to penetrate Cary Grant's impressive emotional defenses. And the press had finally managed to get under his skin with constant questions regarding the thirty-three-year age difference between himself and Ms. Cannon.

"The greatest mistake any man or woman can make is to assume that the more years we live, the less youth we have," Cary said testily. "It just is not true. Yet there appears to be in all of us a mysterious and irresistible urge to believe that because we have existed for a certain number of years, we can no longer be entitled to keep the attitudes of youth.

"It's my opinion that most people don't have the courage to stay young when they damn well could if they made the decision.

And they are always the first to ask those moronic man-of-your-years questions. Age is not measured by a clock or calendar. It is determined by the strength of your heart and the spirit of your soul.

"Besides, it's easy to age," Cary continued. "Just be like all those who get nervous at thirty or forty or fifty. So when they ask me how is it that a man of my age can do this or that, I resent it. I resent it because I know from experience it's their cute way of suggesting that I get lazy about life, and that I should be just as they are.

"The hell with them," he exploded. "I'll live as I please and think what's best for me. And I can't imagine why anyone else wouldn't want to live the same way."

The columnists noted that Cary Grant was being seen more in public than he had been in years. Cary and Dyan frequently attended Dodger games. A longtime baseball fan, Cary had his own box at the Dodger stadium.

At some point during the summer of 1964, it was understood that they'd get married.

"I did a little prompting, of course," Dyan admitted. "What woman doesn't?"

"He didn't really propose," Dyan confessed. "It was like we'd seen all the drive-in movies we'd care to see—so why not get married? It wasn't like any of his movies, with that flash of romance."

From that time on they were together almost constantly, except when Cary went to New York in December for promotion duties in connection with *Father Goose*. During the New York tour he described, for the first time, his personal method of moviemaking:

"I am the producer, the executive producer, but I hire a producer. I can direct, learned during the war when good directors were in service making morale films. Was compelled to help out with many of those films I made for RKO.

"But I wouldn't direct my own production so I get the best director I can find, usually the one I want. I obtain the services of an excellent script writer and request his presence on the set in order to be on the scene if changes for the better are necessary.

"I work along with a film editor but I have the last word on the editing. Naturally, I choose the story and the cast."

Writer Peter Stone, who fashioned the screenplays of both *Charade* and *Father Goose*, has said that what Cary Grant calls "polishing" is actually a complete rewriting of the script. Otherwise, however, Cary Grant is a writer's dream.

"I think the writer should be let alone," Cary said. "If you try to guide a writer, it cramps his style. He needs to be free to improvise, to let his imagination play."

"I'm not a writer or a director," Cary noted. "I'm an improver." (And a damned good one, he might have added, but modestly refrained.)

I have my own office," Cary explained. "Just a secretary and lawyers. No agent. No overhead. Universal—or another company, I change periodically—puts up the money. They take a distribution fee, but after their investment is repaid, I own the picture."

"Chaplin always owned his pictures," Grant observed.

As an actor-businessman Cary Grant's success is unlike anything Hollywood has ever seen. From the time of his 1955 "comeback" in Hitchcock's *To Catch a Thief*, until what has turned out to be his final film, the 1966 *Walk, Don't Run*, Cary Grant made thirteen films, most of which premiered at the nation's flagship theatre, Radio City Music Hall. In many instances he was able to arrange a Christmas opening, traditionally the Music Hall's biggest grossing season. Cary Grant has had more films presented at Radio City Music Hall than any other star. The top grossing movie in the history of the Music Hall is a Cary Grant film, *That Touch of Mink*, with Doris Day. It pulled in $1,885,335 in a ten-week run.

In 1963, before his last three films had been released, twenty-five Cary Grant movies had played the Music Hall for ninety-nine weeks. In recognition of this feat the Music Hall presented Grant with an inscribed silver bowl.

After *Charade* opened later that year, the Theatre Owners of America presented him with another award. They had voted Cary Grant "Star of the Year."

Carefully presenting his movies at the Music Hall was, of course, extremely shrewd planning on Grant's part. But there was more to it than that. Cary Grant likes to make people laugh. He has spoken many times of the pleasure it gave him to stand in the back of Radio City Music Hall when one of his films is showing and "listen to the laughter."

"There's great satisfaction in that," Grant said. "If I can make people with worries and problems forget them for a couple of hours in a cinema, I consider I have achieved something that few politicians can ever do."

When *Father Goose* opened, he was in a very loquacious mood and spoke more candidly about his acting techniques than he ever had before.

"Since I was twelve, I've been entertaining people," Cary pointed out. "I would have had to be nutty not to have acquired some experience along the way. Or nuttier still not to have learned something about comedy technique.

"Eventually, you learn why people laugh," he said. "Don't forget that I was a straight man for years. I played with comedians in vaudeville. A laugh doesn't just happen. A laugh cascades. It goes up, and then it falls off. You talk into that arc of sound from the audience. When it starts to turn downward from its peak, you talk into it again, and it goes up again.

"You shouldn't ask me why I think I've lasted," Cary said, smiling. "But look around you. The ones who have stayed the course are the ones who behave most nearly like themselves. Behave true to yourself and behave in tempo with the times. You have to be true to what you are. The public has an unfailing sense for spotting a fake."

* * * * * *

The pre-wedding year Dyan Cannon virtually gave up acting. She worked hardly at all. She and Cary made several trips to England to visit Cary's mother, now aged ninety-one. Dyan said that Elsie Leach "had a very strong personality."

Dyan remembered that Elsie was very nice to her "except she kept calling me Betsy . . ."

Dyan Cannon and Cary Grant were finally married on July 22, 1965 in Las Vegas. After the public confusion surrounding his marriage to Virginia Cherrill in a London registry office, Cary Grant had always preferred secret weddings. Practice had made him very good at it. Incredibly, it was eleven days before the news leaked out.

Cary Grant and his new bride turned up in Bristol on August 1. He announced his fourth marriage in the London Sunday Express.

Cary said that he had kept his marriage a secret because "marriage is a very private affair, and I prefer to do things quietly, without fanfare or intrusion. In fact, I have not even told my mother yet. That is why we are in Bristol."

About his new wife, Cary said:

"At last I am content. Dyan is a delightful girl and extraordinarily good company."

Then Dyan and Cary promptly disappeared. At least that was the official statement to the dozens of reporters who had camped out in the lobby of the Bristol's Royal Hotel. The hotel staff said that Cary and Dyan had slipped out of the hotel and left for a quiet tour of the English countryside at 6:00 A.M. The reporters knew they were being conned. They noted that a guard was posted at the door of Cary Grant's suite all day. More importantly they also noted that Cary Grant's Rolls-Royce—license plate CG1—was sitting in the hotel garage. Unthinkable that Grant should take his new bride on a country tour in any vehicle other than his beloved Rolls.

They had gone to see Elsie Leach before the story of their marriage had broken in the London Sunday Express. The reporters, unable to find Cary Grant and Dyan Cannon, went in search of Elsie. She was no longer living in her house in nearby Clinton. Cary had recently made arrangements for her to be cared for in a Bristol nursing home, but nobody knew where it was, and the local townspeople were not eager to help them find it.

Bristol was proud of Cary Grant but he was, after all, a hometown boy. He never had a problem walking the streets of Bristol as he did in New York. He had, in fact, simply had to give up the pleasures of a midtown Manhattan stroll, an event that often caused a near-riot. The good Bristol townsfolk would have been incapable of such behavior, nor could they understand why all these newspaper reporters were so hot on Archie Leach's trail. After all a fellow should be able to enjoy his honeymoon without having a guard at his door. It took the reporters a week to find Elsie. She hadn't seen Cary and Dyan either.

"Why haven't they come to see me again?" Elsie wanted to know. "He promised they would."

Finally, when it became clear that Cary Grant was not going to give even a five-minute interview, the reporters left Bristol. Cary and Dyan drove to London in the Rolls, and after a few days of sightseeing, flew back to Los Angeles where Cary began putting together his next movie, *Walk, Don't Run*. It would be his last film.

Walk, Don't Run was a remake of a successful and thoroughly delightful 1943 comedy called *The More the Merrier*, which had starred Charles Coburn, Jean Arthur, and Joel McCrea. The comic rationale of the earlier film was the housing shortage in Washington, D.C. during World War II. Cary Grant's 1966 version used the housing shortage in Tokyo during the 1966 Olympics as its comic base. Grant plays the Charles Coburn part, and Samantha Eggar and Jim Hutton are the young couple in love. At least they are in love by the end of the film, thanks to Cary Grant's expert imitation of Cupid.

When Dyan did not accompany Cary on location in Tokyo, the Hollywood gossips immediately began asking "why"? Was there trouble already in the Grant menage? The answer was soon forthcoming. On October 14, the news leaked out that Dyan was pregnant. Cary Grant's becoming a father made the front page of virtually every U.S. newspaper. The first Associated Press bulletin came over the wire at 10:00 A.M., in time for the final editions of the afternoon papers. Most of them ran the bulletin in its entirety:

> *Hollywood, Oct. 14 (AP)—Cary Grant is expecting his first child next May, when he will be sixty-two.*
>
> *His office confirmed the news. Neither Grant nor his twenty-seven-year-old wife, actress Dyan Cannon, was available for comment. He is in Tokyo to begin a movie, and she was reported resting "out of town." She plans to join him soon.*
>
> *Grant, the screen's top charmer for more than thirty years, was childless in his first three marriages: to Virginia Cherrill, Barbara Hutton, and Betsy Drake. His late parenthood recalls that of Clark Gable, who became a father with his fifth marriage to Kay Spreckels. A son was born after Gable's death at fifty-nine.*

High marks for the best headline should probably go to the old New York Journal-American: *Cary's Fourth Expects First.*

When reporters were able to get to Grant in Tokyo, he simply said that his imminent fatherhood would be "the most important role in my life." He said he was looking forward to completing his work in *Walk, Don't Run* so that he could be with Dyan during her pregnancy.

* * * * * *

The baby arrived early. At about 4:00 A.M. on February 26, 1966, Dyan began having abdominal pains that seemed to fit the description she'd read of what labor pains are like. They got stronger and closer together. There could be no doubt about it. Cary drove her to St. Joseph's Hospital in Burbank.

Dyan's labor was difficult. She had never known that time could pass so slowly. It was evening before they finally took her to the delivery room. Cary was not allowed to witness the birth of his long-awaited first child at 7:41 P.M.

The first glimpse that Dyan had of the child she had just borne was not a cheerful one. The newborn infant had been placed, face down, on a plain metal table.

"I waited for the doctor to pick her up by the feet and go whap! the way they do in the movies, but he didn't. He whapped her right there, lying on the table, and I screamed in protest," Dyan recalled.

Only then did she think to ask a nurse whether she'd had a boy or a girl.

"You have a pretty little daughter," the nurse said. "She weighs four pounds, eight ounces."

They named her Jennifer.

Cary Grant was ecstatic.

"I've waited all my life, hoping for children, and when you've waited for such a long time, you hope like mad that everything will work out all right. In my case, I knew the birth of my baby was the chance of a dream coming true. It's never too late to become a parent," he said.

Of course, everyone wanted to know: whom does the baby look like?

"It's a bit early to tell," Cary said. "I hear that girls are supposed to look like their fathers, so maybe Jennifer will end up looking like me, although sometimes I look terrible. But just now she looks like both of us."

Cary refused to admit that his age—he was sixty-two when Jennifer was born—would be a handicap in his new role of "father."

"I'm no spring chicken," he agreed. "I've been around a few years, and anyway, I think having a child when you're older has its advantages. At my age I reckon I'm about ready for it. You're older, but you're able to understand a child better because you know yourself better.

"To everything disadvantageous, there is an advantage," he added. "One, I am materially able to take care of the child. Two, I'm older and therefore wiser, although perhaps that's too egotistical. I think I'm fitted to teach her spiritual values with more conviction," Cary declared.

"It's true that I may not be able to exert myself strenuously in playing children's roughhouse games or in bouncing a little girl on my knee, but there are other definite advantages.

"I think it's nice for a father to be able to play football with a son, but I'm not sure you should be playing football anyway. You can get your brains knocked out. But I can ride with my children and swim with them. Tennis, I don't even play now. That's too exerting for me."

From his remarks after the birth of his first child, you could assume that Cary Grant was planning to spend the rest of his life preaching the benefits of fatherhood:

"I hope to raise many," he said. "Now we have a daughter, and it's marvelous. But we want dozens—as many as possible. I can now financially afford to give them a good education and a healthful life. I think it's pretty difficult for children today. We are biologically ready to have children at twelve, but can't afford it until perhaps twenty-seven. I think this great rift is perhaps responsible for much of the juvenile delinquency—the inhibition of the life force."

There is no record that anyone asked the recuperating Dyan Cannon how she felt about having "dozens" of children.

Then Cary Grant, the man whose career had been a consuming passion from the time he was twelve years old, announced that he was taking a year off so that he could be with his wife and baby. And he acknowledged that playing romantic leads was something he could no longer do.

"By now, my choice of subjects is very limited," Cary said. "I may wind up playing some old retired banker in a wheel chair. I want to go on and on, like Sir Aubrey Smith."

Cary may have made the statement about going "on and on"

when his energy level was very high. On other days he didn't sound quite so convinced.

"I make no plans," Cary said. "This may be my last film—I don't know." (He was referring to *Walk, Don't Run* which, as we know, *was* Cary Grant's last film.)

"I never make plans," he repeated, almost musingly. "And if I embark on something it'll be because it's too good to turn down. I don't plan things that closely. Then if you find something that interests you, that's the thing to do."

Cary began taking weekly photographs of Jennifer so he and Dyan would have a visual record of her growth. He bought a small tape recorder specifically set aside to capture forever Jennifer's first coos and gurgles. He looked in on her before he left for his office at the Universal Studios, and he arranged to be home in time for her 7:00 P.M. feeding.

"I like to be a part of that," Cary said. "She's the most winsome, captivating girl I've ever known, and I've known quite a few girls."

Cary had arranged for more stringent security measures for his mountaintop hideaway in Beverly Hills. He and Dyan spent most of their time at home. A few friends were invited in from time to time. All of them were sworn to secrecy as to the new baby's looks and routine. One of Dyan's girlfriends told a reporter:

"I could answer all your questions about what the baby looks like and everything else, but I won't. It's forbidden."

Actor Jim Hutton, Grant's co-star in *Walk, Don't Run*, said that Cary often needed someone to talk to when they were on location in Tokyo.

"I have two children myself," Hutton said, "so naturally we talked a great deal about fatherhood. Since Dyan was pregnant, Cary thought it best she stay at home. He seemed lonely and confused, and he would seek me out and talk for hours about what he wanted for his child and what he felt he could do for it. He told me he hopes to have many children. He also said that this might be his last picture, because becoming a father is more important than anything he has ever done."

Sitting in a small Tokyo restaurant, Grant told Hutton:

"Before Dyan became pregnant, I really only had *me* to take care of. I felt free and footloose. And yet, fatherhood will make me freer than I've ever been, because at last I want the responsibility."

Cary also said firmly that his child would not be fed any fantastic stories about Santa Claus or the Easter Bunny. He felt such fantasies were harmful and confusing to a child. He believed the best policy was to teach the child about life's realities from the very beginning.

Tony Curtis, Grant's co-star in *Operation Petticoat*, had, as usual, nothing but admiration for his idol's new role.

"Although Cary has as great a drive as any young man I know," Curtis said, "he has, in becoming a father at his age, shown great courage. It *does* take courage for a man who, for many years, has had a certain way of living—the habit of being alone, of being a free thinker and master of all he surveyed—to give that up. I always felt that Cary was searching for something. Now I think he's found it."

And, of course, Tony Curtis had no doubts that Cary would be just as superb in his new role as he had been in the ones he had played on the screen. Maybe even better.

"This I know," Curtis declared. "Cary hasn't given the so-called philosophy of fatherhood a thought. His child will learn by being given love and through osmosis and not by exposure to theories. This lucky little girl will know more about her parents than most children because they'll be there to answer her questions and kiss away her hurts. That isn't a philosophy of parenthood. It's just *being* parents."

By July Jennifer weighed eleven pounds, and Cary allowed a photo session for the press. The best picture to emerge shows Cary and Dyan holding Jennifer between them. All three are smiling into the camera, but somehow Jennifer managed to upstage both her good-looking parents. It is rare to find a four-month infant with such an intelligent expression, such an engaging grin.

With Jennifer's introduction to press and public behind them, Dyan, Cary, and the baby left to visit Cary's mother. It was a leisurely ocean trip on the *Oriana*. Leaving from San Pedro, their route took them down the west coast, through the Panama Canal, with stops at Lisbon and Le Havre before they finally disembarked at Southampton.

As soon as they were settled into the Churchill suite of Bristol's

Royal Hotel, Cary and Dyan took the baby out to Elsie Leach's nursing home. She had waited a long time to become a grandmother. She looked at the baby carefully and thoughtfully, as if trying to remember and compare. Then her mind was made up.

"Archie," Elsie said, "she looks *exactly* like you did when you were a baby."

Later, Cary Grant said, "Presenting Jennifer to my mother was the proudest moment of my life."

The town fathers in Bristol asked Cary if he would let them honor him with a luncheon. He was very touched and said that yes, he'd be delighted to attend.

After his achievements had been duly noted by the town fathers, Cary made a few informal remarks. He said that he thought marriage was on the way out, that it would not exist in a hundred years.

"Our divorce laws are more relaxed now," Cary observed, "and women are in competition with men."

Dyan Cannon, who had not worked for over two years, applauded.

When they returned to California, Cary rented a secluded house in La Jolla. At this point, if Cary Grant's life had been like a Cary Grant film, they would have lived happily ever after. But life is seldom like the movies, and before the year was out, the marriage was wrecked.

The announcement came on December 28, 1966. Married less than two years, Cary Grant and Dyan Cannon announced they had separated.

A Bitter Divorce and Custody Battles

WHEN DYAN CANNON LEFT CARY GRANT, she took the baby with her. They went to Seattle and stayed with Dyan's parents for two weeks. When Dyan returned to Los Angeles, she took a small apartment and refused to talk to Cary Grant. Friends described him as "distraught" and "heartbroken."

A close friend who would not allow his name to be used described Cary Grant as "deeply upset and doing all in his power to get his wife to return to their home with the baby and nurse."

But if Dyan Cannon was not willing to talk to Cary Grant, she was quite willing to talk to reporters.

"I'm having a ball in my little apartment," she said. "I cook my own dinners—eat what I want when I want it—and fix the baby up how and when I want to."

Dyan apparently felt that in the Cary Grant household she was not taken seriously.

"Cary is such a perfectionist that he takes charge of everything. I never could plan a meal for guests; he even supervised that. And since he's such a big star, the cooks and butlers deferred to him and only to him."

She made it clear that she did not enjoy the kind of stay-at-home life that Cary relished, even though she was well aware of his tastes before they were married.

"Then it didn't bother me, because I was working. But later it became quite a difficult thing to stay at home all day and watch TV at night. But that's not Cary's fault. I can't say I hadn't been geared for that," she admitted.

She had found Cary Grant to be a man of many moods: elated one moment, deeply depressed the next. It was difficult to live with such a person.

"I would say that he is an extremist," Dyan said.

After she married Cary Grant, she lapsed—or was driven—into a state of psychological subservience.

"He dominated me completely and I was so eager to please," she said.

Several times she told him that she wanted to go back to work, and would he help her find a good part?

"But I didn't do it often, because I really had the feeling Cary didn't want it, and I found myself—it was eerie—just living to try and please, to please, to keep going," Dyan confessed.

The months following their separation were a kind of limbo. After several months she met with Cary and agreed to let him see Jennifer. Then they were frequently seen at restaurants and parties. It was like a reprise of his separation from Betsy Drake, except that this time there was a child to consider. Cary Grant wanted very much for his daughter to have two live-in parents, and he spared no effort or argument to convince Dyan to return to their home and rebuild their marriage.

Dyan's feelings were by no means clear.

"I still love Cary very much, and he still loves me. But let's say it is nice to be free for awhile," Dyan said on one occasion.

Weeks later, she told a friend:

"I just had to get away and collect my thoughts. I had to look at things objectively. I am miserable away from Cary, and I hope he feels the same way."

In spite of her ambivalence and professed love for her husband, Cary was not able to get her to come home. On August 22, 1967, nearly eight months after they had separated, Dyan filed for divorce in Superior Court in Los Angeles, charging Cary with having treated her "in a cruel and inhuman manner." She put his financial worth at $10 million, with an annual income of five hundred thousand dollars. She asked for "reasonable support" and said that her monthly expenses for herself and Jennifer came to $5,470 a month. Her only income, she said, was about four hundred dollars a year from television residuals. A temporary support hearing was set for September 12.

The summer was not a total loss for Cary, however. He took Jennifer to her first Dodgers' game where she ate her first hot dog.

Before she filed the divorce action, Dyan had managed to get a part in a play, *The 90-Day Mistress*, that would begin rehearsals in New York the following October. Dyan told the court that she was a "fit and proper" person to have custody of her daughter, and that the best thing for Jennifer was to live with her mother during the time she was working in New York.

The court agreed.

Cary Grant spent most of October and November of that year in New York so that he could be with Jennifer. He spent about five hours a day with her. On one occasion Cary decided that it was time Jennifer was exposed to one of New York's more colorful neighborhoods. He took Jennifer and her nurse, Mimi O'Connell, to dinner at an Italian restaurant, La Groceria, in the heart of Greenwich Village.

Jennifer was then twenty months old and apparently had inherited her father's hearty appetite. She had antipasto, ravioli, and dessert, most of it filched from her father's plate. In place of the traditional Chianti, however, Jennifer had milk.

Before they returned to Cary's chauffered limousine, he agreed to let a Daily News photographer take pictures. There was an uncomfortable moment when a group of teen-agers recognized Grant and began to crowd around him. Jennifer looked frightened. Cary controlled his anger and, instead, pleaded with the girls to move back.

"Please, kids, please," he said. "Jennifer would like to have her picture taken."

A reporter followed him to the limo. "Any chance of a reconciliation with Dyan?" he asked.

"You'll have to ask a crystal ball," Cary replied.

A few days later he was photographed leaving the Biltmore

Theatre with Dyan after *The 90-Day Mistress* had begun its brief run on Broadway. (The play closed after three weeks, although Dyan received critical praise for her efforts in the ill-fated production.) Cary continued to persuade Dyan to give their marriage another try.

Dyan told a magazine writer at that time that leaving Cary, and the intervening months when he was trying to get her to return to the marriage had been "the most devastating experience of my life." Her feelings began to emerge.

"I lost my individuality completely after I married Cary," she said. "I gladly gave up my career, I was so in love, so eager to please. I allowed it to happen to me, but it wasn't helped at all by Cary. He is always the dominant one. If you want to be a piece of lox, that's OK. But I didn't want to be. It just happened."

According to Dyan, after Jennifer's birth, she lost so much weight that her friends hardly recognized her. They thought she was on the brink of a nervous breakdown. One of the first things she did after leaving Cary was to begin seeing a psychotherapist.

"I knew I had to have outside help—to help my insides," she said. What I've learned through analysis is of enormous help. I spent so many years trying to please, and considering myself last, really, in so many cases. I've now learned the importance of my own desires and it's helped. I'm getting back my individuality, and even in the face of this discontent—in spite of the outside factors which are very disturbing—I'm regaining a certain ease, a certain calm. And since I now understand so much more about myself, I understand much more about Cary."

Dyan did not, however, understand Cary in a way that made her want to be his wife again. She was determined to pursue her divorce action, and a court date was set for March 21, 1968.

During the months of their separation, Dyan Cannon frequently discussed their relationship with reporters. Cary maintained his practice, through four marriages now, of saying nothing.

* * * * * *

Even after *The 90-Day Mistress* closed, Dyan stayed in New York, hoping she could land another part in a Broadway play. She kept Jennifer with her. Cary continued to spend most of his time in New York, so he could be near the baby.

In spite of the emotional tension generated by the impending divorce hearing, Cary and Dyan tried to get along amicably for the sake of the child.

"When he comes to see Jennifer and me now," Dyan said, "the circumstances are very much the same as when we were dating. I can talk. We talk a lot about Jennifer. How not to spoil her too much. How wonderful she is. She knows she's loved—she knows that—and if we can continue to have her know that feeling, she'll be okay."

Late in January Cary returned to the West Coast in order to attend to various business and personal matters. When he returned to New York late in February, he accepted a long-standing invitation to stay at the apartment of his friend, public relations executive Robert S. Taplinger on East Forty-Ninth Street. (Taplinger's apartment is across the street from the Turtle Bay townhouse of Cary Grant's former co-star, Katharine Hepburn.)

The divorce was just over a month away. Cary still kept alive a few slim hopes that Dyan would change her mind. As the divorce hearing loomed ever closer on the horizon, however, he realized the possibility of reconciliation simply didn't exist anymore.

He planned to leave for Los Angeles on March 12, eight days before the divorce hearing in Superior Court. He was booked on a late evening flight out of LaGuardia. Taplinger, hoping to cheer him up and provide a show of moral support, held a small dinner party in his honor the night of his departure. Among the guests were Faberge president George Barrie, Barrie's wife, Gratia von Furstenburg, a friend of Taplinger's, and Norman Zeiler, another friend of Cary's. The party broke up rather early. Taplinger and Barrie had to attend a business conference at the New York Hilton. They suggested that Gratia accompany Cary to the airport. Taplinger and Barrie said they would join them as soon as their meeting was over for a farewell drink.

Ms. von Furstenberg and Cary Grant climbed into the back of Zeiler's chauffered Cadillac. He would take a taxi home and make the limousine available to Cary. It was a raw March evening. Clouds had been gathering all day and now a hard rain was falling.

Chauffeur Troy Lindahl expertly maneuvered the car through the rain-clogged Manhattan traffic to the tunnel under the East River at Thirty-Seventh Street. After they had passed through the tollgates on the Queens side of the tunnel, Lindahl noticed the traffic was much lighter than it had been in Manhattan. He headed for LaGuardia.

Gratia and Cary made small talk in the back seat, but Cary found it hard to keep his mind on the conversation. He was returning to California for his fourth divorce. It was a record he was not proud of.

Lindahl had the limo in the inner lane of the Long Island Expressway. He never saw what hit them. But after the endless seconds of the actual impact, he heard Gratia's screams. Then he saw the damaged trailer truck across the highway.

Finally when the police arrived, they pieced together what had happened; Lindahl had been driving east toward the airport. In the westbound lane, Henry Harris of the Bronx had been driving a tractor cab, with no trailer attached, to Manhattan. Harris reported that another truck cut in front of him. He braked sharply. The cab began to skid. At first Harris thought he had skidded into someone else. Then he saw what had happened. The rear wheel assembly on the cab had wrenched loose. It flew across the one-foot metal highway divider and slammed into the left front of the Cadillac limousine in which Cary Grant was a passenger.

The police arrived within minutes to the site of the accident, near Greenpoint Avenue in Long Island City. They immediately radioed for an ambulance, and when it arrived, dispatched Grant, Ms. von Furstenburg, and Lindahl to St. John's Hospital in Elmhurst. As a final exasperation in the whole ghastly incident, the ambulance stalled halfway there, and the driver couldn't get it started. Gratia and Cary were then taken to the hospital in a police car. Troy Lindahl waited in the ambulance. It had stalled when they drove through a huge puddle caused by a backed-up storm sewer. Fifteen minutes later, after the spark plugs had dried off, the engine turned over. Lindahl arrived at the hospital shortly after Gratia and Cary.

Cary's clothes were a bloody mess. He was bleeding profusely from the nose, and doctors were at first convinced it was broken. X-rays, however, showed no bone damage, but the cartilege had been severely bruised. Every time he breathed it hurt, but chest X-rays showed no rib fractures either.

Cary Grant was cut and bruised all over his face and badly shaken up, but did not then seem to be severely injured.

Gratia von Furstenburg and Troy Lindahl were not so lucky. Gratia's right leg was fractured in three places. She also suffered a broken collar bone. Lindahl broke his right kneecap.

After their arrival at the hospital, everyone, naturally, was separated as various examinations and tests were performed. Cary, somehow, felt responsible and constantly pestered nurses, attendants, and doctors for news of his fellow accident victims.

"How are the others? Where are the others?" Cary asked repeatedly.

Shortly after Cary had been installed in a semiprivate room, Bob Taplinger showed up.

"I feel like a Grade B movie," Cary confessed.

After Troy Lindahl's knee was set, they wheeled him in. Strong sedatives were given to both men and a security guard posted outside the door. The next day Cary Grant was offered a private room. He declined.

"We're friends," he said, waving at Troy, "and I'll have someone to talk to."

That evening, Dyan Cannon arrived for a forty-five-minute visit. She had been scheduled to leave for California that day but had delayed her trip in order to visit Cary. She said she was going ahead with the divorce hearing.

When she left, she told reporters, "He's feeling much better."

Cary's chest pains continued. His nose was badly swollen, and the doctors ordered periodic doses of oxygen to ease his breathing. He was fed intravenously the first few days, because his mouth was so swollen it was impossible to chew or swallow.

The day after the accident a hospital spokesman said that Cary's chief problem was "the nurses may kill him with kindness."

The doctors at St. John's, however, were not as enchanted. Cary Grant was not a docile patient. Doctors, of course, expect docility; it goes with the medical degree, they think. One of the St. John's staff physicians was trying to swab Cary's nose with medication designed to reduce the swelling. Cary waved him aside.

"I can't be bothered with that," he said, in an irritated tone of voice.

The M.D. could hardly believe his ears. Sure, Cary Grant was—Cary Grant, but—*he* was a doctor.

He put on his most imperial bedside manner and said icily, "Unless your attitude improves, I would suggest you seek another hospital."

Cary Grant hesitated for a fraction of a second. Was it worth it? No, it definitely wasn't. He had quite enough troubles already, thank you just the same. Cary Grant smiled.

"Okay, Doc," he said and meekly offered his nostrils for swabbing.

* * * * * *

The hospital switchboard was, of course, swamped, with one call coming all the way from Johannesburg, South Africa. One man phoned, said he was a representative of Lloyd's of London and wanted to know how badly Cary's face was injured. It was insured, he said, for five hundred thousand dollars. Dozens of women called saying they were Dyan Cannon. Finally a half-dozen close friends were given a code name for Cary. Callers who didn't have the special name, Count Bezok, were turned away.

A group of student nurses sent Cary an oversized get-well card.

"We haven't had this much excitement here since the blackout," they wrote. "We wish you a speedy recovery."

Cary was in Room 453, and the corridors of the fourth floor were much more crowded than usual as nurses from other wards, student nurses, and other staff members sauntered by, hoping to catch a glimpse of their famous patient.

Three days after the accident Cary was still not feeling well enough to leave. He wrote a personal letter to the hospital staff, saying:

"I am feeling much better, and after seeing photos of the wrecked limousine, I am particularly glad to learn that the young lady who accompanied me and our remarkably level-headed driver have also made good progress.

"The doctors, nurses and staff here at St. John's have been unusually kind and efficient and helpful in every way and I am truly appreciative."

But the chest pains continued. In fact, they were getting worse. Cary's personal physician, Dr. Lester Gabrilove, ordered more X-rays. They showed that Cary Grant did, indeed, have cause for complaint. He had two fractured ribs.

He had been slated to leave the hospital on Monday. (The accident had occurred the previous Tuesday.) The divorce hearing was set for the following Wednesday, March 20. Cary Grant could not possibly appear in court. Strangely he did not order his lawyers to ask for a continuance which, under the circumstances, the court would have routinely granted.

Cary was concerned about what the accident would mean to Troy Lindahl's pocketbook. He told hospital administrators that he would take care of Troy's expenses. That wouldn't be necessary, they said, Mr. Lindahl was covered by Blue Cross.

"What's that?" Cary asked.

* * * * * *

On Wednesday, Dyan went into Superior Court and told her version of her marriage to Cary Grant. It was an incredible tale.

Dyan described Cary as an "apostle of LSD." She said that he had used it for about ten years, and that sometimes when he was under its influence, he would have "yelling and screaming fits." She also said that taking the drug would trigger violent impulses in him, causing him to beat her. According to Dyan, during their brief marriage, he took LSD every week. His doctor would be there, and often she was present as well.

She was on the stand for thirty minutes. She said that on two occasions Grant had yelled and screamed at her when they were dining out. When she was six months pregnant, Dyan said that Cary "made me cry by claiming my doctor was on the make for me and wanted a lot of money because he was Cary Grant."

Once she had planned to attend a dinner party. Cary forbade her to go, took the keys to their three cars, locked the gates to the grounds, barricaded himself in her dressing room, and began reading a book of poetry. But after awhile he was still angry.

"He started to hit me, and screamed. He was laughing as he hit me, and he screamed for the help to come and see what he was doing. I was frightened because he was laughing, and I went to call the police.

"Mr. Grant," Dyan added, "was very much out of control."

She let Cary talk her out of phoning the police. He warned her that the press would descend on them en masse if she made such a call. She phoned her agent instead, Adaline Fiddler Gould. Grant grabbed the receiver out of her hand.

"Addie, stay out of my marriage," Cary yelled. "I'm going to break this girl. She's not going to leave until I break her."

Dyan says she left the baby with the servants, escaped out a window, and climbed the fence surrounding their rented mansion. Waiting for her was her agent, Addie Gould, and her husband. They had driven out to La Jolla right after Dyan's phone call.

On another occasion, Dyan said, she and Cary, several friends, and the domestic staff were watching the Academy Awards in the master bedroom.

"He became violent and out of control," Dyan told the court. "He jumped up and down on the bed and carried on. He yelled that everyone on the awards show had their faces lifted, and he was spilling wine on the bed. This lasted a couple of hours—as long as the awards were on."

She blamed LSD for Cary's strange behavior.

"He asked me to use it many times," she testified. "I did use it once before our marriage, but never after."

Dyan alleged that Cary once told her she was "on the verge of a nervous breakdown and he hoped I would have it so the new me would be a wonderful me—and he told me the new me would be created through LSD."

Dyan said she was revealing Grant's LSD experience and philosophy to justify her petition to the court for Jennifer's custody.

"Mr. Grant is an unfit father because of his instability," she declared.

She told the court that she would allow Cary to see his daughter only if a nurse was present at all times. She did not want Jennifer spending the night at Cary's house.

Cary Grant's attorneys had brought two expert witnesses to court to discredit Dyan's testimony. Both were psychiatrists and had examined Cary the previous autumn.

Dr. Judd Marmor said that he had found no reason to believe that taking LSD had harmed Cary Grant. He said there were no lingering bad effects. His opinion was that Cary was "an emotional individual, but I have often seen that in actors."

Dr. Marmor testified that Cary Grant had told him that LSD had "deepened his sense of compassion for people, deepened his understanding of himself, and helped cure his shyness and anxiety in dealing with other people." Cary had also admitted to Dr. Marmor that he had "spanked" Dyan for what he described to the psychiatrist as "reasonable and adequate causes." On one occasion, Dyan said she was going to a discotheque with friends. Cary told Dr. Marmor that she was wearing a miniskirt and heavy makeup.

"He pleaded with her that it wouldn't be right for his wife to go out alone, and tempers flared on both sides," the psychiatrist told the court. "There was an explosion on his part and he spanked her."

Dr. Sidney L. Pomer, the other psychiatrist who testified on Cary Grant's behalf, stated that he had found no evidence of "irrationality, erratic behavior, or incoherence" when he had examined Cary.

Dyan also told the court that when they had taken Jennifer to visit Cary's mother in England the previous summer that Cary had refused to take along enough of Jennifer's formula to last for the length of their trip.

"The cows in England are just as good as they are in this country," he had said.

As a result Dyan claimed, Jennifer got sick, and the formula had to be shipped to them by air.

Cary Grant's friends immediately came to his defense. Norman Zeilor, in whose borrowed limousine Cary had been injured the week before, said that Dyan's charges were "ridiculous." Another friend, who preferred to remain anonymous, said that it was unthinkable that Cary could have beaten Dyan.

"Cary wouldn't lift a finger to swat a fly," he added.

Hospital spokesmen said that Cary had received phone calls of support from, among others, actor Danny Kaye and from Princess Grace and Prince Rainier in Monaco.

Cary, however, was not allowed to accept any calls the afternoon of the divorce hearing. His doctors had ordered him to take sedatives and had forbidden visitors. He was not even allowed a radio in his room.

The first news he had of Dyan's charges arrived with the morning papers the following day. He took one look at the glaring headlines of the *New York Daily News* and said, "Oh, my God!"

On the second day of testimony, a woman friend of Dyan Cannon's and her agent, Adaline Fiddler Gould, both said that Cary had frequently beaten her, and that he had tried to "break" Dyan and transform her into his notion of what the ideal wife should be. Ms. Gould said that Grant told her:

"I'm going to break this girl. I'm going to break her like a pony."

Describing the evening that Dyan had called her instead of the police, Ms. Gould said:

"She was frightened to death. She called my residence three times that night and I heard Mr. Grant screaming in the background. The baby was screaming, too."

Mary Gries, Dyan's friend, told the court that Cary Grant had said:

"This girl is heading for a nervous breakdown and I hope she has it. That's the only way I can make her into the wife I want."

Cary Grant had prepared written testimony but, for reasons he never disclosed, told his lawyers at the last minute not to present it to the court.

Judge Robert A. Wenke granted the divorce to Dyan and awarded her custody of Jennifer, now twenty-five months old. Cary was ordered to pay fifteen hundred dollars monthly child support plus five hundred dollars for Jennifer's nurse, plus all "extraordinary medical and dental bills." In addition a complicated three-year alimony period was set up: Dyan was to receive $2,250 for the next six months, beginning April 1, then $1,750 for the next eighteen months, and one thousand dollars monthly for the final year.

Judge Wenke refused to limit Cary's visits to Jennifer to daylight hours as Dyan had requested. He said that Cary could have custody of Jennifer for sixty days a year.

Cary was finally released from St. John's Hospital on March 30 after a seventeen-day stay. Hospital personnel lined the main corridor as he slowly made his way to a waiting limousine. They cheered and applauded when Grant shook hands with Sister Thomas Francis, executive director of the Queens hospital.

"I had a remarkably good time here," Cary told reporters.

"I'm obliged to the dear people of the hospital. I enjoyed their company. I hope they enjoyed mine."

He ignored all questions about the previous week's divorce action. He said his only plans at the present were to "keep breathing in and out."

He was driven to Bob Taplinger's house on East Forty-Ninth Street. Later that day he left for Los Angeles in a private jet.

* * * * * *

In the years following their divorce, Cary and Dyan have returned to court many times over the question of Jennifer's custody.

In August, 1969, seventeen months after their divorce, Cary went to court in order to prevent Dyan from taking Jennifer to visit Dyan's parents in Seattle.

"I am quite concerned," Cary told Superior Court Judge Marvin A. Freeman. Jennifer did not like her maternal grandparents, Cary said. He feared that Jennifer would be "just dumped" during the visit, without her mother or a nurse.

Dyan denied that any of Cary's statements were true, but Judge Freeman said that Dyan could not take Jennifer out of Los Angeles, pending another custody hearing already set for October 8. The hearing would deal with Cary's motion that his visiting rights be extended.

They were—from sixty to ninety days a year.

Two years later Cary was back in court again, seeking to extend his period of custody on the basis that Dyan had violated the provisions of the court's custody decree by not making her home in California. Dyan had been living in an apartment in New York during the filming of "Such Good Friends."

Her attorneys said that Dyan had not moved permanently away from California. The court let Cary keep Jennifer for a few weeks longer, but declined to give him permanent custody.

In March, 1972, Cary, who was getting to be something of a courthouse regular, was back fighting Dyan's petition that she be allowed to take Jennifer to New York for four to six weeks while she worked on a new movie.

After a two-day hearing, Judge Jack T. Ryburn ruled that it

was not in Jennifer's best interests to be taken out of school for that length of time. She would stay with Cary while Dyan was out of town working, but Cary was required to take Jennifer to see her mother in New York on two weekends during that period.

In July, 1973, it was Dyan who took the initiative. She petitioned the court for an order that would restrain Cary from living near her. He had rented a Malibu beach house just two hundred feet from hers; she claimed he was spying on her.

"He stood in front of his house, on the beach, with binoculars trained on me and my guests," Dyan said in her petition.

She wanted the court to make Grant move out of the beach house that he had rented the previous October.

Cary said that he had simply wanted to see if Jennifer was taking part in a volleyball game that was underway on Dyan's portion of beachfront. As soon as he saw that she wasn't, Cary said, he took his "opera glasses" away from his eyes. He maintained that he hadn't looked through them for more than "a few seconds." He told the court that he had not moved near Dyan in order to harass her, but because his proximity made it easier for Jennifer to visit him every day.

Dyan did not get her wish. Los Angeles Superior Court Judge Jack W. Swink ruled that Cary did not have to move, but Judge Swink did decree that "each party is restrained from annoying, molesting, or harassing the other."

Dyan also complained that Cary kept a separate wardrobe for Jennifer and required her to change as soon as she arrived at his house. Dyan declared that this custom had led to conflicts in Jennifer's mind. Judge Swink declined to make a specific ruling on the issue of Jennifer's clothing.

But he did rule on who was to have custody of Jennifer's passport. Cary wanted permanent possession of the official document, so that Dyan would not be able to take Jennifer out of the United States without his knowledge or permission. And, of course, if Cary had Jennifer's passport in his possession, he would be able to take his daughter abroad without Dyan's permission.

The judge ruled that Cary Grant would have custody of Jennifer's passport in even-numbered years, and that Dyan Cannon would have custody in odd-numbered years. Either parent, however, must relinquish the passport if the court approved travel for

Jennifer with either parent. A few months later, Judge Swink said that Jennifer should attend the private school chosen by her father and not the experimental school preferred by Dyan.

* * * * * *

In recent years, Cary Grant and Dyan Cannon appear to have arrived at a workable arrangement for sharing their daughter.

"It wasn't easy," Dyan said. "Believe me, it took a tremendous effort, but we had to work something out for the sake of this little girl of ours, so she can grow up without feeling a continued animosity between the two people who love her the most. Both of us have seen so many instances of people separating and the child's being torn—the father coming into the house to visit and the mother hurriedly leaving the room. This isn't the kind of atmosphere in which we want our daughter to grow up."

Cary Grant has said that he believes that, in spite of the once bitter custody struggles, that his daughter is going to be "all right."

"Jennifer and I level with each other. She finds it difficult to leave me, and she also finds it difficult to leave her mother. Any court that can handle the situation has to have the wisdom of Solomon. Her mother and I are trying to handle it the best we can, and I think the love we feel for Jennifer will be reflected."

12

A New Career And a Long Overdue Oscar

CARY GRANT FIRST MET George Barrie in the mid-Sixties. They immediately hit it off and became good friends almost instantly. Barrie was the sort of man who would appeal to Cary Grant. A former jazz saxophonist, he had built a small hair-spray business into an international multimillion concern: Rayette-Faberge. According to published reporters, Cary was the one who first broached the idea of joining Barrie's company in some capacity.

Barrie created a special title, "creative consultant," and offered Cary a job along with a spot on the board of directors. Cary thought about it for a year. During that period, which coincided with his year's estrangement from Dyan before they were divorced, Cary attended sales meetings and visited company laboratories in France and England.

Finally on May 22, 1968, about two months after his divorce from Dyan, Cary Grant once again made news. This time, however, it was on the business and financial pages. He accepted George Barrie's offer and became a member of Rayette-Faberge's board of directors. After the announcement of Grant's election to the board appeared in the papers, Rayette-Faberge's stock promptly went up to points on the New York Stock Exchange. Both Cary Grant and George Barrie assured skeptical reporters that Cary's association with the company was neither a gag nor a publicity stunt.

"We have outside directors who just sit in on meetings, but he's also an employee."

Cary said that in the months prior to his election to the board, he had been consulted by company executives on such things as packaging and promotion. He said that he had convinced them to make substantive changes in a couple of print ads and in two projected television commercials.

"I gave it a great deal of thought," Cary said, "and it is not something I entered into lightly. This is a young, vital company. The products include fragrances and toiletries for both women and men . . . I will act as a consultant in both corporate and product areas here and abroad. I feel it will be a worthwhile endeavor."

"We chose each other," Cary added. "I'm doing this because I enjoy it and it's stimulating. It isn't too different from films. We both make a product, can it, and distribute it."

His salary as "creative consultant" was fifteen thousand dollars. For every board meeting he attended, he would receive two hundred dollars.

Since he obviously wasn't doing it for the salary, why was he doing it? After countless offers to endorse various products and join countless business ventures, why had he, after so many years of saying "no" to such proposals, said "yes" to George Barrie? Part of the answer may lie in the description he gave of his corporate duties:

"Call attention to the products and tour the world on a goodwill basis."

Cary Grant's love of travel must have played a large role in his decision to lend his prestigious name to Rayette-Faberge. More specifically, having the company jet at his disposal must have been a powerful inducement.

Also rumored to be part of Cary's deal with Rayette-Faberge was an undisclosed amount of the company's stock that came to him when his election to the board was announced, plus guaranteed stock options that he could exercise in the future.

One of Cary's pet projects was developing a fragrance that could be used by both men and women.

"Why are flowers only for women? They're for men, too," Cary declared, answering his own question. "I think there ought to be more unity of the sexes. Why are there 'his' and 'hers' towels, twin beds, car gearshifts that separate people? Why shouldn't men use the same hair spray, the same cologne, as women, just as they're using the same soap and deodorants?

"The separation of the sexes is so manifest," he continued. "Why shouldn't we develop things we can all enjoy?"

Two years after becoming creative consultant to the cosmetic firm, Cary Grant, an employee who worked only when he felt like it, sounded as enthusiastic about his first business alliance as he had the day it was announced.

"I have always merchandised my own films," Cary said, pointing out that he had always arranged to have his films shown at Radio City Music Hall because the prestige of that theatre would impress the owners of smaller theatres.

"The same kind of merchandising works for the fragrance business," Cary noted. "If you sell the large department stores, the smaller ones fall in.

"Cooperative advertising is also the same for films as it is for fragrances," Cary said, extending his analogy. "Theatres and movie companies often share the price of advertising. We also share advertising costs with the department stores we do business with. Also there is the researching to consider. We researched Faberge's Brut just as you would research a screenplay. Then we ask ourselves where the raw essence can be found (which would be like finding locations for a movie) and how to get the quantities (the prints) in case we've got a hit.

"In this business, of course, my reviews came out in the shopping columns," Cary said. "Part of my job is traveling around to the department stores meeting executives and sales people. I like to think it helps."

Faberge president George Barrie has no doubts that it helps enormously.

"When we purchased Faberge seven years ago, the company was doing 11 million dollars of business," Barrie said. "Last year (1969) it did about 140 million, and I attribute some of that to Mr. G."

In a marvelous piece of understatement, Barrie added:

"He creates an atmosphere."

Cary Grant freely admits he doesn't spend much time in his office at Rayette-Faberge in midtown Manhattan. But then, nobody ever imagined that he would.

* * * * * *

It had been the talk of the movie industry for years—as well as, according to some insiders, a scandal if not a crime.

Why hadn't Cary Grant ever received an Oscar?

He was, after all, nominated twice: for *Penny Serenade* with Irene Dunne in 1941, and for *None But the Lonely Heart* with Ethel Barrymore in 1944. Both times he lost—in 1941 the coveted Academy Award for Best Actor went to Cary's old Paramount rival, Gary Cooper for *Sergeant York*, and in 1944 Bing Crosby took the prize for his portrayal of a priest in *Going My Way*.

Cary Grant, in fact, appeared in many movies that won Oscars. Leo McCary won Best Director in 1937 for *The Awful Truth*. James Stewart took the honors in 1940 for his work in *The Philadelphia Story*. Joan Fontaine was named Best Actress in 1941 for her role as Grant's wife in *Suspicion*. Ethel Barrymore was named Best Actress in 1944 for playing Grant's mother in *None But the Lonely Heart*. In 1947 Sidney Sheldon won for Best Screenplay for *The Bachelor and the Bobby-Soxer*. Soundman Gordon Sawyer won an Academy Award for his work on *The Bishop's Wife*. This state of affairs was perhaps best described by screenwriter Peter Stone who won an Oscar for Best Screenplay 1964. The movie in question? *Father Goose*.

When he accepted his award, Stone thanked Cary Grant, "who keeps winning these things for other people."

Producer Jerry Wald thought it a disgrace that Cary had never won. He decided to do something about it.

"I wanted to take out an ad (in *Variety* and *The Hollywood Reporter*) reminding the movie industry of this oversight, but Cary found out about my intentions and stopped me," Wald said.

In interviews in the Fifties Grant seemed resigned to the fact that he would never win an Academy Award.

"Light comedy has little chance for an Oscar," he said. "You have to play dope fiends to get noticed these days. But what's more difficult—whomping someone in the belly or making them laugh?"

On another occasion, as Awards night approached, Cary said:

"I won't win it. Not that I'm nominated, of course. But when I say I won't win it, I mean now or any other year. I don't say I should, and I have nothing but respect for the nominees. But 'acting' by today's critical lights has something to do with facial acrobatics and missing teeth. Light comedy has no more chance than the man who keeps his features still. You know, any amateur can black out a tooth, stick on a beard, and pretend he's something he isn't. The tough thing, the final thing, is to be yourself. *That* takes doing," he said.

Finally, the absurdity of Cary Grant not having an Oscar became more than Hollywood could live with. At the forty-second annual presentation of Academy Awards on April 7, 1970, Cary Grant was given a special award by the Academy of Motion Picture Arts and Sciences.

The award covered nearly four decades of continuous achievement. Frank Sinatra presented Cary's Oscar to him. It was inscribed:

TO CARY GRANT
for his unique mastery
of the art of screen acting
with the respect and affection
of his colleagues

"No one," Sinatra said, "has brought more pleasure to more people for many years than Cary has, and nobody has done so many things so well. It was awarded for sheer brilliance of acting," Sinatra added. "Cary has so much skill that he makes it all look easy."

Many people thought that Cary would not show up in person to collect his Oscar. They were wrong. He not only showed up, he accepted his long overdue Oscar with tears, laughter, and a very gracious speech.

He thanked the many directors and writers with whom he had worked over the years.

"This is a collaborative medium," Cary said. "We all need each other.

"Probably no greater respect can come to a man than the respect of his colleagues," Cary concluded.

The entire audience rose to its feet and gave superstar Cary Grant a minutes-long ovation.

Preceding the presentation of Cary's Oscar, the audience had seen a well-done montage of clips from Cary's films. The montage, assembled by Jack Haley, Jr. and Richard Dunlap, showed Cary in scenes that provided a partial history of his film career. Beginning with the also-indestructible Mae West, Cary was seen charming a long list of Hollywood's foremost leading ladies including Jean Harlow, Katharine Hepburn, Jean Arthur, Irene Dunne, Ingrid Bergman, Grace Kelly, Eva Marie Saint, and Audrey Hepburn.

The effect on the crowd was electric. Of course everybody in Hollywood knew that Cary Grant had managed to become an institution. But maybe they had forgotten just how funny, engaging, and just plain superb he had been for more years than practically anyone else in their business.

As an insecure and troubled boy, he had set out to entertain and delight people, to make them laugh. Then maybe they would give him the love and approval he so desperately needed.

That he succeeded in the first half of that equation there can be no doubt. Whether his success brought him enough love and approval to make his efforts and his life worthwhile, only Cary Grant can say.

13

Keeping Busy

RESTING ON HIS LAURELS would no doubt drive Cary Grant to the farther reaches of unbearable boredom. He began working when he was thirteen years old and that kind of background conditions you. Life without involvement is simply unimaginable.

Cary Grant has another reason for keeping busy. It's possible that if he had custody of Jennifer, he would eliminate some of his business concerns. He might cut down on his travel. But these things provide a way of keeping himself occupied during the long weeks when his daughter is not with him.

He still makes goodwill trips for Faberge. A recent public relations journey took him to Monte Carlo where he met, for the first time, England's Prince Charles, and Princess Caroline, the daughter of his former leading lady, Grace Kelly, and her husband, Prince Ranier.

Two other companies claim his attentions these days. Grant was elected to the board of directors of MGM when that company was reorganized in the mid-Seventies. He is also on the board of Western Airlines. For a number of years, he was a board member of Tamboo, a private club on Great Harbor Cay, where he still owns property. He was also involved with several other investors in developing "Shannonside," a planned community on the outskirts of Shannon, Ireland. Cary envisioned the 555-acre site becoming "a kind of Shangri-La."

"I am sincere when I say that this is the most beautiful spot on earth I've seen," Cary said. "The point is that we want to keep it this way. Lovely and esthetically pleasing."

Cary Grant has always had a healthy dose of homesickness for the British Isles in general, and his hometown of Bristol in particular.

"I'm always nostalgic for England and as I grow older I have the same instinct as the salmon. I want to come home more and more and I do find myself coming here more frequently," Cary told a reporter for a London newspaper.

"Anyway, it's so comparatively civilised for an American," he continued. "So is Southern Ireland. I've bought a three-acre plot of land on this little township we are developing, and I'm building a house there for myself and my daughter."

When he wasn't travelling for business or pleasure, Cary Grant also had several lawsuits to keep him busy.

In 1970 a thirty-three-year-old former employee of the film production department at 20th Century Fox, Cynthia Bouron, brought a paternity suit against Cary Grant, then sixty-six. She said that he was the father of her seven-week-old daughter born the previous March 20. The little girl's name was Stephanie Andrea.

Ms. Bouron said that Cary Grant had "failed and refused" to provide support or to pay for medical and hospital expenses.

A week later, Cary filed a counter-suit asking the court to stop Ms. Bouron from claiming that he was the father of her child until the paternity suit was settled. When her daughter was born Ms. Bouron had registered the child in official records as Stephanie Andrea Grant. She listed the father as Cary Grant, actor.

Cary's petition read in part:

"This order is essential to preserve (Grant's) personal status and reputation in the community. Unless (Ms. Bouron) is so restrained, she will continue to represent or publish that Grant is the father, to his humiliation, embarrassment and damage."

Resolution of the case turned out to be anticlimactic. Cary Grant agreed to take a blood test to support his position that he was not the father of Ms. Bouron's baby. Ms. Bouron, however, failed to appear with her daughter for her blood test. The test was re-scheduled. Again she did not show up. Yet another test was set.

When Ms. Bouron failed to appear for the third time, Superior Judge Laurence J. Rittenband threw the case out of court.

* * * * * *

Other lawsuits dealt with business matters. Cary Grant filed an $8 million lawsuit against MCA-Universal charging that it had sold several of his films to television under conditions that were "premature" and "not under best terms."

He claimed that MCA-Universal's handling of the TV deals had dissipated his property rights.

Late in 1973 *Variety* reported yet another Cary Grant lawsuit. This time *Esquire* magazine was the target. Cary charged the magazine had unlawfully used his photograph.

Back in 1946 Cary Grant had appeared in a fashion spread in *Esquire*. In 1971 *Esquire* used the twenty-five-year old shot of Cary's head with another body wearing a Forum sweater. The later piece was designed to show new trends in male fashions. Cary wasn't having any of that. The piece may have looked like a news story, he said, but it actually was an unauthorized use of his likeness to sell Forum sportswear.

The case was eventually settled out of court.

As was Dr. Andrew Salter's case, originally filed in 1970. Dr. Salter was the psychologist whom Dyan Cannon had consulted after she left Cary. According to Salter's petition, he had also seen Cary between February 21, 1967 and January 29, 1968, and had provided "extensive professional services as a psychologist and counselor in lengthy personal consultations." Dr. Salter said that he had seen Dyan on the same basis between July 28, 1967 and January 29, 1968. Dr. Salter said that Cary and Dyan were seeing him in order "to restore harmony to their married life." He claimed that Cary Grant owed him over seven thousand dollars.

Cary said that's not the way it was. He entered a general denial to Salter's suit and charged that he had failed to perform the condition of the contract. Grant's legal reply stated that Salter had "failed in treating and counseling my wife so that the condition of estrangement was not corrected and ameliorated but was in fact aggravated."

Cary's life in the Seventies, however, hasn't been all business and legal wrangling. In 1972 he sold seven of his films to National Telefilm Associates for a sale price described as "in excess of $2 million." The package included *Walk, Don't Run, Indiscreet, Operation Petticoat, That Touch of Mink, The Grass Is Greener, Father Goose*, and *Penny Serenade*.

A much smaller financial bonanza came Cary's way when he and Gratia von Furstenburg shared a $70,000 settlement for the injuries they had received in the March 12, 1968 accident on the Long Island Expressway. They had originally sued both the trucking and the limousine company for five hundred thousand dollars in damages.

In 1974 at the sixth annual Straw Hat awards, underwritten by Faberge and honoring excellence in summer stock productions, New York Mayor Abraham Beame surprised Cary Grant with a special award—a plaque intended to memorialize New York's appreciation of Cary Grant's contributions to the American theatre.

That same year Cary was back in New York for a much more solemn occasion. He took part in the rededication of the Bristol Basin Memorial, a part of Manhattan whose existence is unknown to most New Yorkers.

In the early years of World War II, before America had entered the conflict, American ships carried food, warm clothing, and other supplies to England. Bristol was the major port used on the English end of the lifeline. German submarines had effectively stopped the traffic into England's bigger ports.

On the return trip to the United States, the ships were loaded, for ballast, with the stones, bricks, and other rubble of bombed-out Bristol. The ballast was dumped in the East River near Kips Bay. On top of this landfill was eventually built a portion of the East River Driver, later renamed FDR Drive in honor of America's wartime president.

The area was officially named the Bristol Basin. Mayor Fiorello LaGuardia dedicated the Bristol Basin. A bronze commemorative plaque was set into place—and stayed there until it was removed in the early 70's so that a huge apartment complex could be built. After its construction the plaque was once again replaced and the area rededicated.

Cary Grant spoke briefly at the ceremony.

"My uncle Jack and his wife, Rose, and their children lived in a Georgian house in Bristol, which was their only protection against a blockbuster of a bomb which hit their street directly," Cary said. "When I returned to the site some days later, I composed a prayer. I hoped that humanity would conduct itself hereafter so that this kind of thing would never happen again. I add my hope today that it still will not."

* * * * * *

In recent years Cary Grant has become more candid than ever and less defensive. His laugh is heartier than it ever was. He has even responded, in public print, to the persistent rumors that, in spite of four wives and numerous less serious attachments with women, he is gay.

"When I was a young and popular star," he told a *New York Times* reporter, "I'd meet a girl with a man and maybe she'd say something nice about me and then the guy would say, 'Yeah, but I hear he's really a fag.' It's ridiculous, but they say it about all of us. Now in fact, the guy is doing me a favor. Number one, he's expressed an insecurity about the girl. Number two, he has provoked curiosity about me in her. Number three, that girl zeroes in on my bed to find out for herself, and the result is that the guy has created the exact situation he wanted to avoid.

"Now on the other hand," he continued. "I know I have a happy husband and wife when a guy comes up to me and says, 'My wife just loves you,' and then I give her a little embrace and tell the guy kiddingly, 'Do forgive us.'

"Or a guy will come up to me and say, 'See that girl over there. Please go over and whisper something to her or kiss her on the neck or put your arms around her.' Well, I'll *do* it because I know the guy trusts and loves that girl."

* * * * * *

Estimates of Cary Grant's wealth were put at $10 million in the Fifties. Now the estimates are coming in at $25 million. Cary sums up the most recent estimate this way: "That's nonsense."

He accepts his age with both good grace and common sense. Asked how it felt to be in his Seventies, Grant replied:

"What else can I be? I'd prefer to be younger and know what I know today and be able to apply it to life in every aspect. I'm reminded of what someone said: 'If I had known I was going to live this long, I'd have taken better care of myself.' "

But Cary Grant's most charming story on the age question, concerns his mother. The year was 1971 and Elsie Leach was ninety-three years old, claiming to be only ninety-one. Cary Grant, was visiting her. She enjoyed drives in the country, so Cary had arranged for his driver to bring the Rolls around to Elsie's nursing home right after lunch.

Elsie watched the passing scenery for some minutes, then turned to Cary and said, "Darling, you should do something about your hair."

Cary Grant hadn't the faintest idea what his mother was talking about. He ran his hand over his silver pelt.

"What should I do about my hair?"

Elsie lowered her voice. "Well, dear, it's so *white*. You should dye it; everybody does these days."

"But why should I?"

Elsie looked him in the eye. "If you must know, because it makes *me* look old," she said.

Elsie Leach died in 1973 at the good age of ninety-five. Presently it very much looks as though Elsie passed on her longevity genes to her only child. Which means that Cary Grant could one day become a grandfather. Which is nice to think about.

In the meantime he takes each day as it comes. A reporter once asked him if he wasn't sometimes tempted to take his money and flee to Tahiti?

"This is my Tahiti." Cary said. "I don't put a great deal of effort into my work for Faberge. I get up in the morning, go to bed at night, and occupy myself as best I can in between. I do what I want when I want. Once, in St. Louis, I knew a fellow who ran a whorehouse, simply because it made him happy.

"Well, I do what makes *me* happy."

Jennifer—
His Last Love

WHAT MAKES CARY GRANT HAPPIEST is being with Jennifer. She's almost twelve years old now, an exceptionally pretty child who, in earlier news photographs taken when she was four and five years, bears a quite striking resemblance to her mother, Dyan Cannon.

There are not many photographs of Jennifer available. Cary Grant is haunted by the fear that his daughter could become a target for kidnappers. One time a reporter arrived to interview him in the suite that Faberge maintains for him in Manhattan's Warwick Hotel. She had a photographer with her. She noticed that Cary, anticipating their photo session, had turned over all of Jennifer's pictures in their frames so that none of them could inadvertently appear in the picture of him.

A magazine writer who once met the child reported that Jennifer was "sweet and unspoiled, with a natural grace."

Ironically Jennifer has proved such a delightful experience that she has been the cause of Cary Grant's only regret in life.

"If I had known then what I know now . . . if I had not been so utterly stupid or selfish . . . I would have had a hundred children and I would have built a ranch to keep them on."

He has made her a baseball fan. They are frequently seen at

Dodgers games. Jennifer is probably the only eleven-year old girl in the country who can tell you the Dodgers' starting line-up.

In 1970 when Jennifer was three and a half, Cary sketched, perhaps unwittingly, the tenderness in their relationship to an interviewer:

"We have a great rapport between us. Usually when she won't take her afternoon nap, I lie down with her and we both fall off. It's so heartwarming and restful even if she kicks me in the head once in awhile. She rubs it and says, 'Daddy, I'm making it well.' On another occasion, I fell asleep and snored so loudly it awakened her and she shook me and said, 'Stop it, Daddy.'

"I've been tape recording everything she does with me. I've also shot a great deal of film footage of her so she'll know, when she grows up, how deeply her father loved his little girl. Jennifer's a jealous female, too. One day we were together when I met Deborah Kerr, and we kissed hello. This shook Jennifer up, and she said to Deborah, 'You keep away from my daddy.' "

Humorously, he refers to Jennifer as "my last and best production."

"Jennifer is my life today," Cary has said. "I plan around her, where she is, when I may have her.

"I am not at all proud of my marriage record. But I have wanted a family for years. I finally have one in this child. I will do what I can for her."

Cary Grant shows a charming predilection for fatherly excess. He now owns a Cadillac Coupe DeVille in cobalt blue, because General Motors had named the color "Jennifer blue" in the Cadillac catalogue.

"I don't know why I didn't (have more children). I've come to the conclusion that it's the only real reason we're here—to procreate," Cary said recently.

Cary Grant has said that he has never known a happy actress. "Happy actors, yes. Happy actresses, never."

He would not stand in Jennifer's way, however, if movies and the theatre interested her.

As parents always do, he hopes that Jennifer will learn from his mistakes.

"I pray that she will get married and have children. I hope she has a fair start. I'll do everything I can, but it would have been better for her if she had united parents," Cary said.

"I want Jennifer to give one man love and confidence and help," Cary has said. "It has taken me many years to learn that. I was playing a different game entirely. My wives and I were never one. We were competing. I will advise Jennifer to love someone and to be loved. Anything else she may get in her life is a bonus."

How astonishing, how touching, and somehow appropriate that Cary Grant, screen lover of the world's loveliest women, a man who is the world's standard of urbane and civilized charm, a man whom Grace and Ranier regularly invite to Monaco, whom Ari and Jackie invited to Skorpios, a man who has been everywhere and is known by everyone—how tender, human, and nourishing that the deepest pleasure he has known in a rich and textured life is the one that is available to all of us: bringing a child into the world and watching the miracle of life unfold.

The Films (1932-1966) of Cary Grant

1. **THIS IS THE NIGHT.** Paramount, 1932. Director: Frank Tuttle. Cast: Lily Damita, Charlie Ruggles, Roland Young, Thelma Todd. Marital musical chairs. Or is it beds?

2. **SINNERS IN THE SUN**. Paramount, 1932. Director: Alexander Hall. Cast: Carole Lombard, Chester Morris, Adrienne Ames, Alison Skipworth. Poor working girl tries social climbing. Learns her lesson.

3. **MERRILY WE GO TO HELL**. Paramount, 1932. Director: Dorothy Arzner. Cast: Sylvia Sidney, Fredric March, Adrienne Allen, Skeets Gallagher. Hard-drinking newsman marries rich girl. His booze drives her home to papa.

4. **DEVIL AND THE DEEP**. Paramount, 1932. Director: Marion Gering. Cast: Tallulah Bankhead, Gary Cooper, Charles Laughton. Sea-going sex triangle. Cary says no. Gary says yes . . . to Tallulah.

5. **BLONDE VENUS**. Paramount, 1932. Director: Josef von Sternberg. Cast: Marlene Dietrich, Herbert Marshall, Dickie Moore, Gene Morgan. Dietrich embraces a life of sin to pay her husband's medical bills.

6. **HOT SATURDAY**. Paramount, 1932. Director: William A. Seiter. Cast: Nancy Carroll, Randolph Scott, Edward Woods. Local rake reforms his errant ways when Ms. Right happens by.

7. **MADAME BUTTERFLY**. Paramount, 1932. Director: Marion Gering. Cast: Sylvia Sidney, Charlie Ruggles, Sandor Kallay, Irving Pichel. American naval officer behaves like a cad to lovely Japanese woman.

8. **SHE DONE HIM WRONG**. Paramount, 1933. Director: Lowell Sherman. Cast: Mae West, Gilbert Roland, Noah Beery, Sr., Rafaela Ottiano. Saloon lady takes a liking to religious gentleman. Or is he?

9. **THE WOMAN ACCUSED**. Paramount, 1933. Director: Paul Sloane. Cast: Nancy Carroll, John Halliday, Irving Pichel, Louis Calhern. Lady kills ex-lover to insure he'll have a permanently zipped lip.

10. **THE EAGLE AND THE HAWK**. Paramount, 1933. Director: Stuart Walker. Cast: Fredric March, Jack Oakie, Carole Lombard. World War I as seen from the air.

11. **GAMBLING SHIP**. Paramount, 1933. Directors: Louis Gasnier and Max Marcin. Cast: Benita Hume, Roscoe Kearns, Glenda Farrell. Gangsters, molls, and a floating (literally) crap game.

12. **I'M NO ANGEL**. Paramount, 1933. Directors: Wesley Ruggles. Cast: Mae West, Edward Arnold, Rolf Harolds. Jilted circus queen won't take "no" for an answer.

13. **ALICE IN WONDERLAND**. Paramount, 1933. Director: Norman Z. McLeod. Cast: Charlotte Henry, Richard Arlen, Roscoe Ates, Gary Cooper, and just about everybody else in the Paramount stable. Grant plays the Mock Turtle. The Lewis Carroll classic as butchered by Paramount.

14. **THIRTY-DAY PRINCESS**. Paramount, 1934. Director: Marion Gering. Cast: Sylvia Sidney, Edward Arnold, Henry Stephenson, Vince Barnett. Newsman falls for princess who really isn't.

15. **BORN TO BE BAD**. United Artists, 1934. Director: Lowell Sherman. Cast: Loretta Young, Jackie Kelk, Henry Travers. Rich man adopts baby. Mother wants it back.

16. **KISS AND MAKE UP**. Paramount, 1934. Director: Harlan Thompson. Cast: Helen Mack, Genevieve Tobin, Edward

Everett Horton. The beauty business in Paris. Not all it's made up to be.

17. **LADIES SHOULD LISTEN**. Paramount, 1934. Director: Frank Tuttle. Cast: Frances Drake, Edward Everett Horton, Rosita Moreno. Payboy spreads himself too thin among his lady friends.

18. **ENTER MADAME**. Paramount, 1934. Director: Elliott Nugent. Cast: Elissa Landi, Lynne Overman, Sharon Lynne, Paul Forcasi. Spouse of temperamental diva calls it quits.

19. **WINGS IN THE DARK**. Paramount, 1935. Director: James Flood. Cast: Myrna Loy, Rosco Kearns, Hobart Cavanaugh, Dean Jagger. Blinded aviator invents instrument for blind flying. Tests it himself. It works.

20. **THE LAST OUTPOST**. Paramount, 1935. Directors: Louis Gasnier and Charles Barton. Cast: Claude Rains, Gertrude Michael, Kathleen Burke. Lawrence of Arabia under another name. And with a love interest.

21. **SYLVIA SCARLETT**. RKO, 1936. Director: George Cukor. Cast: Katharine Hepburn, Brian Aherne, Edmund Gwenn. Sex disguise, on the lam, and the absurdities of true love.

22. **BIG BROWN EYES**. Paramount, 1936. Director: Raoul Walsh. Cast: Joan Bennett, Walter Pidgeon, Lloyd Nolan, Alan Baxter. Manicurist turned "sob sister" catches jewel thieves.

23. **SUZY**. MGM, 1936. Director: George Fitzmaurice. Cast: Jean Harlow, Franchot Tone, Lewis Stone, Benita Hume. American showgirl marries French flying ace, vintage World War I.

24. **WEDDING PRESENT**. Paramount, 1936. Director: Richard Wallace. Cast: Joan Bennett, George Bancroft, Conrad Nagel, Gene Lockhart. Wacked-out newsman gains an editor's job and loses his girlfriend.

25. **THE AMAZING QUEST OF ERNEST BLISS**. Grand National (England), 1936. Director: Alfred Zeisler. Cast: Mary Brian, Henry Kendall, Peter Gawthorne. Rich man takes job to cure his boredom.

26. **WHEN YOU'RE IN LOVE**. Columbia, 1937. Director: Robert Riskin. Cast: Grace Moore, Aline MacMahon, Henry Stephenson, Thomas Mitchell. Opera star and artist marry for convenience.

27. **THE TOAST OF NEW YORK**. RKO, 1937. Director: Rowland V. Lee. Cast: Edward Arnold, Frances Farmer, Jack Oakie, Donald Meek. Story of robber baron Jim Fiske.

28. **TOPPER**. MGM, 1937. Director: Norman Z. McLeod. Cast: Constance Bennett, Roland Young, Billie Burke, Alan Mowbray. Ghosts do good marital works.

29. **THE AWFUL TRUTH**. Columbia, 1937. Director: Leo McCarey. Cast: Irene Dunne, Ralph Bellamy, Alexander D'Arcy. Divorce in haste, repent at leisure. And who gets custody of the dog?

30. **BRINGING UP BABY**. RKO, 1938. Director: Howard Hawks. Cast: Katharine Hepburn, Charles Ruggles, May Robson, Walter Catlett, Barry Fitzgerald. Heiress recruits paleontologist to help her look for pet leopard.

31. **HOLIDAY**. Columbia, 1938. Director: George Cukor. Cast: Katharine Hepburn, Doris Nolan, Lew Ayres, Edward Everett Horton, Binnie Barnes. Two sisters in love with the same man.

32. **GUNGA DIN**. RKO, 1939. Director: George Stevens. Cast: Victor McLaglen, Douglas Fairbanks, Jr., Sam Jaffe, Joan Fontaine. British troops in India back in the days of the white man's burden.

33. **ONLY ANGELS HAVE WINGS**. Columbia, 1939. Director: Howard Hawks. Cast: Jean Arthur, Richard Barthelmess, Rita Hayworth, Thomas Mitchell. Daredevil pilots deliver the mail in South America.

34. **IN NAME ONLY**. RKO, 1939. Director: John Cromwell. Cast: Kay Francis, Carole Lombard, Charles Coburn, Helen Vinson. Another triangle.

35. **HIS GIRL FRIDAY**. Columbia, 1940. Director: Howard Hawks. Cast: Rosalind Russell, Ralph Bellamy, Helen

Mack, Ernest Truex, Gene Lockhart, Regis Toomey. Editor tricks ex-reporter into covering just one more story. Remake of *The Front Page*.

36. **MY FAVORITE WIFE**. RKO, 1940. Director: Garson Kanin. Cast: Irene Dunne, Randolph Scott, Gail Patrick. Presumed-dead wife turns up just as husband plans to wed again.

37. **THE HOWARDS OF VIRGINIA**. Columbia, 1940. Director: Frank Lloyd. Cast: Martha Scott, Sir Cedric Hardwicke, Alan Marshal, Anne Revere. Love story set in Revolutionary times.

38. **THE PHILADELPHIA STORY**. MGM, 1940. Director: George Cukor. Cast: Katharine Hepburn, James Stewart, Ruth Hussey, John Howard, Roland Young. Ex-husband turns up for wife's next wedding.

39. **PENNY SERENADE**. Columbia, 1941. Director: George Stevens. Cast: Irene Dunne, Beulah Bondi, Edgar Buchanan. Couple loses adopted child.

40. **SUSPICION**. RKO, 1941. Director: Alfred Hitchcock. Cast: Joan Fontaine, Sir Cedric Hardwicke, Nigel Bruce, Dame May Whitty, Leo G. Carroll. Man plans to kill his wife. Or does he?

41. **THE TALK OF THE TOWN**. Columbia, 1942. Director: George Stevens. Cast: Jean Arthur, Ronald Colman, Edgar Buchanan. Glenda Farrell. Innocent murder suspect hides out in schoolteacher's house.

42. **ONCE UPON A HONEYMOON**. RKO, 1942. Director: Leo McCarey. Cast: Ginger Rogers, Walter Slezak, Albert Dekker. Newsman tells former American showgirl her husband is a Nazi.

43. **MR. LUCKY**. RKO, 1943. Director: H.C. Potter. Cast: Laraine Day, Charles Bickford, Gladys Cooper, Alan Carney. Gambler displays heart of gold.

44. **DESTINATION TOKYO**. Warners, 1944. Director: Delmer Davies. Cast: John Garfield, Alan Hale, Dane Clark, Warner

Anderson. Submarine on a secret World War II mission.

45. **ONCE UPON A TIME**. Columbia, 1944. Director: Alexander Hall. Cast: Janet Blair, James Gleason, Ted Donaldson, Howard Freeman. Theatrical producer is saved from ruin by a performing caterpillar.

46. **ARSENIC AND OLD LACE**. Warners, 1944. Director: Frank Capra. Cast: Priscilla Lane, Raymond Massey, Josephine Hull, Jean Adair, Jack Carson, Edward Everett Horton, Peter Lorre. Two spinsters practice imaginative euthanasia.

47. **NONE BUT THE LONELY HEART**. RKO, 1944. Director: Clifford Odets. Cast: Ethel Barrymore, Barry Fitzgerald, Jane Wyatt, June Duprez. Life in the east London slums just before World War II.

48. **NIGHT AND DAY**. Warners, 1946. Director: Michael Curtiz. Cast: Alexis Smith, Monty Woolley, Ginny Sims, Jane Wyman, Eve Arden. Purports to be the life of songwriter/composer Cole Porter.

49. **NOTORIOUS**. RKO, 1946. Director: Alfred Hitchcock. Cast: Ingrid Bergman, Claude Rains, Louis Calhern. Nazi spies in South America.

50. **THE BACHELOR AND THE BOBBY-SOXER**. RKO, 1947. Director: Irving Reis. Cast: Myrna Loy, Shirley Temple, Rudy Vallee. Man must "date" teen-ager until her crush is cured.

51. **THE BISHOP'S WIFE**. RKO, 1947. Director: Henry Koster. Cast: Loretta Young, David Niven, Monty Woolley, James Gleason, Gladys Cooper, Elsa Lanchester. Angel helps bishop with marital woes.

52. **MR. BLANDINGS BUILDS HIS DREAM HOUSE**. RKO, 1948. Director: H.C. Potter. Cast: Myrna Loy, Melvyn Douglas. Manhattan couple eager for joys of country living.

53. **EVERY GIRL SHOULD BE MARRIED**. RKO, 1948. Director: Don Hartman. Cast: Betsy Drake, Franchot Tone, Diana Lynn, Eddie Albert. Girl chases pediatrician until he catches her.

54. **I WAS A MALE WAR BRIDE**. 20th Century Fox, 1949. Director: Howard Hawks. Cast: Ann Sheridan, William Neff, Eugene Gericke. French officer marries American officer.

55. **CRISIS**. MGM, 1950. Director: Richard Brooks. Cast: Jose Ferrer, Signe Hasso, Paul Raymond. Vacationing surgeon operates on ailing South American dictator.

56. **PEOPLE WILL TALK**. 20th Century Fox, 1951. Director: Joseph L. Mankiewicz. Cast: Jeanne Crain, Hume Cronyn, Walter Slezak, Sidney Blackmer. Mysterious professor marries woman about to have someone else's baby.

57. **ROOM FOR ONE MORE**. Warners, 1952. Director: Norman Taurog. Cast: Betsy Drake, Iris Mann, Lurene Tuttle. Woman can't say "no" to the patter of little feet.

58. **MONKEY BUSINESS**. 20th Century Fox, 1952. Director: Howard Hawks. Cast: Ginger Rogers, Charles Coburn, Marilyn Monroe. Youth potion gets into the drinking water.

59. **DREAM WIFE**. MGM, 1953. Director: Sidney Sheldon. Cast: Deborah Kerr, Walter Pidgeon, Betta St. John, Buddy Baer. Man decides fiancee too independent minded. Turns to geisha type.

60. **TO CATCH A THIEF**. Paramount, 1955. Director: Alfred Hitchcock. Cast: Grace Kelly, Jessie Royce Landis, John Williams. Jewel thief returns to old profession in new role.

61. **THE PRIDE AND THE PASSION**. United Artists, 1957. Director: Stanley Kramer. Cast: Sophia Loren, Theodore Bikel, Frank Sinatra. Guerrillas against Napoleon.

62. **AN AFFAIR TO REMEMBER**. 20th Century Fox, 1957. Director: Leo McCarey. Cast: Deborah Kerr, Richard Denning, Neva Patterson, Cathleen Nesbit. An almost tragic love affair that starts on board ship.

63. **KISS THEM FOR ME**. 20th Century Fox, 1957. Director: Stanley Donen. Cast: Jayne Mansfield, Leif Erickson, Suzy Parker, Ray Walston. Navy heroes prove boys will be boys.

64. **INDISCREET**. Warners, 1958. Director: Stanley Donen. Cast: Ingrid Bergman, Cecil Parker, Phyllis Calvert, Megs

Jenkins. A love story for grown-ups.

65. **HOUSEBOAT**. Paramount, 1958. Director: Melville Shavelson. Cast: Sophia Loren, Martha Hyer, Harry Guardino. Widower lives on houseboat with passel of kids. Hires governess.

66. **NORTH BY NORTHWEST**. MGM, 1959. Director: Alfred Hitchcock. Cast: Eva Marie Saint, James Mason, Jessie Royce Landis, Leo G. Carroll, Martin Landau. Mistaken identity, intrigue, murder, sex, and a chase scene across the faces of Mt. Rushmore.

67. **OPERATION PETTICOAT**. Universal, 1959. Director: Blake Edwards. Cast: Tony Curtis, Joan O'Brian, Dina Merrill, Arthur O'Connell. Taut ship loosened by contingent of nurses.

68. **THE GRASS IS GREENER**. Universal, 1960. Director: Stanley Donen. Cast: Deborah Kerr, Robert Mitchum, Jean Simmons. Wife of English earl falls for American millionaire.

69. **THAT TOUCH OF MINK**. Universal, 1962. Director: Delbert Mann. Cast: Doris Day, Gig Young, Audrey Meadows, Alan Hewitt. The Eternal Virgin meets Mr. Charm.

70. **CHARADE**. Universal, 1963. Director: Stanley Donen. Cast: Audrey Hepburn, Walter Matthau, James Coburn, George Kennedy. A quarter of a million dollars lost in Paris. Everybody's after it.

71. **FATHER GOOSE**. Universal, 1964. Director: Ralph Nelson. Cast: Leslie Caron, Trevor Howard, Jack Good. Beachcomber turns baby-sitter.

72. **WALK, DON'T RUN**. Columbia, 1966. Director: Charles Walters. Cast: Samantha Eggar, Jim Hutton, John Standing. The Tokyo housing shortage during the 1964 Olympics.

Index